Those Who Face Death is a gripping, first-hand account of one of the most consequential but overlooked campaigns of the Iraq War by one of America's true experts in unconventional warfare. More than a war story, this book is filled with history that cannot be read anywhere else, dramatic and humorous anecdotes, and lessons that have timeless relevance. This is a must read for any military professional. It should be mandatory for every Special Forces student in the qualification course.

COL (Ret.) DAVID MAXWELL
Vice President, Center for Asia Pacific Strategy
Senior Fellow, Global Peace Foundation
Editor, Small Wars Journal

Mark Grdovic is one of the greatest warrior-thinkers of his generation and the intellectual engine behind the plan to conduct unconventional warfare in Northern Iraq in 2003. Reminiscent of the Operational Groups of the Office of Strategic Services in World War II, *Those Who Face Death* is a must read for anyone interested in gaining a better understanding of Special Forces and unconventional warfare.

CHRISTOPHER MILLER
Former Acting US Secretary of Defense

Those Who Face Death is the incredible story of how 10th Special Forces Group transformed the Kurdish militias into a "fifth column" in support of the US-led invasion. Mark is without question one of the leading subject matter experts on unconventional warfare. He makes the reader feel like they are a part of the operation while weaving in critical lessons.

STU BRADIN
President/CEO
Global SOF Foundation

PRAISE FOR *THOSE WHO FACE DEATH*

History is replete with stories of soldiers doing the seemingly impossible in the face of overwhelming odds. Mark has created a riveting account of this critical piece of US Army and special operations history, finally providing some long overdue context and perspective.

DR DENNIS WALTERS, Director
US Department of Defense, Irregular Warfare Center

Mark Grdovic, one of the most thoughtful and searingly honest Special Forces officers I've met, tells a little-known story of US Army Special Forces during the Iraq War. Listening to one's partners and heeding the realities on the ground are, he shows, the only way to succeed in war or peace.

LINDA ROBINSON
Author of *Masters of Chaos* and a Senior Fellow
at the Council on Foreign Relations

Published by Copper Mountain Books
www.coppermountainbooks.com

ISBN:

eBook	978-1-963781-07-6
Paperback	978-1-963781-06-9
Hardcover	978-1-963781-05-2

Those Who Face Death
The Untold Story of Special Forces and the Iraqi-Kurdish Resistance
First Edition

MARK GRDOVIC

THOSE WHO FACE DEATH

THE UNTOLD STORY OF SPECIAL FORCES
AND THE IRAQI KURDISH RESISTANCE

COPPER
MOUNTAIN
BOOKS

For the men and women of 10th Special Forces Group (Airborne),
for their courage, dedication, and professionalism.

For the brave men and women of the Iraqi Kurdish resistance,
for their courage, sacrifice, and perseverance in the face of
overwhelming hardship and oppression.

For my wife, Gretchen, for always supporting me.

TABLE OF CONTENTS

Insurgents' actions are similar in character to all others fought by second rate troops: they start out full of vigor and enthusiasm, but there is little level-headedness and tenacity in the long run.

—CLAUSEWITZ, On War

It was a critical task of the Special Operations Executive (SOE), to make sure that where level-headedness and tenacity were lacking (among resistance forces), these characteristics were made available by first rate organizers, so these forces could be brought into combat.

— M.R. FOOT, The SOE 1940-1946

KEY PARTICIPANTS

Joint Special Operations Task Force (JSOTF-North) and 10th Special Forces Group Commander - **COL Charles Cleveland**

3rd Battalion, 10th Special Forces Group - **LTC Ken Tovo (BN and ODC 103 CDR)**

BN S-3 (Operations Officer) – **MAJ Mark Grdovic**

076 (Pilot Team) (under battalion control)

CW3 Andy Gronlund (ODA CDR)

Jack - Air Force Special Tactic Squadron (STS) member

A Co (ODB 070) - MAJ Tye Connect (Company CDR)

ODA 071

ODA 072

ODA 073

ODA 074

ODA 075 - CPT Pat Bekurs (ODA CDR)

B Co (ODB 080) - MAJ Pat Roberson (Company CDR)

ODA 081 - CPT Brian Rauen (ODA CDR)

ODA 081 - MSG Rich Sanders* (ODA Team Sergeant)

ODA 081 - SSG Mark Giaconia

ODA 081 - SSG Chris Crum

ODA 081 - SSG Ken Gilmore

ODA 081 - SSG Blake Kramer

ODA 082 - CPT Tim Fuller (ODA CDR)

ODA 082 - MSG Tim DeNio (ODA Team Sergeant)

ODA 083 - CPT Joe Lock (ODA CDR)

ODA 083 - MSG Jim Donovan (ODA Team Sergeant)

ODA 083 - CW2 Mike Santoro (ODA XO)

ODA 084 - CPT John Holevas (ODA CDR)

ODA 085 – MSG Eddie Licon (ODA Team Sergeant)

ODA 085 - SFC Kelly Hornbeck

---

* At the individual's request a pseudonym has been used in place of their actual name.

C Co (ODB 090) - MAJ George Thiebes (Company CDR)

ODA 091 - CPT Erich Fellenz (ODA CDR)

ODA 091 - MSG Keven Cleveland (ODA Team Sergeant)

ODA 092

ODA 093 - CPT Steve Stowell (ODA CDR)

ODA 093 - MSG Chris Hartnett (ODA Team Sergeant)

ODA 094 - CPT Pete Russo (ODA CDR)

ODA 094 - CW2 Scott Fleming (ODA XO)

ODA 095

Patriotic Union of Kurdistan (PUK)

Jalal Talabani - Secretary General of the Patriotic Union of Kurdistan

Bafel Talabani - son of Jalal Talabani

Lahor Talabani - nephew of Jalal Talabani

Wahab - PUK personnel security detail

Dr. Barham Salah - Senior Advisor to Jalal Talabani

Kok Mustafa - CDR, PUK forces

Kok Usman - PUK CDR collocated with ODA 084

Kok Abizaid - PUK CDR collocated with ODA 075

Kok Hewa - PUK CDR collocated with ODA 083

Kok Abdulla - PUK Yellow Prong CDR

Kok Seamond - PUK Red Prong CDR

Mullah Bakhtiar - PUK CDR collocated with ODB 090

INTRODUCTION

There is another type of war, new in its intensity, ancient in its origins—war by guerrillas, subversives, insurgents, assassins. War by ambush instead of combat; by infiltration instead of aggression; seeking victory by eroding and exhausting the enemy instead of engaging him. It requires a wholly new kind of strategy, a wholly new kind of force and therefore a new and different kind of military training.

—PRESIDENT JOHN F. KENNEDY, 1962

NO ONE KNOWS THIS STORY—AT LEAST NOT THE WHOLE STORY.

Not the military commands, not the military historians, not even the Special Forces soldiers who were a part of the events. In the spring of 2003, the 10th Special Forces Group tied down 60 percent of the Iraqi Army north of Baghdad while US and coalition forces attacked from the south. That may sound like an exaggeration, but it's true. I wish I could tell you the reason this story is unknown is because it was conducted under the utmost secrecy and only recently declassified, but that's not the case. Although it was a highly sensitive and classified operation at the time of its execution, the real reason is more due to the fact that it was conducted out of sight of the larger campaign and in the most remote regions of Iraq.

When the operation abruptly came to an end, the majority of the participants quickly moved on to other assignments, so even the 10th Special Forces Group itself had piecemeal, secondhand knowledge of what it had just done. Regrettably, before the Army could capture the history and reflect on the lessons and implications, it was forced to contend with a rapidly devolving situation in Iraq and Afghanistan that was compounded by an apparent lack of counterinsurgency doctrine and training among the force.

In 2002, I was the Operations Officer (or S-3) for 3rd Battalion, 10th Special Forces Group. I was a major and it was my second assignment with the Group. That spring was when I first learned of the plan to invade Iraq and remove Saddam Hussein from power. As the S-3, I was responsible for developing a viable plan for special operations in support of the pending invasion and oversee its execution. The concept seemed simple: enable the existing Kurdish resistance to fight against the Iraqi regime and military, creating a second front that would tie up Iraqi combat forces. The reality was not so simple.

First, the two main Kurdish groups, the Kurdish Democratic Party (KDP), and the Patriotic Union of Kurdistan (PUK) were in a fragile state of ceasefire from their recent internal civil war. The KDP had to contend with periodic cross-border violent incursions from the Turkish military in pursuit of their own Turkish-based Kurdish insurgents from the Kurdistan Workers' Party (PKK). The PUK, whose territory was below the Northern No-Fly Zone, established after the 1991 Gulf War, was consumed by a radical Islamist group that had taken refuge in their territory along the mountainous border with Iran. On top of all of this we faced additional challenges with an Iraqi regime with vast experience in crushing resistances, a Turkish ally wavering in its support due to fears of Kurdish nationalism, and Kurdish factions still leery from the unfulfilled promises by the US government that led to unsuccessful and costly uprisings in 1991 and 1996. We needed to contend with all these competing factors prior to enabling any effective resistance.

Additionally, developing and integrating our plan with the US conventional military forces presented its own challenges. Within the Department of Defense, enabling resistance movements or insurgencies in support of US objectives is referred to as unconventional warfare, or UW. While Army Special Forces was created in 1952 specifically for UW, the opportunities to conduct it have been rare, particularly since the end of the Cold War. This dynamic has at times placed Special Forces, who claim their *raison d'être* to be UW, in an awkward position.

In the 1990s, it was not uncommon to see other types of special operations miscategorized as UW or to hear it described in overly generic terms—almost as a more of a mindset or some nebulous form of warfare, whose secrets were known only to the Special Forces community. As a result, a clear and common understanding of the topic within the broader military and special operations community, specifically regarding capabilities, limitations, and prerequisite conditions, has often been lacking.

Lastly—if the task at hand weren't already complicated enough—the entire operation also needed to occur quickly enough to still be of value to the US military attack from the south—the exact date of which remained a closely guarded secret, known only to a handful of senior commanders and planners at the highest levels of command.

I can say from my own experience that when senior planners and decision-makers are faced with executing large-scale combat operations, their willingness and capacity for conceiving, and incorporating unfamiliar niche special operations against competing conventional ground, air, and sea campaigns is minimal. This is the story of a rare occurrence when the conditions aligned to make UW a desirable and viable option for the Department of Defense, meaning we were suddenly expected to put theory into practice. It would have been easy for the higher commands to discount this operation as unfeasible or too risky; and, in fact, there were numerous times when circumstances seemed to suggest the same.

It was our challenge to put theory into practice and transform potential resistance into reality. However, prior to enabling any effective resistance, we needed to navigate and contend with all these competing factors.

Looking back on my career as a Special Forces officer, I am indebted to the men who came before me and took the time to document their experiences. Their stories inspired me and provided me the benefit of their hard-learned lessons. I regard these men as my mentors, many of whom were veterans of the Office of Strategic Services, Special Forces, and the Central Intelligence Agency. I am indebted to many: Frank Lindsay, Roger Hilsman, COL (Ret.) Aaron Bank, COL (Ret.) Wendell Fertig, BG (Ret.) Russell Volckmann, Sir Robert Thompson, Bernard Fall, William Colby, T.E. Lawrence, LTC (Ret.) Charles Simpson, COL

(Ret.) Ben Malcomb, COL (Ret.) Francis J. Kelly, MAJ (Ret.) John Plaster, and COL (Ret.) Al Paddock, to name a few. It's my hope that this story will contribute to their collective wisdom. I aim to provide some context to the history of the Iraq war and the role of Special Forces and continue the tradition of passing on our hard-earned lessons to the next generation.

To fully comprehend the lessons of this operation, we first need to appreciate the complexity of the situation that planted the seeds for this conflict and placed the United States on a trajectory for war with Iraq.

CHAPTER 1
THE ROAD TO WAR

The Kurds have no friends but the mountains.

—KURDISH PROVERB

ZAKHO, IRAQ, AUGUST 1996

"Prepare for imminent evacuation."

The message surprised US Army Captain Pat Roberson, a tall, fit, calm officer with a dry sense of humor. He was in Iraq, serving as the Special Forces Detachment Commander of Operational Detachment Alpha (ODA) 076. CPT Roberson compared the message he received to the reaction of his local Kurdish contingent, who didn't seem overly concerned about the Iraqi military. Unfortunately, the message from his higher command wasn't asking for his opinions or insights; it was an order. The instructions were clear: leave the majority of the computers and office equipment behind to maintain an appearance that US forces might return. This pretense was done to avoid creating a panic among the Kurds and any perception that they were being abandoned. Nonetheless, the Kurds understood exactly what was happening. Many of the Kurds pleaded with Roberson, in many cases with tears in their eyes, to stay—or at least not leave them behind.

* * *

NORTHERN IRAQ

The environment of Northern Iraq circa the 1990s was complex, to say the least. In August of 1990, Iraqi dictator Saddam Hussein shocked the world when he invaded Kuwait. Seven months later, a coalition led by the United States liberated Kuwait. During the war, commonly referred to as Desert Storm, Iraq suffered one of the most devastating defeats in modern history. Some estimates calculate that the Iraq military lost roughly 40–60 percent of its overall forces during the conflict. As a result, the combined Kurdish and Shia populations in Iraq, which accounted for roughly 60 percent of the overall population, saw this as an opportunity to rise up against a weakened Iraqi regime.

Like gasoline on a fire, President George H.W. Bush exacerbated the situation when he made several statements suggesting that the people of Iraq should take matters into their own hands and remove Saddam from power. The US broadcast this message a few days before the war ended and again the day after the formal ceasefire on February 28, 1991. It's not hard to imagine how the population might have misinterpreted Bush's message as a sign of pending US support.

In the days immediately following the ceasefire, various Kurdish and Shia groups started to challenge the existing Iraqi security forces. In the south, numerous soldiers returning from Kuwait defected and joined the uprising. These rebellions came to be known as the Iraqi *Intifada*, from the Arabic word for "uprising" or "shaking off." At its height, the Intifada gained control of 14 of Iraq's 18 provinces.

However, the initial success was short-lived. In a characteristically deceptive and defiant move, the Iraqi military requested permission from the coalition to use Iraqi helicopters in early March 1991, to transport government officials into the ethnic enclaves, since so many bridges and roads in southern Iraq had been destroyed or damaged during the air campaign. Although this usage was prohibited in the ceasefire agreement, General Schwarzkopf, the coalition commander, approved the request. The Iraqi military immediately put their available helicopters to use, bombing and strafing crowds of protestors and convoys of refugees fleeing toward the neighboring borders. Soon after, Saddam's elite Republican Guard units that survived the onslaught in Kuwait were able to regroup in southern Iraq.

Within a few weeks of the start of the Intifada, Saddam demonstrated his regime's experience at crushing resistance. He quickly recaptured most of his provinces and reestablished control.

THE IRAQI KURDISH PEOPLE'S STRUGGLE

The Kurds were all too familiar with Saddam's capacity for brutality. In 1988, the last year of the Iran-Iraq war, Saddam initiated what was known as the *Anfal* campaign, a term derived from the Qur'an that translates to "the spoils of war." Saddam intended to use the Anfal campaign to break the Kurdish resistance as well as punish them for their support and assistance to Iran during the war. During the campaign, hundreds of Kurdish settlements were literally erased off the map. He attacked dozens of villages with chemical agents. He lured military-aged males with false promises of amnesty, then executed them en masse. He placed women and children who were not killed in the attacks in detention camps. During the campaign, the Iraqi military deliberately blocked the main highway to the Turkish border to prevent the population from escaping. While it's difficult to confirm the number of Kurds killed in the campaign, conservative estimates place the number between 50,000 and 100,000 people.

In 1991, the Iraqi forces were able to push the Kurds back from the major cities of Kirkuk and Mosul, but were unable to control areas where the terrain transitions into foothills and mountains—more specifically, the cities of Dahuk and Erbil. This time, the Kurdish guerrillas, referred to as Peshmerga, fought a series of brutal battles with Iraqi forces to prevent a repeat of the 1988 campaign that prevented refugees from escaping to the safety of the mountains and eventually to Iran and Turkey.

Ad hoc camps housing tens of thousands of Kurdish refugees rapidly appeared along the Iraqi border. The fleeing refugees in the camps had no means to sustain themselves and nowhere to go. Soon, hundreds of Kurds started dying each day from malnutrition, exposure, and exhaustion. In response to the rapidly worsening humanitarian crisis along the border, the United Nations Security Council adopted Resolution 688, condemning Iraq's political repression of its citizens. However, the remoteness of the area coupled with the potential for additional hostilities with Iraqi forces created a unique challenge for a humanitarian mission. To mitigate some of the risk, the US, Great Britain, and France established the Northern No-Fly Zone under the auspices of Resolution 688. In reality, the No-Fly Zone was created to protect the refugee camps and the humanitarian aid efforts along the Turkish border more than the Kurdish population since it only covered the northern half of the Kurdish region.

Initially, the operation, named Provide Comfort, attempted to address the situation with a minimal commitment. The US Air Force made several humanitarian air drops, only to have the bundles smash apart and scatter supplies across inconsequential locations in the mountains. In the few cases where bundles successfully landed in the vicinity of the camps, mobs of panicked refugees ransacked the supplies. In several tragic instances, refugees attempting to reach the bundles first were inadvertently crushed by the pallets that, despite drifting down by parachutes, still weighed several tons. It quickly became evident that to avert the crisis, the US needed to place ground forces inside Iraqi territory.

While most of the US military's forces reside inside the United States, a small portion are stationed overseas. This enables the five US Geographic Combatant Commands to respond to situations quickly with their assigned organic forces, without relying on the time required for the Pentagon to work through the process of staffing a request to deploy and attach forces to their commands. In this case, European Command (EUCOM) and Special Operations Command Europe (SOCEUR) requested the 10th Special Forces Group be deployed forward as soon as possible to support their plan. Simultaneously, SOCEUR turned to their assigned special operations assets, the 39th Special Operations Wing and the 1st Battalion of the 10th Special Forces Group, both of which were stationed in Germany, and ordered them to immediately deploy to a Forward Staging Base (FSB) located at Incirlik Air Force Base in Turkey.

While the majority of the Group's forces were still in transit or assembling at the FSB, the 1st Battalion started to insert its teams into the refugee camps via MH-53 helicopters from the 39th Special Operations Wing. The mission was somewhat ambiguous: Stop civilians from dying in the camps. Fortunately, Special Forces are accustomed to operating in complex environments and under ambiguous circumstances.

THE ONGOING CRISIS IN NORTHERN IRAQ

The Special Forces teams quickly brought order to the chaos once they were on the ground. They met with the local Kurdish leadership and assessed the situation, then coordinated air drops of food and material for shelters, conducted medical triage, directed and supervised the establishment of field sanitation procedures, and controlled the distribution of supplies. They were comfortable working in small teams, isolated from established military lines of communications. They were also a force that wasn't easily intimidated by Iraqi forces or a Kurdish mob. Subsequently, the Kurdish leadership recognized and respected this attribute.

In October 1991, seven months after the uprising began, the Iraqi military withdrew its forces from much of Northern Iraq. Most of the Kurdish refugees had returned to their homes and the majority of conventional military forces started to redeploy back to Europe or the United States. A small contingent of US, UK, French, and Turkish Special Forces maintained a presence inside the No-Fly Zone. The Kurds were able to declare an autonomous zone and established what would later become known as the demarcation line of Iraqi control, or "the Green Line." The Green Line generally started a few kilometers west of the Harbur Gate crossing point on the Iraqi-Turkish border and continued in a southeasterly direction for approximately 200 kilometers until it intersected the Iranian border. While technically still Iraqi sovereign territory, this delineation enabled the Kurds to establish their own local governments and lucrative system of legal and illicit commerce with Turkey, Iran, and Iraq across the Green Line.

Operation Provide Comfort was considered a success for bringing an end to the crisis in the north. Based on the success of the Northern No-Fly Zone, a similar, much larger no-fly zone was established in the southern part of the country in 1992 for the Shia population. When it was over, the Intifada resulted in an estimated 20,000 Kurds and between 30,000 and 60,000 Shia killed and roughly two million displaced refugees in Turkey, Iran, and Saudi Arabia.

However, before long, Saddam started to demonstrate his defiance to the conditions outlined in the ceasefire agreement, the No-Fly Zones, and various United Nations resolutions and sanctions. At the same time, a series of international events started to create a perception that the US government was either incapable or unwilling to employ its military in an effective manner. Two specific events were at the forefront of this issue: military operations in Somalia in 1993 that resulted in disaster and the deaths of 19 Special Operators and an ignominious withdrawal from the country; and, at home, Islamic terrorists detonated a car bomb at the World Trade Center in New York City.

In April of 1994, two US Air Force F-15 fighter aircraft on patrol in the Northern No-Fly Zone misidentified two American UH-60 Blackhawk helicopters. The helicopters were carrying the outgoing and incoming commanders for the Task Force operating the coordination center at Zakho. In addition to the crews on board, there were two members of 10th Special Forces Group, representatives from UK, French, and Turkish Special Forces, as well as one member of the US State Department and several Kurdish representatives. In a series of procedural mistakes that compounded on each other, the F-15s shot down the two UH-60s, killing all twenty-six people on board.

The situation wasn't improving for the US military. Because of other events taking place elsewhere in the world, namely the Rwandan genocide and the terrorist bombing of the US military barracks at Khobar Towers in Saudi Arabia, American audiences increasingly grew weary of intervention abroad and questioned US military involvement. The US military attempted to navigate this new normal by balancing operational involvement while accepting minimal risk. The new framework looked to address most problems with standoff airpower and no ground troops. While the US military seemed blissfully unaware of the negative long-term effects of this new paradigm, the opportunities it presented were not lost on Saddam Hussein and he increased his defiance.

AN ATTEMPTED COUP AND KURDISH CIVIL WAR

The first weeks of June 1996 saw a failed coup to oust Saddam with the support of the Kurdish Democratic Party (KDP) and its southern neighbor, the Patriotic Union of Kurdistan (PUK). As Saddam had done numerous times before, his security apparatus detected the coup prior to its execution. The Iraqi forces moved quickly. Soon after the initial plan was compromised, the pending Kurdish support from the PUK and KDP was also exposed. The focus now shifted from countering the coup to punishing not only the perpetrators, but also the surrounding populations as a message and warning to future conspirators. Iraqi forces advanced from their static defenses and pushed forward into the controlled Kurdish territory. Saddam was making it clear: even without the benefit of air cover, that he could exercise control over his territory if he chose to do so. The current state of Kurdish "autonomy" decreed by the West over the Kurdish territory was merely an illusion and temporary inconvenience that he had been willing to tolerate—until now.

The KDP were aware that the plan for the coup had been compromised, and they had been in contact with elements of the Iraqi military and reached a mutual "understanding." Subsequently, the majority of the retaliation would be focused farther south against the cities of Erbil and Sulaymaniyah and their rivals, the PUK. Although the US had long-standing contingency plans put in place after the Gulf War in 1992 to reinforce at-risk positions with quick response forces staged in Turkey, the military did not employ those plans. By sunrise on August 25, 1996, CPT Roberson and the American forces were evacuating Iraq.

A week later, on August 31, a force of 3,000 PUK Peshmerga clashed with 30,000 Iraqi soldiers in the battle for Erbil. Eventually, the Iraqi Army overwhelmed the defenders, seized control, and executed 700 prisoners in a field outside the city. After the battle, the Iraqi Army turned control of the city over to the KDP and continued their campaign to drive the PUK from their strongholds. A month later, the Iraqi Army captured Sulaymaniyah. The American mission to provide situational awareness from inside Northern Iraq was over.

Although relations between the KDP and PUK had deteriorated prior to the attempted coup, the two factions were now in an open civil war with each other. Eventually the PUK were able to expel the Iraqi military and the KDP from Sulaymaniyah and the surrounding territory, allegedly with the help of the Islamic Revolutionary Guard

Corps (IRGC) from Iran. In exchange for their support, the PUK allowed the Iranian military to enter their territory to attack elements of the Kurdish Democratic Party of Iran (KDPI), which had taken refuge in the mountainous tri-border area of Turkey, Iraq, and Iran. If the situation were not complicated enough, the Turkish military also conducted incursions through the KDP territory to attack their adversaries, the Kurdish Worker's Party (PKK), who had established sanctuary bases in the same area. The region, now immersed in continuous violence and instability, posed little to no threat to Saddam or his regime's survival.

In September 1998, the United States brokered a formal peace treaty between the KDP and PUK. The two parties agreed to share revenue, share power, deny the use of Northern Iraq to the PKK, and not allow Iraqi troops into the Kurdish region. The peace treaty was part of a broader effort that became the Iraq Liberation Act, which stated that "it is the policy of the United States to support democratic movements within Iraq." The justifications cited in the bill were that Iraq had committed various and significant violations of international law, failed to comply with the obligations to which it had agreed following the Gulf War, and continued to ignore resolutions of the United Nations Security Council.

On December 16, 1998, President Clinton ordered United States Central Command (CENTCOM) to execute Operation Desert Fox, a major four-day bombing campaign. The operation targeted and struck 97 separate sites with 415 cruise missiles and 600 bombs. While the president made a compelling case that the evidence indicated Iraq was circumventing the inspections in order to maintain some remnants of its biological and chemical weapons programs, critics were quick to raise the question of timing, as the strikes coincided with the opening of the president's impeachment hearing related to his alleged sexual misconduct. After the strikes, many in the US government thought any weapons capability that Saddam may have had was now most likely crippled. In any case, the weapons inspectors did not return, and the Special Forces and CIA bases in the north had been abandoned two years earlier during the evacuation in August of 1996. What little fidelity the US may have had regarding the actual situation inside Iraq was significantly degraded. Saddam was slowly breaking away from the control measures enacted after the 1991 Gulf War. This seemed to be a dynamic that all sides involved were starting to accept—until the events of September 11th, 2001.

CHAPTER 2

RUMORS OF WAR

All the revision in the world will not save a bad first draft:
for the architecture of the thing comes, or fails to come, in
the first conception, and revision only affects the detail and
ornament, alas!

—T. E. LAWRENCE

FORT CARSON, COLORADO, JULY 2002

Since the terrorist attacks of September 11th a year earlier, we had all watched the war in Afghanistan develop into a full-scale counter-insurgency. Afghanistan was to be the first in a series of campaigns to destroy the terrorist organization, known as al-Qaeda, in its various safe havens. We knew they had clandestine networks in Yemen, Somalia, the Philippines, Algeria, Georgia, Syria, and the Balkans. As a result of this new focus, the United States was no longer willing to tolerate the commitment of resources required to contain Saddam Hussein while the threat of al-Qaeda loomed around the world.

I had recently relinquished command of B Company, 3rd Battalion, 10th Special Forces Group to MAJ Pat Roberson (previously mentioned and now promoted) and assumed the position of the Battalion Operations Officer, or S-3. One of my first functions as the S-3 was to travel to CENTCOM at MacDill Air Force Base in Tampa, Florida. For several months we had heard bits and pieces about plans for a possible invasion of Iraq. Now, for the first time, I was hearing the actual plan. In theory, the problem of Iraq had to be resolved before the US military could effectively deal with al-Qaeda in Afghanistan and other locations around the world.

The command maintained a standing operational plan for war with Iraq, known as OPLAN 1003v, (pronounced "ten-oh-three-victor").

The plan was essentially a continuation of the Gulf War in Kuwait in 1991. The updated version, code named DELIBERATE START, due to the unrealistic concept of starting with 20 US divisions in theater, was based on the state of things at the end of the war in 1991. The problem was, in 2002, the US military only had a fraction of the force structure that existed in 1991. To make matters worse, Iraq is roughly twenty-five times the size of Kuwait.

Secretary of Defense Donald Rumsfeld became aware of a concept that favored a small ground force supported by air power. The new plan was called RUNNING START. In simplest terms, this was the light and fast version with roughly two divisions of ground troops supported by precision bombing. Eventually, a growing number of planners expressed concerns and the RUNNING START planning effort overcompensated. This led to a third (simultaneous) planning effort, referred to as HYBRID. The final decision was for seven divisions: six would attack from the south and one would come from the north.

THE ENEMY SITUATION

The Iraqi Army consisted of twenty-four divisions and a handful of special brigades. Most were undermanned and ill-equipped with 1980s-era equipment. Of the twenty-four, seven were elite Republican Guard divisions. In addition to these, there were also five Special Republican Guards brigades, the Fedayeen and Quds forces. The Special Republican Guards were responsible for protecting Saddam Hussein and key government sites. The Quds Force functioned much like a national guard, protecting their local areas with an estimated 30,000 members, while the Fedayeen operated like secret police under the direct control of Saddam's oldest son, Uday.

Iraq's army was essentially defending in three distinct groups: seven divisions south of Baghdad, four divisions in and around Baghdad, and thirteen divisions north of Baghdad. Conventional doctrine has long been that attackers should have a 3:1 ratio with defenders. In an urban setting, this ratio can increase to as much as 9:1. This doctrine is based on decades of experience, documenting the forces required to achieve a degree of superiority. Without this, attacks either fail or become costly stalemates. Even if CENTCOM's math was based on attacking the three defensive groups one at a time, their calculations didn't make sense. From my perspective, it became immediately evident that success was going to require preventing Saddam from maneuvering and massing his forces at the time of his choosing.

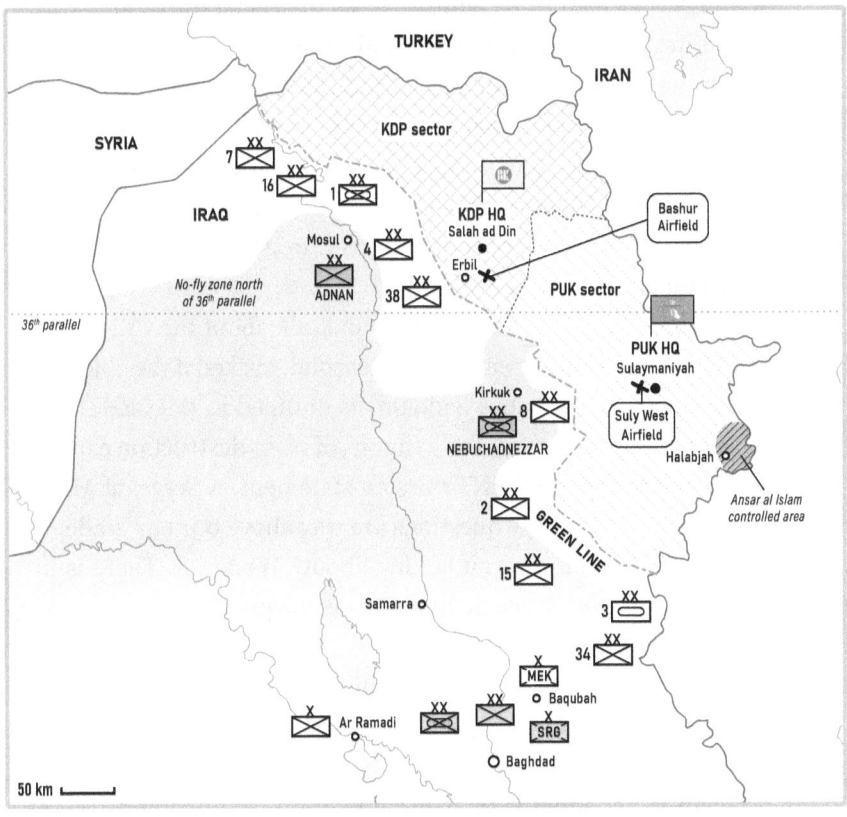

Map 1. The Disposition of Enemy Forces

THE CONCEPT FOR SPECIAL OPERATIONS

Within CENTCOM is Special Operations Command Central (SOC-CENT), which has responsibility for all special operations within the Middle East theater. The SOCCENT staff were the primary planners running the conference, but the planning resembled more of an auction house with people shouting out ideas and unit planners agreeing or declining to accept them:

"Someone needs to seize Haditha dam. Who wants to take this?"

"Someone needs to seize oil platforms off the southern coast. Who wants it?"

SOCCENT seemed to be naming types of special operations without any strategy to it all. There was significant focus on SCUD missile hunting in the western desert. This struck me as odd since the reason for the SCUD-hunting mission in 1991 was to prevent missiles from hitting Israel. Saddam's intent was to trigger an Israeli response which would have caused the Arab portion of the coalition to collapse. His strategy was very sound—in 1991. However, in 2002 this had little to no bearing on the current conflict.

I asked if we could take a step back and talk about the CENTCOM and SOCCENT mission statements for a second. I asked if the objective of the invasion was to remove Saddam, as outlined in the CENTCOM mission statement, or remove the weapons of mass destruction capability, as outlined in the SOCCENT mission statement. A Sergeant Major in the room said, "Sir, those questions are way above our pay grade."

I said, "SGM, what are you talking about? We are it. There is no other room with smarter people in it. This is the plan."

My questions were never resolved.

The SOCCENT planners kept saying our mission was to "conduct unconventional warfare (or UW) with the Kurds." They told 5th Special Forces Group the same thing, but with the Shia in the south. The problem is, "conduct UW" is not a mission as much as a type of special operation. You could see the planners hadn't considered what they wanted these operations to contribute or accomplish. Meanwhile, the CENTCOM planners kept saying we were to "fix" the enemy in the north. While I understood what they meant, I questioned the use of this term, "fix."

"Fix means to forcibly hold an enemy in place," I explained. "You do understand that technically, we can't physically 'fix' the enemy from going south?"

"What do you mean?" the planners asked.

If I'm geographically on the other side of them, northeast of the Green Line, in military terms, I can't fix their forces from going south, if they choose to do so. I was trying to get them to acknowledge that to do what they were asking was more nuanced than "fix," and it would occur from the east side of the Green Line. Both CENTCOM and SOCCENT planners were somewhat dismissive, along the lines of, "Whatever, just go do your special operations or UW, whatever you call it." I understood what they wanted, but I don't think they understood what it would require. While frustrating, I was sympathetic to their situation. The guys were struggling to plan a ground and air war beyond the scope of anything any of us had experienced in our careers.

By the end of the conference, the concept for 10th Special Forces Group was to establish Joint Special Operations Task Force North (JSOTF-N) in Turkey. Two battalions would work with the Kurdish resistance and a third battalion would conduct harassment operations in the western desert between the Euphrates River and the Syrian border. COL Cleveland, the 10th Group Commander, assigned the task of supporting the KDP to his 2nd Battalion and supporting the PUK to his 3rd Battalion. Despite his best efforts to get the 1st Battalion from Germany, they remained under the control of USEUCOM and SOCEUR. As an alternative, US Special Operations Command (USSOCOM) attached the 3rd Battalion, 3rd Special Forces Group to JSOTF-N, ideally to conduct the harassment operations in the western desert. While the exact date of the invasion remained a compartmented secret, we were told to expect to deploy sometime in the next couple of months.

EATING THE ELEPHANT

As soon as I got back to Fort Carson, I sat down with the battalion commander, LTC Ken Tovo, and went over what was discussed at the CENTCOM planning conference. Although we had only known each other for the last year, we had developed a very strong working relationship and rapport. Tovo was a particularly calm, collected, and intelligent officer who was well-liked by the men. As we sat alone in the battalion's conference room, we discussed the situation.

Iraq wasn't our normal area of responsibility, but we had a fair number of guys in the battalion with experience in Northern Iraq from the years supporting operations Provide Comfort and Northern Watch. The Group had also developed a considerable amount of valuable operational experience over the past six years of rotation in Bosnia and two years in Kosovo. Overall, we knew our guys very well and had a high degree of confidence in them.

Regarding the enemy situation, the Iraqi Army wasn't a world-class fighting force, but Saddam compensated for this with his ruthlessness. At any time, if our signature on the ground became obvious, Saddam could target our positions with rockets, artillery, air, or a ground attack and there would be little we could do about it.

Both the KDP and PUK had reasons to distrust us, particularly after the events of 1991 and 1996. Tovo and I knew this was a unique opportunity at a second chance. We had both grown up in the 1990s in 10th Group and were very attuned to the underlying resentment among the guys who served in Northern Iraq previously. This was a chance to correct our history with the Kurds and we intended to make the most of this opportunity. While we understood they wanted to work with us, we were smart enough to realize it was based on their own calculus of the potential risk versus gain. We were also well aware that the two factions still harbored a deep mistrust for each other after the recent civil war, which added an additional level of complexity.

The enormity of what we were talking about wasn't lost on either of us. Air support wouldn't be available before the official start of the conflict, there would be no extraction or medical evacuation, no quick reaction force, no chemical decontamination, and we'd be backed up against the Iranian border. We would be operating inside Iraqi territory well below the protected No-Fly Zone, which was largely defunct at this point anyway. If things went badly, we would largely be on our own.

Nonetheless, I felt like we both had an unusual degree of clarity, coupled with a surprisingly odd calmness. Tovo made an analogy of eating an elephant: "We'll do this one bite at a time."

We agreed the first problem was time. We needed time to plan and prepare as well as time on the ground with the PUK to implement our plan. Unfortunately, in both cases, how much time we had was unknown.

We talked about each Operational Detachment Alpha (ODA) and its strengths and weaknesses. We had three companies (Alpha, Bravo and Charlie), each with five ODAs. On paper, all Special Forces companies had six ODAs. In reality, they only maintained five ODAs each, because the Army—and consequently, Special Forces—were unable to recruit and retain sufficient personnel to maintain the size of the force.

Complicating the situation, we had just deployed Alpha company to Kosovo for a six-month rotation. To mitigate this, we would be receiving a National Guard company from 20th Special Forces Group. While this made the numbers balance better on paper, we didn't know these guys, their leadership, or their level of readiness or training.

The Special Forces Team or Operational Detachment Alpha (ODA) is the cornerstone unit within Special Forces. It is comprised of twelve men and specifically designed to be self-sufficient and capable of infiltrating and operating in remote locations without the benefit of established lines of supply and communications. Each ODA has two members trained in each military occupational specialty (MOS), which enables the team to function in an austere environment. These specialties are communications, weapons, demolition and engineering, and medical. In addition to these members, the team also has an intelligence sergeant, an operations sergeant who serves as the senior noncommissioned officer (NCO) for the team, a warrant officer who is the deputy commander, and a captain who is the team leader and commander.

TEAM NUMBERS

It's worth explaining team numbers. There are five active-duty Army Special Forces Groups: 1st, 3rd, 5th, 7th, and 10th. Each Group has three battalions (labeled 1st, 2nd, and 3rd) with three companies each (labeled Alpha, Bravo, and Charlie). Each company has six teams, also called Operational Detachment Alphas or ODAs (pronounced "oh-dee-ays"). In 2001, Army Special Forces units were denoted by a three-digit number. The first number was based on the Special Forces Group (with zero denoting 10th Group). The second number denotes the company (1, 2, or 3 for the first battalion, 4, 5, or 6 for the second battalion and 7, 8 or 9 for the third battalion). The third number is the specific team within that company (1 through 6). So, when a Special Forces soldier says, "I was on ODA 083," he is saying he was in 10th Group, in the eighth of nine companies (meaning the second company or Bravo company, in the 3rd Battalion) and the third team (of five) in that company.

This also applies to company and battalion headquarters in Special Forces. Company headquarters are referred to as Operational Detachment Bravos (ODBs) with their corresponding number (e.g., ODB 070, a.k.a. A Company, 3rd Battalion, 10th Special Forces Group) and the Battalion Headquarters is sometimes referred to as the Operational Detachment Charlie or ODC (i.e., ODC 103). The terms ODB and ODC are generally used when those headquarters have tactical responsibilities in addition to their normal command and control functions.

THE NORTHERN IRAQ LIAISON ELEMENT (NILE)

About a week after I got back to Fort Carson in July 2002, we had our first meeting with two representatives from the CIA, Tom and Randy. Their team, the Northern Iraq Liaison Element, had recently revitalized the relationship with the KDP and PUK and intended to reestablish a base of operations in Iraqi Kurdistan. They explained that the KDP had an estimated 30,000 Peshmerga while the PUK was estimated to have 22,000.

Tom explained that both the KDP and PUK absolutely wanted to work with the US. However, the threat posed by a group called Ansar al-Islam was the greater problem for the PUK. Ansar al-Islam was a fanatical violent extremist organization affiliated with al-Qaeda that established themselves in the PUK territory near the town of Halabja, not far from the Iranian border. Ansar al-Islam had come to the attention of the US intelligence community due to their affiliation with al-Qaeda and reports that they were experimenting with chemical and biological weapons. They were estimated to have anywhere from 600–1,000 fighters.

Of the PUK's 22,000 Peshmerga, 10,000 were arrayed near the border with Iran to contain the threat from Ansar al-Islam. Eight thousand Peshmerga were positioned along the northern side of their sector, defending against the KDP. The final 4,000 were positioned along the Green Line protecting against a potential incursion by Saddam Hussein. While Ansar and the Iraqi regime weren't allies, Saddam did keep tabs on them through one of his intelligence officers embedded with the Ansar forces. Keeping the PUK more concerned about their border region with Iran and their northern border with the KDP was exactly the situation Saddam wanted to preserve.

The CIA was interested in having some of our guys augment their CIA team in Iraq. Coincidently, in the days immediately following the attacks of September 11th, 2001, 10th Group had sent a handful of guys with specific skills and experiences to augment the CIA's paramilitary teams in Afghanistan. It was an easy decision to use some of the same guys since they already had a strong working relationship.

In 2002, 10th Special Forces Group had two six-man teams, designated as pilot teams. These ODAs (066 for 2nd Battalion and 076 for 3rd Battalion) were specifically selected and trained to infiltrate an environment, confirm the situation, and set conditions for the follow-on forces. The team's leader for ODA 076 was Chief Warrant Officer (CW3) Andy Gronlund. Andy was an incredibly experienced and proficient Green Beret, known for his sense of humor and seemingly carefree demeanor. Tovo and I both had a strong relationship with Andy and about half of his team from our time in the 1st Battalion in Stuttgart several years earlier.

Within a month, the first members of the pilot team infiltrated Northern Iraq and linked up with the NILE team already on the ground.

WE'VE GOT 60 DAYS

We had only received a short, half-page warning order from the Group headquarters with little to no real details. Everyone was telling us to expect to deploy in thirty to sixty days. In their defense, they hadn't received a plan from SOCCENT, who, in turn, hadn't received a plan from CENTCOM. In my experience, it's not uncommon for units at all levels to wait until they have all the information to develop their plan. Unfortunately, the trickledown effect is that the subordinates receiving the plan don't get the time they need to prepare. Tovo and I agreed that we would not continue the cycle.

We put out our own warning order, giving the teams and companies a heads-up on what was coming in the month ahead. We were going to write our own plan and get the teams into isolation planning as soon as possible. Fortunately, I had an incredibly strong operations section in the headquarters that included CPT Derek Jones, CW3 Jay Klein, SFC Mike Oppedal, CPT Jim Holder and CPT Josh Potter— amazing guys who seemed able to do anything I asked of them. I told them simply that "everyone is telling us we go in a month. Maybe so, but we need to write a battalion order, prepare for isolation planning for the teams, and come up with four to five months of training concepts, just in case we have time. We'll prioritize and work through the list as far as we can until we deploy. Oh yeah, and set up some training for our new National Guard company, (which we renamed D Company), so we can get a sense of their levels of skill and readiness."

We got to work.

CHAPTER 3
THE PLAN STARTS TO COME TOGETHER, KIND OF

If language is not correct, then what is said is not what is meant; if what is said is not what is meant, then what must be done remains undone.

—CONFUCIUS

WHILE WE DILIGENTLY MADE OUR PREPARATIONS IN THE FIRST WEEK OF August, three Kurdish men had made the pilgrimage from Chicago to Fort Carson. When they arrived, they were somehow granted entry to the post and inquired about the location of the 10th Special Forces Group. Someone directed them to the compound on the other side of the berm with the buildings with the bright green roofs. The men made their way to the Group Headquarters and asked for CPT Pat Roberson. It was a coincidence that Pat, now a major, had recently returned to 10th Group. These Kurdish men had all worked for the US forces during Provide Comfort and remembered Pat. A member of the headquarters directed them to the 3rd Battalion headquarters across the parking lot, explaining, "It's the one with the door propped open with the cinder block."

As I knelt on the four-by-eight-foot map marking enemy locations and boundary lines with CW3 Jay Klein, we both paused when we saw the three Middle Eastern–looking men standing in our doorway. One of the men snapped to attention and rendered a British-style salute with his palm facing upwards and said, "Sir! Reporting for duty."

Jay quickly covered the map. "Maybe they didn't see what we are working on," he muttered.

Another one of the men pointed to the map and said, "Ah, Kirkuk, my hometown."

I looked at Jay and calmly said, "I think they saw."

Over the next few months, the battalion was only able to identify and vet a small handful of Kurdish interpreters—fewer than ten in all. Saul and his two compatriots became the first members of that group.

The more time I spent thinking about the situation, the more it solidified my understanding. I felt like I was starting to see Saddam's strategy on the map. My impression was that Saddam intended to allow the south to be taken at a high cost, bloodying the American forces along the way. Then he would counterattack somewhere near or in Baghdad, ideally creating a mass casualty event and a stalemate. He could withdraw to Tikrit if he needed to, but remain in control of a smaller Iraq and call for a ceasefire, while the American population grew impatient and frustrated. It wasn't a bad plan given his options.

The Iraqi defenses in the north were composed of three layers. The first two layers were understrength divisions manned at 50–75 percent and faced east. The third layer was composed of the Nebuchadnezzar Republican Guard Division and the 3rd Armored Division, both at or near full strength. These were the units that Saddam would reposition. Our strategy had to focus on affecting this layer of his defense.

I thought about the debate over the terminology of "fixing the enemy," as CENTCOM kept saying. More accurately, we needed to compel Saddam to keep his forces in the north. We would accomplish this by creating a viable second front. While this might seem like semantics, the distinction becomes more obvious when considering the details of how we might accomplish this task. Compelling or coercing Saddam to keep his forces static in the north would require a wider range of efforts beyond just collocating with the Kurds or even attacking the Green Line, and I wasn't sure CENTCOM, SOCCENT, or even the Group HQs fully understood this distinction.

We needed to threaten something he cared about, and that wasn't the first two layers of his defense. The answer was Kirkuk—not his forces, but, more specifically, the Baba Gurgur oil fields on the north side of the city. This was going to require us to coordinate with the Kurdish underground inside the city for acts of subversion and sabotage in conjunction with the Peshmerga guerrilla attacks. Attacking his forces along the Green Line defenses alone wasn't going to cut it.

This value of this operation also had an expiration date. We would need to transform the PUK from a defensive to an offensive posture and to do this would require destroying Ansar al-Islam first. If that task weren't monumental enough on its own, it would need to be accomplished in time to reposition the PUK forces to the Green Line. If we failed to do this before Saddam repositioned his forces in the south, the purpose of a northern front would have been for nothing. Underpinning all of this was the fact that the date of the invasion—D-day—remained unknown.

ISOLATION PLANNING

The Group maintained a facility for isolation planning: the ISOFAC. Isolation planning is a technique for compartmented planning, developed by the Office of Strategic Services (OSS) during WWII. Tovo and I suspected if we tried to conduct planning in the ISOFAC the teams were going to get inundated with distractions. Instead, we decided to use a satellite training area three hours from Fort Carson called Piñon Canyon. This site had absolutely no facilities other than some dilapidated barracks and a few classrooms. It was perfect.

Each week, we put five ODAs into isolation planning. On Tuesdays, Tovo and I got up at 0400 and drove the three hours to Piñon Canyon. We spent two hours with each team, making sure they understood the mission, his intent and guidance, and then made the drive back to Fort Carson. While these were some brutally long days, we needed to get the teams to a point where they felt comfortable talking to us, asking us questions, and telling us their concerns. I told the teams these briefings weren't auditions. We didn't want them performing for us, we wanted them to talk to us—and they did.

During one of the brief backs, ODA 081's team sergeant, MSG Rich Sanders insisted on briefing the bulk of his team's plan himself. What the briefing lacked in clarity, he made up for in its emotional intensity. It was, to say the least, a confusing mess. Afterwards, several of the team members cornered Tovo and me, trying to convince us not to scrap the team and its mission.

I looked at the concerned NCOs and said, "Guys, I'm not going to sugarcoat this: that sucked." Then I smiled and said, "Thank God we aren't sending you guys to Iraq to conduct briefings." Immediately, I could see their relief. "I told you guys; this isn't an audition. You suck at briefings but you're a great team. It's still your mission."

We repeated this process on Fridays to receive the teams' final plan. The briefs were in no way perfect, but we were all on the same page. These were our teams and we knew them well. If we hadn't been comfortable with them beforehand, we wouldn't have tasked them with the missions to plan.

We did this for three weeks in a row.

PRE-MISSION TRAINING AND REHEARSALS

Our methodology was paying off. In fewer than thirty days, we had gotten all the ODAs through isolation planning and into the pre-mission rehearsal and training phase. We started by addressing things the teams had briefed as part of the plans. During their brief backs, the teams described how they would load their equipment onto non-standard vehicles—in this case, pickup trucks. My operations team had filled numerous containers with the equivalent weight of common items, such as ammunition, ammunition cans, crew-served weapons, mortars, and tripods. If they wanted to take ten ammo cans of .50-caliber ammunition, they loaded up ten boxes that matched the space and weight. Then, they'd load the crew-served weapons and other team gear. What we found was every single team underestimated their weight by 500 to 1,000 pounds. That much extra weight on a truck axle will break it, so the teams adjusted their plans accordingly.

Once they got their vehicles configured, we launched them for a week in the field with a series of specific tasks each day. The terrain around Fort Carson is surprisingly like Iraqi Kurdistan with its vast rolling plains, washout canyons, rocky foothills, and backdrop of mountains. The training included long-range navigation, off-road vehicle recovery, low signature radio communications, close air support training, advanced first aid training, NBC training, a staged media ambush, aerial resupply, and familiarization with mortars, anti-tank weapons, and Soviet weapons. It was a lot of training packed into a short amount of time.

The training was also an opportunity for the ODAs to experiment with their own techniques and procedures. They were always looking for ways to improve. One new piece of gear was the Blue Force Trackers—secure transmitters that depicted your location with an icon on a digital map back in the headquarters. They also had four buttons that could be used to transmit precoordinated signals. Pressing all four buttons sent an emergency distress signal. None of us had ever seen or used these before. They were about the size of a typical hardback novel and used a specific, oddly-shaped military battery. The 18E commo sergeants went to Radio Shack—a now-defunct retail outlet that sold consumer electronics—and bought components to rewire the devices to run off a vehicle's cigarette lighter plugs. They found ham radio operator antennas that were lighter and better than the ones we'd been issued and rigged up makeshift telescoping poles with five-foot sections of PVC pipes to raise them twenty feet in the air.

Almost everyone had purchased a Garmin Etrex handheld GPS, which was a relatively new piece of technology at the time. The Garmin, which could fit in the palm of your hand, was significantly smaller than the Army's GPS, which was about the size of a hardback textbook. After testing them in the field, one of the teams contacted Garmin and they sent us custom software for planning aerial resupplies, surveying drop zones, and converting latitude and longitude into military grids. Watching the teams, I couldn't help but grow more confident as they instinctively innovated and adapted to the situation with ease.

ODA 076, THE PILOT TEAM

In October, one of the pilot team members, a sergeant named J.C. whom I knew well from my time in 1st Battalion years earlier with him, was being exfiltrated because his daughter was scheduled for emergency brain surgery. The emergency provided a unique opportunity to debrief him. We requested permission to meet with him for over a week, only to have our requests denied by the Group HQs. The reason for the denial was that he was officially under the control of CIA.

Finally, a few hours before his departure to return to Iraq, I made the decision to meet with J.C. During our meeting, he asked if I had been reading their reports. I told him I had not seen a single one. I was furious that someone somewhere thought they needed to filter, correct, or sanitize the information I was getting. I was now learning that most of what I had been told by our Group Intelligence section, the S-2, in the previous months had been wrong.

I proceeded to break out a yellow notepad and go through my seemingly endless list of questions. At the end of the meeting, we developed a back channel to start communicating via encrypted iridium phones. This was a game changer for our planning. I started getting very detailed information directly from the team leader, CW3 Andy Gronlund. He explained that over the last few months he had written approximately sixty reports specifically for me. Now, I was getting folders on each PUK commander and their units and a survey of the Sulaymaniyah airfield. I had a clear picture of how negotiations were going with the PUK leadership, what was important to them, and an overview of their concerns. Andy told me he had started writing "For MAJ Grdovic" on the top of his reports, but for whatever reasons they still weren't getting to me.

A few weeks later, I went back to the Group S-2 and asked a series of questions to which I already knew the answers.

"What uniforms do the PUK wear?" I asked. They told me desert fatigues, but the correct answer was the same green battle dress camouflage worn by the US Army.

"Is the airfield in the PUK area serviceable?"

"No, it's cratered," they said. "You shouldn't plan to use it."

Most of the answers I got were flat-out wrong. I stopped wasting my time asking the S-2 for help.

Although the airfield wasn't cratered, the pilot team did determine there was a problem. Saddam began building the runway in 1988 during the Iran-Iraq war, but the war ended, and the runway was never completed. Until the team could test the thickness of the asphalt, they couldn't render a determination. Testing required a special device called a penetrometer. Unfortunately, the penetrometer the team brought with them broke as soon as they tried to use it. The solution was to infiltrate an Air Force special operator—Jack, from the 321st Special Tactics Squadron in England—into the team with a new penetrometer.

"It's going to require several more layers of asphalt," Jack told the team after testing the thickness.

One of the team members turned to the PUK counterpart and asked who laid the original asphalt. He pointed to a small industrial building with a smokestack about three kilometers from the airfield. The team went to work, coordinating with the Kurdish family that owned the asphalt plant to add the required layers. Fortunately, as it was a family operation with a single dump truck and steam rollers, it drew little to no attention.

As we entered the holiday season, it was amazing to look back on what we had accomplished. We had developed and issued a fairly solid plan and all of our detachments completed their own planning and rehearsals. Not only had we integrated our National Guard company but in fact developed a very strong working relationship with them. As the rumored date for deployment kept slipping further to the right, we successfully worked all the way through our list of training events. The pilot team was sending me great information and, although the airfield wasn't functional yet, they were working on it. Overall, everything seemed to be on a good trajectory. Little did I know how quickly that was about to change.

CHAPTER 4
THE PLAN STARTS TO UNRAVEL

The basic assumption in our work is to prepare in the best possible fashion, so that we may stand quietly on the day of judgement, when it comes, in the knowledge that we did everything we could in the time we had.

—LT. COL. YONI NETANYAHU,
Commander of the Entebbe Raid, killed in action, July 4, 1976

ONE AFTERNOON I WAS IN THE BATTALION CLASSROOM DOING SOME training with the Javelin anti-tank and Stinger simulators we had set up for the teams. One of the NCOs came up to me. "Hey, sir," he began. "Is this for real?" He gave a vague nod to the equipment around us. His unspoken question was clear: are we *ever* deploying?

I knew where he was coming from. With as much understanding in my voice as I could muster, I said, "Well, the battalion commander and I are hanging out in the classroom room at 1800 on a Friday. I've got this ridiculous mustache and we're playing with Stinger and Javelin simulators. What do you think?" I didn't wait for a response before answering my own question. "I'd say it's real."

The were a couple of times I gave into peer pressure and shaved off my mustache. I hate having just a mustache. Without fail, as soon as I would shave, we would get called in for another secret briefing.

"I know we told you last month we were leaving," they'd tell us. "This time it's different. I can't say why, but we should be getting alerted this weekend, so stay near a phone." So I'd start growing it back. It's emotionally exhausting to be in that constant state of uncertainty with your left foot ready to go into battle and your right foot still firmly planted at home. Your brain is split between what you think you're about to do next week halfway across the world and all of the important things happening in your personal life too.

Over the past few months, Tovo and I had attended several planning conferences. Sometimes together, other times apart, we traveled to Germany, Turkey, England, Italy, and Qatar. In each case, we would leave our deployment gear and bags in our office and say goodbye to our families, with the reality in the back of our minds that we might not be able to come home before we had to deploy. In each case, we returned home, only to repeat this cycle again a few weeks later. Each trip took an emotional toll.

Back at Fort Carson, it seemed like there was always some odd new requirement. We got the anthrax vaccine, which was a fairly painful series of shots, and a smallpox vaccine, which came with the bonus caveat of no physical contact with your family for a week. We were told to start taking mefloquine for malaria, which causes mood swings and disrupts sleep patterns. Finally, we were told to start taking the anti-nerve agent pills that were still considered experimental and caused massive controversy during the Gulf War. The uncertainty was starting to fray everyone's nerves a bit.

SOME BAD NEWS AND WORSE NEWS

Right before Christmas, we were notified that we would be losing our National Guard company, as their mobilization orders were set to expire in January. It was hard to reconcile that we were likely deploying to war while, in the same meeting, being told we were about to lose one-third of our forces. About the same time, we got the news that Turkey decided that, at least for the time being, they didn't want to interfere with Iraq. Turkey had massive concerns that anything that fueled Kurdish nationalism had potential to bleed over to their own Kurdish population.

Now, Turkey was no longer an option for the forward staging base. Up to this point we had assumed our ally was merely stalling. This was a major blow to the viability of our plan. Over one hundred Land Rovers had been quietly purchased and painstakingly shipped to Diyarbakir, Turkey, along with all of our equipment and ammunition by SOCEUR over the course of the last five months. We had originally thought we were going to infiltrate half of our teams by ground from Turkey and half by air landing at Sulaymaniyah airfield. None of that was viable without Turkey.

THE INCIDENT AT GURDI DROZNA

Around the same time, in Iraq, Ansar forces attacked the Kurds at a PUK outpost on a hilltop known as Gurdi Drozna, not far from the Iranian border. The Kurdish fighters on the position eventually ran out of ammunition and were overrun. In a brutal show of depravity, Ansar fighters mutilated the dead Peshmerga, burning the bodies and cutting off their heads, recording everything for later use as online propaganda.

During an attack by the PUK to retake the hilltop, the Ansar fighters started to repel the Peshmerga assault force. As it happened, two members of the pilot team were up near the hill and found themselves in an advantageous position to spot for the single PUK D-30 artillery piece and direct the fire. Although they were taking fairly accurate fire from the enemy, they remained in place and were able to help the adjust fire onto the enemy. Their efforts essentially saved the battle from turning against the Kurds and enabled the PUK to retake their former position on the hilltop. While the pilot team already had strong rapport with the PUK, this elevated their relationship to a new level of trust and credibility.

FIND A WAY IN

Fortunately, COL Cleveland had grown increasingly concerned by Turkey's stalling in the previous months. At his direction, the Group tasked three ODAs from 2nd Battalion, along with three ODAs from 3rd Battalion (081, 082, 091), to push forward to Germany as an advance force. MAJ Pat Roberson was chosen to command the advance force. The original concept was to pull Kurdish members out of Iraq, come to a third country where we would train them up on M47 Dragons and TOW missiles, and send them back into Iraq. That concept quickly fell apart, but the six teams were still sent forward to Stuttgart, Germany.

From Germany, MAJ Roberson's headquarters and the six ODAs moved to Turkey under the pretenses of a training deployment. The

Turkish forces were openly hostile toward them and put them under what amounted to house arrest. The Turks harassed the teams by insisting they conduct a layout and inventory to inspect all their equipment each day. ODA 082's commander, CPT Tim Fuller, who was coincidentally trained as a Turkish speaker, pushed back about the necessity of the search but also used the interactions to build rapport with the Turkish guards.

As the relationship continued to deteriorate, the Turkish guards somewhat accepted the story that they were there for training but specified that no Special Forces were allowed to go into Iraq under any circumstances. SOCEUR and the Group HQs decided to create an opportunity to cross the border into Iraq, albeit under the pretense of being a short excursion. They used the cover of an American general who needed to travel to just inside the border in Northern Iraq to meet with a Kurdish delegation: an odd but plausible story. Of course, the general would need a security detail and MAJ Roberson and his ODAs would provide it. The Turks didn't stop them.

Although the Turkey/Iraq border looks long on a map, there are only three border crossings, and two of them are essentially dirt roads. That leaves the main checkpoint, Harbur Gate, as the single viable crossing point. When the first of Roberson's teams crossed the border into Iraq, journalists videotaped some of the team members and the networks broadcast the footage of American Special Forces sneaking into Iraq. The Turkish government was furious and increased the level of scrutiny, accounting for every person who crossed the border. MAJ Roberson decided that the group needed to break up and cross as split teams to maintain a lower signature and regroup on the Iraqi side. For whatever reason, the team leader of ODA 091 told Roberson that he was unwilling to split his team, and it was everybody or nobody.

MAJ Roberson was in no mood to debate the merits of his plan and without missing a beat, told the team leader, "Okay. Grab your gear. You and your team can all travel back to Romania. Together."

Over the next twenty-four hours, some of the teams crossed the border in rental cars, while others traveled in a bus escorting the general. When the general returned later that day with a largely empty bus, the Turks blew a gasket. They sealed the border entirely and declared that no one else could cross.

Meanwhile, the three ODAs from 2nd Battalion started heading to their area. The other two teams from 3rd Battalion (ODAs 081 and 082) started to drive to Sulaymaniyah, farther south in the Kurdish sector. Since the highway headed south from the Harbur Gate is very close to the Iraqi front lines—actually in clear view from some spots—the teams agreed to drive farther east into the mountains before heading south. As it was wintertime, the mountains were completely snow-covered. It ended up being a twenty-hour drive from the Turkish border to Sulaymaniyah, often in whiteout conditions on secondary mountain roads with the team members walking in front of the vehicles.

Once the teams linked up with the CIA and pilot team, Roberson tasked the advanced force teams to expand the area assessment efforts started by the two pilot teams. The ODAs met with individual Peshmerga units, surveyed potential targets, and coordinated for the arrival of the follow-on ODAs. The teams purchased what few vehicles they could from the black market. Perhaps most importantly, they brought the $50,000 fee for adding the additional layers of asphalt to the airfield. While not necessarily a deliberate plan, the fact that it was a single-family operation with one truck and a steam roller drew no undue attention to the effort. We stayed completely under the radar.

While the teams did what they could to minimize their profile, word was out that US Special Forces (and CIA) were in the region. The PUK leadership told them that Saddam had a bounty on their heads. When they asked how much, the PUK leaders told them they weren't sure, but the phrase Saddam used was "you will be able to live like a king." The following week, the PUK killed a team of infiltrators attempting to access their compound posing as Peshmerga.

ONE PROBLEM AT A TIME

Meanwhile, back at Fort Carson, my team attacked the issue of integrating Alpha Company to assume the sector and portion of the plan formerly tasked to our recently demobilized National Guard company as quickly as possible. Although Alpha Company had been deployed for the last six months in Kosovo and four months in Uzbekistan previous to that, they got the week of Christmas with their families and then it was straight into isolation planning followed by a compressed rehearsal and pre-mission training block.

The larger problem was Turkey's reversal of their position as part of the coalition. Coincidentally, SOCEUR had just been working with Romania for a theater-wide exercise that was going to happen in a few months. The good news was that Romania agreed that we could use their territory for our Forward Staging Base (FSB). The bad news was the new FSB was going to be in Romania, adding 1,000 miles to our infiltration plans. The even worse news was that none—and I emphasize *none*—of our equipment would be in Romania.

FINALLY DEPLOYING

On Friday, February 28, 2003, we received word that we would be deploying to Constanta, Romania on Monday morning. President George W. Bush made his case on television and forces were assembling in Jordan, Saudi Arabia, and Kuwait. By all appearances, the war was starting with or without a northern front. When we were told we would be headed to Romania, everyone thought the same thing: what do we do from there? Nevertheless, it's closer than Colorado. We accepted solutions in steps. *Let's get closer and we'll figure the rest out from there.*

CHAPTER 5

FORWARD STAGING BASE CONSTANTA

When you have exhausted all possibilities, remember this: you haven't.

—Thomas Edison

I would have welcomed sleep to momentarily escape the impending reality and have a chance to rest and be at peace before facing what lay ahead. But no sleep came that night. I was in bed with my wife next to me. Both of us pretended to sleep, but neither one of us was actually sleeping. My brain just continued to race. Finally, it was time to get up. I felt horrible.

My wife had been doing this for a while and was remarkably supportive. When it was time for me to leave the house, we were both holding back tears—more or less successfully depending on the moment. We both acknowledged the importance of what I was doing. I was racking my brain for something to say to make things better, but what can you possibly say in those moments? I debated making promises I knew I couldn't keep because I had no control over things, but ultimately decided against it. I wanted to say something that would make sense, but the reality was, this was unlike any of my previous deployments. Finally, after what felt like a long time but was only a few minutes, it was time to go. I didn't want to leave, but I accepted it, as did she, and I walked away. It was one of the worst things I've ever had to do.

It wasn't that I didn't want to go to Iraq. I did. I just didn't want to put us through that parting dance and charade.

We all arrived around 0500. It was dark and cold, as you'd expect for an early February morning in Colorado. The high mountain air was crisp as everyone walked into my office. I looked around at my belongings there and wondered if there was anything I should take with me. Of course, there was absolutely nothing I would need, not to mention the fact that I was already packed, but my brain was reminding me that everything I would have for the next however many months was contained in my bag. It was an odd feeling.

I wondered if anyone would be in my office later with a box to collect my things because I was gone. Is my office prepared for someone to come in and clean it out? Because I wouldn't be coming back next week—or maybe not even at all. I hoped my space was clean enough and all the what-ifs crept in my mind as I closed my door behind me. We all walked out toward the parking lot.

As I looked around and made eye contact with the guys, we all mutually understood that we'd all just experienced the same hellish goodbye partings without anyone needing to verbalize it. The most painful part was not the fear of death, or whether I'd be coming back. *It was the pain we might cause our families.* We left it unsaid, but we all knew we'd been in tears an hour ago. That's one of the shared experiences of soldiers that brings you closer together.

I fumbled for something to say and asked LTC Tovo, "How are Suzanne and the boys?" But it was a weird and somewhat ridiculous question, because of course I knew how his wife was. She was the same as my wife: distressed and downhearted that her husband just left their home to go halfway across the world into danger. It was a horrible situation and we didn't need to talk about it. We assessed that everyone was as all right as they could be given the circumstances, and then we flipped the switch to work mode in our brains. We became mechanical and focused on the task at hand. We loaded the gear, got the bags on the bus, and the bus took us to the airfield.

We flew on several flights: somewhere in the US, somewhere in Europe, and finally arriving in Romania. In many ways, our arrival mirrored the experience we had leaving Fort Carson: it was cold and dark, with buses outside the plane. Except this had a completely different feeling. It was cold and remote. It felt like it might as well have been in the Arctic, but at least for our purposes we were closer to our final destination.

We had no idea how we would actually get in country, or even what we were doing next, but we'd taken the first step. While in Romania, a handful of Air Force Joint Terminal Attack Controllers (JTACs) arrived. JTACs are a part of the Air Force special operations community that specialize in controlling aircraft and fire support. They were a welcome addition to the teams. Ultimately, we were able to attach a JTAC to about two-thirds of the ODAs.

We quickly considered our options from Romania. It seemed unlikely that we were going to get into Turkey and have access to our vehicles, so we started to plan for everyone going in by air. Our original plan had been to fly half our team in over a couple of nights while the other half drove across the border. All of the 2nd Battalion teams had prepared to drive in country. Now, instead of seven of my southernmost teams, the entire JSOTF would need to infiltrate by air—assuming Turkey would eventually allow the use of their airspace.

WE NEED TO PROVE WE ARE STILL COMMITTED

Not long after our arrival, we learned that MAJ Roberson had made it in country with five of his six advance force teams. The reports we were getting from our pilot team and Roberson's element both indicated that the KDP and PUK were starting to question if we would be able to fulfill our promises. The JSOTF commander, COL Charles Cleveland, wanted to do something to demonstrate our commitment. He decided to infiltrate the two battalion commanders and two operations officers—including me—in that night.

COL Cleveland was an exceptional officer. Truth be told, his leadership style was not unlike that of John Wayne's character, Colonel Kirby, in the iconic movie *The Green Berets*. He served in 10th Group as a lieutenant at the heart of the Cold War, and as a captain and a major with 7th Special Forces Group in Central and South America in the 1980s. He returned to 10th Special Forces Group in the 1990s as a battalion commander and Group XO before assuming command of the Group in 2001.

He was the son of an Army NCO and grew up living in multiple overseas locations. As a result, he spoke excellent Spanish, passable

German, and some Russian. He always sought out and valued the perspectives of the NCOs, and his soldiers respected him for that quality. He was what the Special Forces community referred to as "old school."

LTC Tovo and I immediately started planning what we needed to do in the next few hours. We had discussed this possibility months earlier based on some events in the first months of the Afghanistan campaign. We deliberately planned and prepared for a small team from the battalion to function tactically as an Operational Detachment Charlie. Although only two of us going forward wasn't what we had envisioned, the idea was still the same. We were not going to take over the teams. LTC Tovo was still going to exercise command and control over the SOTF, albeit with a slightly lighter team than we anticipated, but he was primarily infiltrating into Iraq to be the US counterpart advising and coordinating with the PUK leadership.

I needed to gather my equipment. My first stop was the J-6, the communications office. I went to the base station, where they maintained communications. I quickly noticed that all the radios were stacked in one corner of the room while all the guys were on the completely opposite side building miscellaneous furniture like nightstands and weightlifting benches.

I asked if they could hear the radios on the other side and they all assured me they could, but I seriously doubted it. I asked about getting the radios I needed, and they decided to send me in with two satellite phones. As soon as they issued them to me, I asked for the phone numbers to the JSOTF so I could use them for their actual purpose of communicating. The young communications NCO told me that they plug the radios into the telephones, but they don't know what the actual numbers are.

I couldn't believe what I was hearing and started arguing with the J-6, telling them I was leaving in a few hours and I needed these numbers. The JSOTF J-3 heard the argument and came over to see what was going on. I explained that I was issued the satellite phones but no one seemed to know the phone numbers.

"That's bullshit," he said. I agreed. It *was* bullshit. Except I misunderstood him. I thought he meant it was bullshit that they didn't have the numbers and couldn't help me. That wasn't what he meant. Rather, he thought what *I* was saying was bullshit.

"You are just trying to make us look bad," he said

"Are you kidding me?" I asked. "Let me get this straight. We are arguing whether or not you actually have a phone number. You think I'm lying to make you look bad, and in fact you have the numbers, but for some unknown reason, you won't just produce them and end this debate. Did I get that right?"

At some point, LTC Tovo came over and pulled me away. I complained that this was ridiculous.

"It is," he agreed. "What would these guys do for us even if we did call them? They don't have capabilities or assets that could support us inside Iraq."

"Fair point," I concluded, and we ended the whole heated exchange by walking out. To add insult to injury, I found out later in country that one of the two phones they gave me had the wrong chip in it. It only worked in Europe, not the Middle East.

I now had in my possession two satellite phones: one that worked where I was heading, and one that would be an expensive paperweight, albeit with sensitive crypto and zero phone numbers to use to communicate with my higher headquarters.

My next stop was the J-3 Personnel Recovery cell. I was anticipating collecting a pretty large amount of cash and perhaps some gold coins, since they work as currency anywhere in the world. Both items are common for an infiltration like this. When I arrived, I was told the money guy was working out and they didn't know where he was.

Great. I also needed special instructions (SPINS). SPINS are part of communications procedures and every theater has a unique book of special instructions and code words and numbers specific to the date you infiltrate. They are a contingency for communication during an evasion event. Just as had happened in the J-6 shop, a debate arose. This time, it was less heated, but they couldn't figure out if they were supposed to give me SPINS for EUCOM (specific to Romania) or CENT-COM (specific to Iraq). They gave me an answer and I wrote down and memorized my SPINS. It turned out they were wrong. I didn't find out until a few weeks later, when I called from Iraq to confirm the SPINS, that the previously issued ones were incorrect.

The J-3 shop apparently wasn't done with their mishaps, however. Personnel infiltrating into denied territory would normally get issued what are called blood chits. Basically, it's a waterproof document written in several languages local to the region. It explains that you request assistance in exchange for a reward. I asked for mine from the senior warrant officer.

"We haven't gotten any guidance on who to give those to yet," he replied. "We only have five hundred."

"I hear you," I replied. "But I'm leaving for Iraq in a few hours. I think I'm on that list."

But he was adamant that he could not give me a blood chit. He absolutely refused. Finally, I conceded the blood chit. Thankfully, eight months prior, I was at a bazaar in Incirlik, Turkey, and I bought two fake novelty blood chits. Those were what Tovo and I carried into Iraq in place of actual blood chits.

Novelty blood chit that I carried (left) and an actual blood chit with a serial number (right).

Next, I needed evasion maps. These are typically large-scale maps that cover, for example, all of Northern Iraq. In 2003 the maps now had military grid lines on them, which made them a lot more valuable. The grids made it far easier to communicate because you could more precisely reference your location.

Wouldn't you know it—they insisted that they didn't have any, apologized, and said they were all going to dinner. I knew these guys, I had known them for years, and I needed those maps. When they left, I decided to go through their bags. Sure enough, I found two copies of the evasion maps that people were keeping as souvenirs. I now had two encrypted satellite phones (but no numbers to call), no money, two Turkish bazaar blood chits, and some stolen evasion maps.

LTC Tovo and I met up. We were discussing everything we had and what we were taking in country.

"Are you taking a rucksack?" LTC Tovo asked.

"Nope," I answered quickly.

"You're not taking a rucksack?" He sounded a little incredulous.

"Sir, there is no scenario where I will have a rucksack on my back. I'm taking a small backpack for inside of a vehicle in case we have to run, but I will never be running with a full-sized military rucksack."

He agreed with my logic and we both packed civilian-looking kit bags with our equipment.

"Did you hear the J-3 guys say we shouldn't take uniforms, dog tags, or ID cards?" he asked next.

"That's insane," I countered. "That's the stupidest advice I've ever heard. There's a point in this conflict we are going to want a uniform on."

He agreed.

The plane was waiting for us. I rushed into the arms room. I could see my rifle standing out among all the others as soon as I walked in. I had spray painted it with a camouflage pattern several months prior at Fort Carson. At the time this was not a commonly accepted practice. But I knew from experience that in lieu of carrying an AK-47, a spray-painted weapon generated a much lower signature against your body, which would help me stand out less as an American. The young soldier behind the counter handed me a brand-new, clean black gun without my optics or laser pointer on it.

"What's this?"

Without missing a beat, the kid proudly declared, "That's your rifle, sir."

"No, it's not."

"Well, we had to submit serial numbers to the Turks and we didn't know which one was yours. So, we just submitted this one. You're a staff officer, so I didn't think it would make any difference," he offered, as though he were a server who just brought me Coke instead of Pepsi.

After everything I'd been dealing with, and with the stakes at hand, I got pretty mad. The new rifle wasn't even zeroed with its iron sights. I calmly said, "Hey, do you see that tan and green spray-painted rifle right there? Can I see it for a second?"

He complied. Both rifles were M4s, which have two pins. When pushed, they separate the upper and lower portion of the rifle. The lower half is the part with the serial number on it. I proceeded to break both rifles in half as the plane roared its engines to life outside. I matched the old, spray-painted upper receiver with all of my optics and laser pointer on it and matched it to the new lower half with the serial number known to the Turks.

The kid was freaking out, looking at me in disbelief. "Sir! You can't do that! You're going to get in trouble!"

I locked my eyes with his and deliberately retorted, "I think I'll be okay." I turned to CPT Derek Jones and said "Hey, when you come in country, if I'm still alive, bring the other half of my rifle."

I met LTC Tovo back out on the tarmac along with the 2nd Battalion commander and his operations officer. We all boarded and flew to Incirlik, Turkey. As soon as we landed, we deplaned and the aircraft practically vanished behind us. The four of us stood on the runway in the middle of the airfield with no one around. We had no idea what the plan was or what we were supposed to do.

Finally, we saw a golf cart coming at us with flashing red and blue lights. In the cart were a Turkish private and an American Air Force private, who looked at all of us like we were aliens, wondering where on Earth we'd come from. The four of us stood there awkwardly. "Uhhhh," we stammered, not knowing the protocol for this scenario.

"Get in and we'll take you to the customs shack," they offered.

We all cursed under our collective breaths, asking "Okay, now what? What the hell are we supposed to do?"

Someone shot back with, "I don't know!"

When we arrived, a Turkish official asked for our passports. The Turkish officials were scanning our passports and we were looking around, independently wondering if we were going to end up in a Turkish prison.

Suddenly, a guy nearby called out, "Hey, Ken," as though he knew us. We both assumed he was with the CIA. We called the guy over and explained the situation, and he told us to step out of line and go with him.

It sounded like a good proposition, except the Turkish officials had our passports on the scanner. Our new best friend authoritatively walked into the booth and grabbed the passports. The Turkish private was noticeably agitated as he called for his supervisor, and we quickly walked out of the building. Now we were certain we were going to jail. Surely, they would make an example of us, throw us in prison, and put our pictures on TV.

Thankfully, that didn't happen. We were officially on Incirlik Air Base in Turkey and they took us to get a quick meal. They explained they would put us in a billet room for a few hours and then drive us to the Turkey–Iraq border. After our meal, I had a piece of chocolate cake that I didn't finish. Tovo, usually the straight man counterpart to my funny man, leaned in and deadpanned, "You're going to regret not finishing that cake when we're in an Iraqi prison next week." His dark humor struck me, but I had to agree.

We were set up in a room with one twin bed to rest. LTC Tovo and I lay back to back, feigning sleep for three hours, until it was time to get up and into the vans for our twelve-hour drive to the Iraqi border. I'm not sure what I expected, but it wasn't this. As we got in the van, our new friends offered us peanut butter and jelly sandwiches and Cokes in a Styrofoam cooler.

At some point before we reached the border, one of them asked if we could take some stuff into the country for him. I wasn't really in a position to say no, so I agreed. He reached down on the floor and pulled up an entire duffel bag of cell phones and satellite phones. He casually said, "Here, just take this."

I eyed him questioningly. "Are you freakin' kidding me? You're so going to get me thrown in Turkish prison."

"No," he assured me. "We have an agreement with the Turks. They won't search your personal bags, so just put all this stuff in your bag," he explained. "Put them in a shoe and then put a sock in front of it," he offered.

"Come on, man," I protested. "Where's the shaving cream canister with the false bottom?" Smiling, he handed me a bag of thirty phones, which I reluctantly added to my bag.

We finally reached Harbur Gate, the border crossing into Iraq, which looks like any tollbooth in the States. Once you get past it, you can see the bridge that crosses the Khabur River that divides Turkey and Iraq. No sooner did we get to the checkpoint than my concerns were validated. The Turkish border agents immediately started demanding to go through our bags rather than our vehicles. We exchanged some heated discussion with them, demanding to know what they were doing. Things were not going well. The border agents started going through the bags, and they were conducting a thorough search.

As the heated inspection continued, I noticed some of the guys from the pilot team from 2nd Battalion were in their car on the bridge past the checkpoint on the Iraqi side of the border. They casually walked over and started talking to us. I told them I didn't think our plan was going to work. I saw one of two things happening:

1. The border agents were going to arrest us and confiscate all of our equipment, or
2. They would confiscate all of our equipment and send us back to Incirlik.

Since both options involved our equipment getting confiscated, I decided I wasn't going to let them take my encrypted radio and phone or my pistol. I went into my bag, removed the phone, radios, and my pistol, and tucked my pistol under my shirt. LTC Tovo and our two other traveling companions saw what I was doing and followed my lead. Then it dawned on us that if we were taking stuff out of our bags and the agents weren't even noticing, we could potentially just take our bags and walk across the border. We figured they wouldn't chase us, so we told the pilot team guys to bring the car closer. We planned to just throw the bags in the car and take off.

To help us out, our escorts started to deliberately argue with the Turks, drawing a lot of attention. We executed our plan brilliantly, tossing our stuff in the car and quickly departing. After the fact, someone informed me that when the Turks noticed we were missing, they asked, "Where are the other four guys?"

To which our escorts casually responded, "What four guys?" Our infil caused quite an explosion in Turkey, and we joked that our faces would be on Turkish milk cartons as the missing Americans, but we made it inside Iraq.

From the border, it was about a three-hour drive to Salah al Din, a fortress near the city of Erbil, where the pilot team and the CIA were set up for the 2nd Battalion in the KDP sector. While we were driving, the 2nd Battalion commander was complaining that his pilot team leader had not been communicating with him enough and he intended to crush him as soon as we arrived. I happened to know the team leader from my time in Stuttgart when he was an NCO, and I considered him a friend.

Intending to help him and head off any conflict, I pulled aside one of the pilot team NCOs—who was riding in a different vehicle—and explained the situation, relaying that his battalion commander planned to make an example of his team leader as soon as he saw him. That NCO was able to clandestinely relay the message to his captain, who was there to meet us at our arrival. The first words out of his mouth were an immediate apology to the lieutenant colonel for being out of contact. The whole situation was immediately defused.

A VERY AWKWARD GAME OF TELEPHONE

While we were driving, LTC Tovo suggested we send up an ANGUS report—the code name for an entry report to let your higher headquarters know you made it in country safely. An ANGUS report is one of those unconventional warfare skills we don't often utilize because we don't frequently operate in enemy territory.

"Sure, I'd love to send up an ANGUS report, sir. How do you suggest I do that?" I joked, reminding him that we had no phone numbers thanks to our unhelpful interactions with the J-6 back in Turkey.

LTC Tovo thought for a minute. "Why don't you call Fort Carson and see if they can hook flash [transfer] us to the 10th Group at Carson?"

I agreed to give it a try. I knew I had to be very careful about not revealing sensitive information, so, I called the Fort Carson general operator and asked him to transfer us to 10th Group, which he did with no issue.

"I think this is actually working," I told LTC Tovo as I waited for someone to pick up the line. I recognized the voice of the guy who answered. "Hey, don't say anything, just listen to me for a sec. It's Mark." I knew he would know who I was. I proceeded, "I need you to try to hook flash me to the guys in Romania."

"We don't know those numbers, sir. We don't have that information," he replied.

Dammit! I thought.

"But," he continued, "I can push you to the guys in Stuttgart if that would help."

I agreed it was worth a shot and he connected me. When the duty NCO answered the phone, I started the same way.

"Please listen and don't say anything. It's Mark. I need you to connect me to Cleveland," I said clearly, meaning COL Cleveland in Romania at the JSOTF. "Can you do that?" I asked.

"Sure, sir. Stand by."

As it turned out, this was another NCO that I had served with during my time in Germany and we knew each other. I was glad he could transfer me, but I started to doubt this would work at all. I had been on the phone for probably fifteen minutes at that point. Further, I was getting increasingly agitated at the fact that we hadn't generated a five-digit code name for LTC Tovo or myself, which should have been standard procedure in a mission. Now I was trying to navigate an open, unclassified phone line and communicate sensitive information without giving myself away since I couldn't call the JSOTF directly either. To make matters worse, the young kid who picked up the phone in Romania couldn't hear me because there were a myriad of background noises, ranging from what sounded like a power saw to frat-party levels of dance music, accompanied by people shouting to be heard over the noises.

Obviously, the kid couldn't hear me at all. I kept asking to speak to Cleveland, but he finally conveyed he wasn't there. "Can I leave a message?" I asked.

"Sure," he half-shouted.

"Tell him Grdovic and Tovo made it in country."

"Say that again?"

I repeated myself several times, increasingly loudly, so he could hear. Finally, he acknowledged he heard me when he replied. Much to my dismay, I heard him on the other end of the line bellow out, "Sir, I think Grdovic and Tovo are in Iraq." So much for our covert open line communications.

After I hung up, I looked at Tovo and said, "I'm sure the CIA does this the same way." We laughed, hoping the leaked information wouldn't be too detrimental to our mission. We used to sarcastically joke in training that Group was doing a great job of keeping us trained by replicating the enemy in its absence. I thought that certainly seemed to be the case that night.

From Salah al Din, their team had to drive LTC Tovo and me an additional hour to a coordinated crossing point between the KDP and PUK. The crossing point was referred to as The Painted Rocks because for years, people have been painting graffiti on these big rocks to memorialize people who died in the civil war. This location was the Kurdish equivalent to Germany's Checkpoint Charlie crossing in the Berlin Wall.

As our vehicles stopped, Kurdish Peshmerga appeared from the darkness on both sides. I was immediately struck by the contrast of the KDP Peshmerga— wearing relatively standard uniforms with their red berets and red and white scarves around their necks—and the PUK Peshmerga who had a distinctly more guerrilla-like, ragtag appearance. MAJ Roberson stepped up to our vehicle. It was good to see Pat, since we hadn't seen him since December back in Colorado.

Pleasantries aside, Pat explained, "We need to keep this moving. This is not a routine event. The longer we stay here the better the chances that someone is going to start shooting." The tension between the two factions was obvious.

LTC Tovo and I switched cars and got into a vehicle with MAJ Roberson for the three-hour drive to the PUK's headquarters in Sulaymaniyah. It had been approximately forty-eight hours since we departed Romania, and the day was just starting.

CHAPTER 6
CHANGE OF PLANS

In preparing for battle, I have always found that plans are useless, but planning indispensable.

—General Dwight D. Eisenhower

The sun was just rising as we arrived in Sulaymaniyah on March 10, 2003. I was immediately struck by the beauty of the city and the surrounding ring of green mountains with small patches of snow. The dawning of a new day felt symbolic of the opportunity to get our plan back on track. Without missing a beat, the PUK leadership came out to meet us. Jalal Talabani and five of his top Peshmerga commanders arrived to greet us, including his son, Bafel, and his nephew, Lahur, both of whom spoke fluent English with a British accent. In Kurdish, the term of endearment and respect is Kok, pronounced "cock." The term is used in front of a person's name. For example, I was Kok Mark and Tovo was Kok Ken. As you can imagine, when we first learned this back at Fort Carson, we acted with all the professionalism of a bunch of immature high school kids. After a few days of hearing it, though, I didn't even think about it anymore.

Another important gesture among the Kurds is their standard greeting by placing their hand on their heart, similar to the origins of saluting. It's a sign of greeting and respect. By the end of our deployment, we had all been fully indoctrinated to this gesture as second nature. Jalal Talabani went by Ma'am Jalal, which means "uncle" in Kurdish. He was the founder and secretary-general of the PUK, which had broken away from the larger KDP in 1975.

We moved inside and started with the standard tea and pleasantries. About five minutes into the meeting, Ma'am Jalal started talking about Robert Baer, a former CIA case officer, who had recently written a book published in 2002 called *See No Evil*. Jalal was upset that Baer was on TV claiming he didn't have a hand in the 1996 coup attempt against Saddam. As it happened, I had recently read the book prior to arriving in country. It wasn't particularly useful other than that if I hadn't done so I would have had no idea what he was talking about.

Thankfully, Talabani assured us of the promise that lay ahead for our association, saying, "All of that was in the past and this is now. This is a new start. We're fully committed."

LTC Tovo and I were feeling quite optimistic, despite our lack of sleep. LTC Tovo was doing a great job, discussing the direction of our relationship, our objectives, and our perspective on the situation. He was charismatic with a calm demeanor, both of which worked in our favor. He shared the one-bite-at-a-time elephant analogy and explained to Jalal that we were also fully committed and would work through things together.

Prior to the meeting, we had linked up with the two ODAs that were part of the advance force, 081 and 082. I knew both teams quite well from my time in command of B Company. All of a sudden, the team sergeant from 081, MSG Rich Sanders, literally forced open the door to the room. His body armor was half slung over his shoulder as he shouted, "We've got to get the hell out of here! There's Iraqi jets over our position."

None of the Peshmerga flinched. I made eye contact with Tovo and calmly said, "I've got this." I quietly got up and stepped out of the room.

Meanwhile, Sanders, a highly competent and aggressive guy by nature, was adamant. "We gotta go! We've got to go *now*."

"Hey, take it easy," I said, gesturing. "Look at them. None of them are concerned. It's just the way it is."

He pushed back. "We're loading the vehicles. We're getting ready to go." I knew we had to take our cues from the Kurds. They weren't running, so why would we?

"Rich, I hear you," I told him. "But just stay calm." Without waiting for another response, I walked away. Before I returned to the room, I bumped into CPT Tim Fuller and MSG Tim DeNio, the team leader and team sergeant from ODA 082. Both were super calm. As soon as I saw them, I said, "Hey, you guys hear about the planes?"

"Yeah," CPT Fuller affirmed. "I was coming to tell you."

I looked him over and touched his chest. I could tell he was wearing his body armor under his shirt. Clearly, he was concerned, but maintained a completely calm demeanor. I noted the stark distinction of the two personalities of the two teams. Tim agreed with me and said they would keep the vehicles prepared if we needed to go. However, we were not running simply because there were Iraqi aircraft flying over our position. The Kurds looked at us and explained that happens from time to time.

Talabani's son Bafel explained, "They fly over to just see what we are doing."

Fortunately, we didn't have anything outside that would have had an American signature like a Humvee or anything that would indicate something out of the ordinary.

Overall, the meeting went extremely well. Afterwards, Kok Mustafa, the senior PUK commander, proposed we visit the front lines with Ansar in Halabja. Although we were tired, we didn't miss a beat in accepting their invitation. We stepped outside and the teams gave us a quick orientation to the area. They showed us the two emergency rally points: the asphalt factory to the north, and another structure about three kilometers to the south. While we oriented ourselves to our surroundings, some young Peshmerga handed us our Kurdish uniforms. They explained it was safer if we traveled dressed as PUK. We put on the traditional garb—a drab uniform with big baggy pants, a waist sash, and the traditional black and white headscarves.

The headscarves are an important part of the Kurdish culture. Known as a *kaifiya* in Arabic, Kurds call it a *jamani*. Unlike the Arabs, the Kurds wear it more like a turban or around their necks, not like a headscarf. The colors denote your affiliation. PUK's scarf is traditionally black and white, to show alliance to the political party, similar to the Palestinians (e.g., Yasser Arafat). By contrast, the KDP wear red and white jamani to denote their affiliation to the Barzani family, which is more of a monarchy, similar to the Saudis and Jordanians.

Tovo noted that every commander had a mustache, and said, "Call back and tell everyone to start growing mustaches."

I half-smiled. "Ya think?"

Once we had donned our Kurdish uniforms and scarfs, the PUK loaded us into some SUVs for the two-hour trip from Sulaymaniyah to Halabja. Halabja is approximately fourteen kilometers from the Iranian border and is sadly best known as the site of the 1988 chemical attack where Saddam and Chemical Ali (Ali Hassan al-Majid) killed between 3,200 and 5,000 people in retaliation for their support to Kurdish Peshmergas during the Iran-Iraq war.

Upon arriving, the PUK brought us to their headquarters in Halabja—a pretty simple, nondescript one-story building. Once inside, they served us some tea, as is the custom at the start of any meeting, and eventually began discussing the attack on the Ansar positions and the suspected chemical facility at Sargat. The PUK commanders in attendance were the ones who would be leading the attack. These were serious men who earned their positions by surviving decades of fighting and demonstrating their skill in battle as guerrilla fighters and commanders. These men had been fighting various enemies since they were young boys—the Iraqi Army, the Turkish Army, the PKK and KDP Kurdish guerrillas, and now the Islamic extremists in their mountains.

As Tovo took out his map and laid it on the table, the PUK commanders awkwardly looked at him, wondering why half of his map was blank. As hard as it may be to believe, in 2003, the United States did not have map coverage of this part of Iran. The attack that we were talking about went up to the Iranian border, but our maps were literally blank beyond that. The group eagerly listened to what Tovo had to say. It was a challenging discussion given the fact that most of what we had hoped to provide hadn't materialized. We only had a fraction of the Special Forces and air support we expected, and none of the lethal aid or money. Nevertheless, Tovo stayed positive and conveyed our commitment to this fight.

Following the meeting, the PUK commanders asked if we wanted to drive to the front to actually see the Ansar positions. We said, "absolutely," wrapped up our meeting, and headed to the vehicles waiting on us just outside.

We exited the building to the see roughly four hundred Peshmerga milling about in the street. Some were there because they heard Americans were here, while others were waiting to drive the group to the front lines. As we stood outside in the crisp mountain air, a dozen vehicles tried to simultaneously make three-point turns. All of a sudden, there was a loud, strange noise followed by an explosion. *Twang. BOOM!*

To my surprise, my first response was, "Huh. That's weird." I thought a transformer on a telephone pole had blown up. Instead, a 107-millimeter Katyusha rocket fired by the enemy hit a transformer. As the rocket hit, it made the metal twang sound, followed by an explosion.

Before I could fully process everything, a second Katyusha rocket came a second later and struck the side of the building that we just exited, blowing a hole in the wall that decimated the room where we had been standing with that map five minutes prior. The second round woke everybody up and sent them scrambling in every direction, jumping in whatever vehicle they could catch.

The young Peshmerga drivers all had instructions to take us to the front line, specifically the hilltop called Gurdi Drozna, which had been overrun and then retaken in December.

We all jumped in the trucks, screaming, "Go! GO!" The driver, a kid of about seventeen, mashed the gas and sped off. He followed his earlier instructions and did exactly as he had been told, heading toward the front and source of the incoming rounds. He put the engine to the test, driving the pickup truck at top speed with six of us holding on in the open back bed.

In a series of somewhat surreal events, I gripped the side of the truck, which was jinking and slaloming all over the place to avoid the mortar rounds hitting just to our left and right. As we drove, one of the CIA guys introduced himself along with Jack, the previously mentioned American Air Force special operator who brought the penetrometer to assess the airfield. I shouted it was nice to meet them as we barreled along at sixty miles per hour.

We finally got up to the position (alive, thankfully) and the truck jerked to a stop. We all jumped out and the Kurds, ever helpful, said they were going to show us where the enemy was located.

I thanked them and dryly remarked, "I think I got it. I can see where they are."

Gurdi Drozna was a medieval-era man-made hilltop defensive fortification about 200 feet high. The Kurds built it perhaps 600 to 800 years ago to defend the nearby plains from invaders because it gives an advantage of high ground. There was a series of similar mounds that ran north to south. This area of the world had seen Alexander the Great, the Romans, the Persians, and the Mongols—all of whom attacked through this corridor—making these very ancient fighting positions. There's an incredible mountain range to the east about 8,000 feet tall that looks like Rocky Mountain National Park in Colorado. The ridgeline is the Iranian border. Between that mountain range and me was a five-kilometer flat plane. Because of the terrain, we had a pretty good bird's-eye view and could see the enemy as clear as day. The PUK went on to explain all the enemy positions.

I understood and knew exactly what we were dealing with now. When we drove back through town, I was able to see the monument, which is a statue of a dead woman clutching a dead baby based on photographs from the Halabja massacre. Finally, we loaded back up on regular vehicles and drove back to Sulaymaniyah. I was pretty exhausted by this point. It was a long March 11th for me. I finally got some food—though no chocolate cake. It's an interesting dynamic to not know where your next meal is coming from. Even though we were helping them and it was a good relationship, I was very cognizant that we were relying on them to house and feed us. I didn't want to become more of a burden than I had to, and they were great hosts. I finally got some long-awaited sleep that night.

The next day we went to see the Green Line and the Iraqi defenses. This time we drove sixty kilometers west, to a small town called Chamchamal. Contrary to what some may think, the Green Line is not located where it is because that's the limit of historical Kurdish territory. It's there because that's where the defendable terrain for the Iraqi Army ends.

The Iraqi Army can't hold rolling terrain with foothills because guerrillas would take advantage of it to attack them. Therefore, the Green Line exists where the foothills flatten, and that's where these Iraqi static positions are.

We stopped at a small Peshmerga unit defending the ridgeline outside of Sulaymaniyah and got a firsthand look at the state of their equipment and defenses. They were a mix of old men and young boys, all carrying AK-47s, but with minimal ammunition. They had no heavy weapons that could stop an Iraqi mechanized advance other than the narrow chokepoint the ridgeline created for the highway. Despite their shortcomings, their morale was high and it was great to spend time talking and drinking tea with them.

As we continued on into Chamchamal, the Peshmerga took us to see the Iraqi defenses on the west side of the town. As we headed back to Sulaymaniyah, we passed through about twenty kilometers of what looked like a deserted no-man's land. This was an area that once had dozens of small villages, all of which had since been razed during the 1988, 1991, and 1996 incursions by the Iraqi Army. It wasn't lost on me that the local Iraqi Army had experience attacking along this highway into Sulaymaniyah.

LOST IN TRANSLATION

Later that afternoon, back at the PUK headquarters in Sulaymaniyah, we met with representatives of the underground in Kirkuk. They were surprisingly candid, showing us a map of the city depicting their various cells of operatives. We discussed their potential capabilities and ideas for how to incorporate their efforts.

Because of the culture—whether Arab or Kurdish—the Kurds gave us signs that they were concerned about something, but wouldn't come out directly and tell us. They kept saying things like, "We know you don't like the Iraqis, but we just don't understand why you're doing that."

We didn't know what "that" meant though. Obviously, we asked, "What are you talking about?"

But they would dismiss it with, "It's just...we wouldn't do that."

Finally, we pieced together enough information to figure out they were talking about surrendering. As in, "Why are Americans telling the enemy Iraqis to surrender like that?"

CENTCOM had been transmitting a message to tell the Iraqis they should surrender. In typical US fashion, the message was crafted to be professional, bordering on polite. Unfortunately, the translation came across as deliberately effeminate and degrading to them, and basically implied they seemed like the kind of men that might *want to* consider surrendering, given a choice. The Kurds explained that because of Iraqi culture, it was disgraceful that you would phrase surrender language that way to a man. Instead of inviting him to consider, which they viewed as an offhanded insult, you should instead explain to him that he has no options, and they *must* surrender, or they will be killed. A self-respecting man can accept that.

Our language conveyed a message more along the lines of "I think surrender would suit your lifestyle, because that strikes us as the kind of men you are." So the Kurds explained that even if the Iraqis wanted to surrender, we had made it impossible for them to accept it, because it was so disgraceful. We tried to explain that it was a mistake, and the message wasn't intended to be insulting, or for surrender to be disgraceful. The Kurds had a hard time believing that our language and offhanded insult was unintentional; to them, the US was so knowledgeable and powerful that we couldn't possibly make a mistake like that.

We got further insight into the Iraqi mind when the Kurds explained that when Colin Powell made his speech at the UN about giving Saddam one more chance that no one was going to rise up against him at that point. Of course, the Iraqis wanted him gone, so imagine the US is coming in and the men are accordingly preparing to join the fight. They're pulling up the floorboards in their house to access the gun they've been hiding. But then, they heard that Saddam had one more chance. The gun went back under the floorboards.

It terrified them because Saddam had been so notorious for surviving coups and attacks. Suggesting that Saddam had a way out ensured no one would rise up. Remember, Saddam did stand up to the US in the Gulf War, so to hear the United States say diplomacy had one more chance, they figured they would all get slaughtered.

Donald Rumsfeld, then-Secretary of Defense, came on TV and declared that Saddam was done. He indicated that the US was coming for him and he was as good as dead, and so was his family. As crazy as that may sound, that actually resonated with the Iraqis, who gave Rumsfeld a fond nickname and told us they liked him.

We included the feedback in our situation report (SITREP) which went up through the channels. We received a message from Condoleezza Rice the next day telling us how useful the information had been. They also told us that some of the American messaging was telling the Iraqis to bury their equipment. We later learned this was a CENTCOM translation mix-up of the word "bury" when they really meant "abandon."

ACT NOW, TIME IS RUNNING OUT

We developed a plan with the CIA to utilize the underground to facilitate an offer to capitulate. The idea was we were going to pitch the offer to the Iraqi commanders, who would then hopefully call in to coordinate their surrender. We deliberately used the term capitulate rather than surrender. By the international Law of Armed Conflict, if a unit surrenders, they have to be demobilized. We wanted Iraqi units to stay Iraqi units in the future establishment.

It was surprisingly easy to communicate with the Iraqi Army. Every leader in the PUK had multiple contacts in the Iraqi Army. We intended to spread our message through this unofficial network but also more formally through the underground. We wrote a letter targeting multiple Iraqi commanders. The intent was to get some of them to surrender, but also to spread a warning that they should not follow orders to destroy any oil infrastructure or harm the population. The CIA printed the letter for us, with English on one side and Arabic on the other, laminated it, and we sent it on its way into the Iraqi network. This is what it said:

Dear Sir,
The purpose of this communication is to provide you an opportunity to serve your nation in this time of crisis. The moment of liberation of the Iraqi people is at hand. You have an opportunity to participate

in that liberation and help save your nation's resources so that Iraq may once again enjoy the peace and prosperity it deserves. You can be a part of Iraq's future and enjoy personal prosperity with a timely decision now.

I am contacting you because you are a well-respected professional military leader within the Iraqi Army who has the confidence of the officers and the people. The influence you exert over your forces will allow you to determine your future, as well as that of your [Corps/Division/ Brigade]. As the [Corps/Division/Brigade] Commander, you are in a position to protect resources that are vital to Iraq's economic future. I ask that you direct your forces to secure the oil wells and refining facilities and prevent their destruction. Arrest and control the agents of Saddam Hussein who would enact his plan to destroy these facilities and Iraq's future. Maintain order in the city of Kirkuk and safeguard all its Iraqi citizens, whether they are Arab, Kurd, Turkoman, Assyrian, or any other minority group. Continue all these actions until coalition forces link up with you and provide additional guidance.

There are certain actions on your part that will make an arrangement between you and coalition forces unlikely or even impossible. You must not attack the Iraqi Kurds to your north. You must not allow the employment of chemical or biological weapons, and must safeguard these types of weapons within your area.

The time remaining to determine your future is short. In order to prevent the destruction of your forces, I encourage you to decide now to be a part of a democratic and economically powerful Iraq. Once the conflict begins, communications will become more difficult to establish. I would like to open a direct dialogue between you and my personal military representative currently in Northern Iraq. Procedures for establishing contact with him are enclosed with this correspondence.

Unfortunately, we had not anticipated the adaptations Saddam had implemented since his experience in the Gulf War. He made it clear that if anyone surrendered, he would exterminate their entire extended family. He also made it clear that he would severely punish anyone who suspected but had not warned the authorities. While this proved to be a surprisingly effective tactic that did in fact disrupt our efforts, it also triggered a culture of complete fear and paranoia among his officers, which would offer us some additional opportunities to subvert his authority in the weeks ahead.

Perhaps more than ever before, Saddam was losing his grip on the population and the Army.

CHAPTER 7
STILL IN THE FIGHT

A good plan violently executed *now* is better than a perfect
plan next week.

—GENERAL GEORGE S. PATTON

I'LL NEVER FORGET LOOKING THROUGH THE DUSTY SIDE WINDOW OF OUR
black SUV and seeing the Kurdish man standing near the street, holding his daughter in his arms, and watching as tears of relief rolled
down his weathered cheeks.

Our team had continued to refine our understanding of the situation with several more meetings with PUK leadership, underground
representatives, and trips around the sector. While driving through a
small village on our way back from Halabja, we rolled into an intersection, and I was looking out at about a dozen people. I made eye contact
with the older man holding his child. I knew I looked like a member of
the PUK with my mustache and scarf, but I could see he was curious
about our convoy of three vehicles. I was particularly frustrated that
we had not come through with the promises we had made to the PUK,
but now I was getting a firsthand perspective of how desperate the
situation actually was for these people. Only a small portion of our
forces were here, and we hadn't provided the lethal aid or air support
we intended. It felt like fate was unfolding in a way that was setting us
up to let the Kurds down yet again and I couldn't stop it.

I reached into my vest and ripped open a pocket where I kept a
slightly oversized Velcro United States flag. In a seemingly small gesture of solidarity, I pulled it out and pressed it against the windshield.
The small crowd immediately erupted into joyous celebration. The
man with his daughter in his arms covered his mouth with his hand
and emotion overflowed as tears welled up in his eyes. The Kurds had

lived in constant fear under Saddam and now they also had to contend with the extremists along the Iranian border. That moment galvanized my commitment to do whatever I could to accomplish our mission.

It was hard to believe we had only been in country for seventy-two hours. In that time, we had met with the PUK leadership and learned that Saddam knew American special operators were in country and had a bounty on our heads, had Iraqi jets fly over our position, visited the Ansar front and been rocketed and mortared, visited the Green Line and seen Iraqi defenses, and met with the underground to discuss plans for subversion.

Tovo sat down and wrote his Area Assessment. It was a seven-page document that succinctly outlined the situation. We had developed a high degree of fidelity in a short amount of time. Most of our former planning assumptions had been confirmed as correct. Perhaps most importantly, Tovo was able to convey the seriousness of the situation and the likely ramifications of not following through with the PUK.

11 Mar 2003. Summary. The situation in the PUK sector is a complex and dangerous one; however, the PUK is an extremely willing partner. Initial assessments indicate that they possess significant potential to assist U.S. operations. Both in the vicinity of the Green Line and potentially all the way to Baghdad. Much of this potential will be unrealized if the rear area insurgent threat posed by Ansar al Islam is not neutralized early in the campaign. Underground capability in Kirkuk offers the possibility of significantly assisting in achieving U.S. aims of securing oil infrastructure and facilitating the introduction of conventional forces but carry significant risk of Turkish intervention. This risk might be manageable with intensive information operations. To highlight the multi-ethnic "Iraqi" nature of any indigenous operations. With no U.S. oversight, these indigenous activities will most likely occur spontaneously and could possibly spiral out of control, guaranteeing an unwelcome Turkish response.

We were all getting increasingly frustrated as it felt like our plan was evaporating before our eyes. We hadn't come through with forces, lethal aid, funds, or close air support. We did have roughly forty personnel in country, all of whom required housing and food from the PUK. On the morning of March 16th, three of the NCOs from ODA 082 asked if they could go to Halabja to spend time with the PUK. They thought more Peshmerga seeing Americans would be good for everyone's morale. They also wanted to go assess PUK capabilities.

While in Halabja, the NCOs got a firsthand look at the PUK's mortar crews. They were old Soviet 82 mm mortars with Iranian sights hose clamped to the tube. The ammunition was Chinese. Mortar rounds are propelled through the air by what are called "cheese charges." These are small, foam-like donuts made of an explosive propellent. The gunner places the charges around the base of the round that ignites when dropped into the tube. The number of charges is a critical part of the firing calculation. Since the charges were old and dried out, the PUK compensated by squeezing extra charges onto the rounds. Such was the life of guerrillas, improvising and making do with what they had.

The NCOs asked about their procedures and quickly sensed the Peshmerga generally fired some rounds back at the enemy in response to when they are fired upon—a routine that took place once or twice a day without any conclusive results. Of the three Special Forces NCOs, all were 18B weapons experts. One had previously been an 11C (infantry mortarman), one a 13F (Artillery Forward Observer), and the third a former 18B (mortar instructor). They asked if the PUK would mind if they fired at the enemy position clearly visible on the ridgeline in the distance. The Peshmerga explained, "They will shoot back if you fire."

The Green Berets, dressed in Peshmerga uniforms, took control of the mortar. The Peshmerga moved to their bunkers, intrigued by the Americans' apparent boldness or complete naïveté. The first round landed short and to the left. As the crew made the required adjustments, an enemy round landed, also short and to the side. The Special Forces soldiers didn't waver. The crew quickly made some adjustments and fired their second round. Still slightly over and to the side, but closer. A moment later, a second enemy round exploded nearby but just out of effective range. The NCOs, intensely focused, quickly sighted the enemy position, adjusted the tube's angle and prepared the next round. A few seconds later, the crew leader shouted, "Hang it!" directing the gunner to drop the round into the tube. The round impacted onto the enemy position, instantly killing the enemy crew. The Peshmerga erupted from their bunkers, cheering. The position that had harassed them for months was now dead.

THE SHOCK AND AWE CAMPAIGN

On the evening of March 19th, the United States announced the start of the air campaign. Various special operations forces infiltrated into the south and western desert to strike targets and harass Iraqi forces. Several hours later, in the early hours of the 20th, conventional ground forces crossed the border from Kuwait and began the ground offensive in the south. This came to be known as the Shock and Awe campaign. I was at a meeting with the CIA at their house in Quala Chulan, just outside of Sulaymaniyah, when we learned from an international news broadcast on television that the invasion had begun. Although we expected the attack any day, none of us had any advance warning.

Tovo, the CIA team, and I gathered and compared information. After a brief moment of everyone expressing the shock and awe we were feeling, we shook it off and got down to work. I've often been asked what's unique about Special Forces compared to other components of the special operations community. Is it their physical and mental toughness? Is it their specialized training? Those are important aspects, but the distinctly unique characteristic of Special Forces is their ability to think. We approach problems and handle stress differently than others. Special Forces deliberately recruits, selects, and—to a degree—trains guys to be adaptable and not shut down during ambiguous situations. Special Forces also trains guys *not* to modulate their effort based on their own estimation of success. *That's* the differentiator. In the end, it comes down to not letting yourself shut down when things look bad. Because a lot of times the solution to the problem is literally around the corner, but you can't see it—yet.

We all acknowledged the less than ideal circumstances but agreed we were going to do what we could. The JSOTF had unsuccessfully tried to fly the teams in through Turkish airspace but had been turned back the last few nights. Our alternative plan was to use the three ODAs that we had—076, 081, and 082— to maximum effect. We assessed that the best we could do would be to have 076, the CIA, and me focus on the capitulation efforts, 081 to focus on the Halabja mission, and 082 would try to hold the Green Line if the Iraqis chose to attack.

To give an idea of how desperate we were, the CIA guys had a single AT-4 anti-tank rocket, which isn't that big of a deal, but it was the best we had. We traded them some small arms 5.56 ammunition for their AT-4. I handed it to ODA 082 with instructions to defend the Green Line. In typical fashion, they responded, "Okay, boss." Their response was emblematic of the teams. We all knew the situation was bad, but no one complained or felt a need to point out the obvious ridiculousness of the task. They were going to do what they could to the best of their abilities.

FIRST CONTACT WITH THE IRAQI ARMY

ODA 082 moved as far south as possible along the Green Line to a city called Kalar. They had been surveying numerous positions along the Green Line over the previous week, coordinating with the local PUK units for the arrival of the ODAs. From their current position near the Green Line at Kalar, there was no vantage point to see the Iraqi defenses. Using the recently issued new satellite imagery software known as Falcon View, they determined a potential location with better line of sight to the west. The terrain past Kalar transitioned from rolling hills to wide-open flat plains that offered little cover. The ODA, along with their contingent of Peshmerga, drove to the last concealed position and then dismounted to move the last 500 meters.

As they approached the position, three artillery rounds exploded around them. The patrol took cover on the backside of a small berm and called for air support. The area they had crossed into was a deserted no-man's-land and the Iraqis likely fired at anyone who tried to cross. To the team's surprise, now that the air campaign had officially started, an Air Force F-15 was available and responded. As the aircraft came on station, the team struggled to identify the target as the enemy fire continued to close in on their position. CPT Fuller and his JTAC were able to pinpoint the targets and direct the close air support. The F-15 quickly responded, hitting the target on the first pass. The initial blast triggered several secondary explosions, silencing the incoming fire.

SIXTY-FOUR TOMAHAWKS

Soon after the start of the ground campaign, we were notified that sixty-four cruise missiles had been allocated for a strike on Ansar al-Islam. However, we needed to use them on the night of the 21st or risk losing them. Each missile carried a 1,000-pound explosive warhead. We wanted to use them primarily against the enemy's defensive positions. However, we kept submitting lists of targets up the chain of command, but they repeatedly came back with completely different targets. CENTCOM was evidently very focused on the Sargat chemical facility, which Colin Powell had mentioned in his speech to the United Nations. We were more focused on the general defenses across the entire area. The last list we got back from the JSOTF was, again, different than what we requested. When we plotted the new targets, we discovered the PUK headquarters in Halabja had been added.

Looking to avoid a fratricide event, I spoke with the JSOTF. They assured me the correction would be made. As assurance, I asked the for the name or initials of the targeting officer who was coordinating the final list. I wanted proof and accountability that the correction was indeed made. We never got a straight answer, and so we didn't feel confident that PUK headquarters wasn't still part of the strike package. To counteract that possibility, LTC Tovo decided to go to Halabja with two of the NCOs from 081, and stand on the roof of the PUK HQs with his Blue Force Tracker during the strike. He felt about 60 percent confident he wasn't going to get killed by a cruise missile, but we felt it was important for the mission.

March 21st also happened to be LTC Tovo's birthday and very close to the date of the 1988 Halabja massacre (March 16th) so the Kurds did not see it as a coincidence, but rather a positive omen.

We had requested that the Tomahawks hit all sixty-four targets simultaneously or near-simultaneously. We anticipated it would be spectacular and truly put some fear into the Ansar forces and told the Kurds to expect as much. Tovo, the NCOs, and a handful of Kurds stood on the roof, watching the distant ridgeline and began to count down from ten. Tovo got to zero and nothing happened. About a minute later, it sounded like a jet plane flew overhead, and then they heard an explosion distant in the mountains. It took about two hours as they spread the strikes out five to ten minutes apart. In reality, it was completely underwhelming but the PUK were still very excited. It wasn't exactly what we had hoped for or needed, but it was something. More importantly, we were quietly grateful that the PUK headquarters hadn't been struck.

The situation was bad, but we were still in the fight.

CHAPTER 8
THAT IS ONE UGLY BABY

The bravest are surely those who have the clearest vision
of what is before them, glory and danger alike, and yet
notwithstanding, go out to meet it.

— THUCYDIDES

OUR MAIN BODY WAS STILL STUCK IN ROMANIA. THE JSOTF HAD SIX
MC-130 Talon aircraft for their infiltration of the ODAs. The aircraft
were from the 7th Special Operation Squadron (7th SOS), which is
part of the 352nd Special Operations Group (352nd SOG) stationed in
Mildenhall, England. The 352nd is the dedicated Special Operations
air component for Special Operations Command Europe (SOCEUR).
Sometime prior, around February 14th, the 7th SOS started considering
options other than Turkey to infiltrate the force into Iraq. The idea of
considering an infiltration from the west from Jordan was seen as a
somewhat ridiculous option due to the risk. Nevertheless, the crews
and planners started to develop plans to execute. They reviewed the
available intelligence for Iraqi air defense positions, which, not surprisingly, was significant.

After two nights of launching and flying for several hours, only to
be turned away inside Turkish airspace by Turkish F-16s, the JSOTF
sent the western option to SOCCENT and CENTCOM for consider-
ation. This option involved all six planes flying to Jordan and then
infiltrating Iraq across enemy-defended territory. Previously, the plan
of flying from Turkey meant they could go near the Iranian border
and stay in the tip in the mountains where there would be minimal air
defense threats. Now they were actually talking about flying through
the Iraqi air defenses. Upon reviewing the plan, someone commented,
"That is one ugly baby," and the code name for the operation stuck.

GEN Franks, the CENTCOM Commander, would comment after the war that deciding to use Jordan as the western option was one of the toughest decisions he made. Nevertheless, the plan was approved.

By this time, the 7th had two of their planes down for maintenance. As a result, they were augmented with an additional crew and two aircraft from the 15th SOS from Eglin Air Force Base, Florida. Headquarters decided to load the maximum number of ODAs with their equipment and ammunition and fly to Jordan.

On March 21, 2003, the Ugly Baby mission finally got permission to go. Of the six aircraft, three were allocated to 3rd Battalion, and three were allocated to 2nd Battalion with a reduced JSOTF headquarters package accompanying them on one of their aircraft. COL Cleveland intended to establish his JSOTF (forward) in the proximity of the 2nd Battalion's airfield due to its central location. The aircraft arrived in Jordan, took on additional fuel, and made final preparation for the infiltration. In order to determine an accurate weight for the aircraft, the crews had the passengers each step on a scale with their body armor, weapons, ammunition, and radios. The average weight of an individual's gear on their body was roughly fifty pounds. Their rucksacks were weighed separately, averaging around 100 pounds each. As a result, the crews had estimated 270 pounds for each passenger.

The team sergeant for ODA 083 was MSG Jim Donovan. He was a no-nonsense hulk of a man of Scottish descent. As he stepped on the scale, the crew member called off, "350." Several other members of ODA 083 were also well over the estimated weight. The crew members frantically recorded the totals.

"You guys weigh too much," the member told Donovan. Always quick with a comment, Donovan turned to his fellow team sergeant from ODA 085, MSG Eddie Licon, and said, "Hey Eddie, we're gonna use some of the weight from your team, the skinny scuba team." Donovan just laughed in his usual fashion and walked aboard the aircraft. As the only two scuba teams in the battalion, they had a strong rivalry.

The teams loaded the aircraft, which had been stripped on the inside so there was nothing extra. Even the jump seats were removed and the ammo boxes and rucksacks were tied down in the middle of the floor. The guys all linked into either the anchor points or a common nylon cord on the floor.

The plan was for the six aircraft to take off and assume a single file, staggering the space between each aircraft. On the runway, while taxiing, the first aircraft experienced a complete malfunction with its communications. The aircraft pulled out of the formation and the team on that aircraft was in disbelief, thinking they were missing their chance to go. Fortunately, some of the 18Es on board jumped up to help as the crew worked frantically to overcome the malfunction. After a few frantic minutes, everyone on board breathed a sigh of relief as they fixed the issue. The plane revved its engines to maneuver, rejoining the formation on the runway, now in the number six position.

On the 22nd of March, the aircraft launched just as the sun was setting. It was a particularly clear night. The first hour or so of the flight was uneventful. As the formation approached the Iraqi border, the commander declared "tactical"—an order for all planes to drop to 250 feet, turn off all lights, switch to night vision goggles, and go to radio silence. Inside the cargo area, small green, fluorescent lights provided a minimum amount of illumination. The aircraft's onboard systems enabled them to fly at low altitudes in uneven terrain. In fact, they were flying so low that the guys on board could see the dust the engines were kicking up flying through the air because they were so close to the ground. At times, they flew as low as fifty feet. Imagine a full-sized plane, 100 percent blacked-out with no lights, flying through uneven enemy terrain, about fifteen feet above a two-story house, making its own dust cloud as it goes. Now multiply that by six.

Inside the planes, the floor was a complete mess of explosives and ammunition strapped down between the passengers. Some of the guys were praying, some were throwing up, some were sleeping, and others were rightfully anxious.

The MC-130 has enhanced capabilities to detect and counter enemy positions attempting to lock on to their position. The electronic warfare officer (EWO) in each crew scanned their instrument panels for any indications of enemy radars being alerted. The crews had plotted a route that took advantage of the terrain to mask the aircrafts' radar signature. The six aircraft had staggered their spacing to be thirty minutes apart. This would reduce their signature in the air and provide enough time at the landing zone for each aircraft to land, offload, and take off.

CPT Pete Russo, the team leader of 094, noticed the navigator and crew chief acting slightly frantic and running around. They were shouting to each other and looking at computer display screens. The EWO monitoring the radar started to see an increase in radar activity. One of the crew chiefs suddenly shouted, "We've got a lock!" They had been spotted by Iraqi radar.

There's not much you can do in a situation like that. The guys were quiet. The EWO yelled, "Brace for impact!" which meant the enemy had just fired on the plane.

A combination of tracers and flak filled the sky all around the aircraft as it abruptly started to take fire from ground positions. The pilots immediately took evasive action. They switched off the terrain-following controls, set to 250 feet, in order to take the aircraft lower. In manual flight mode, the pilots would have better control of the aircraft to evade ground fire. A burst of 57 mm flak exploded outside the windshield of aircraft number five (callsign Harley 37), cracking the cockpit's glass.

The pilot instinctively reacted to the EWO's warning to brace for impact by banking to one side as hard as possible, throwing everyone up into the air like rag dolls. They weightlessly floated in space, illuminated by an eerie green hue. While their brains were still registering what had just happened and determining how to react, the plane corrected and then banked hard to the other side, slamming everyone back to the floor with the force of gravity. One of the team guys watched helplessly as his rifle went flying out of his hands, and he spent the next several minutes chasing it down. CPT Joe Lock, the Team Leader of 083, had prioritized comfort over safety when he strapped into the floor upon takeoff. Intent on taking a nap during the flight, he left about two feet of additional slack on his tether. He now bitterly regretted his decision as he flew those same two feet higher than everyone else.

Every crew member was calling out threats as they identified them. Through the few small windows, they could see tracer rounds coming at the aircraft from all directions. The pilots banked the aircraft hard right, then hard left again. Bullets zipped through the aircraft. Miraculously, no one got hit, but soldiers saw bullets zoom through the fuselage and up out of the ceiling. They were concerned about getting shot, but had a bigger concern about the tons of explosives in the middle of the floorboard.

The planes were now flying between 50 and 150 feet to evade the fire. Crew members could make out cigarettes in the Iraqi soldiers' mouths with their night vision goggles, something that is only possible at 100 feet or below. As rounds and shrapnel struck the fuselage, the men in the back could hear the clang of metal hitting metal. They could see the insulation inside the cargo bays tearing as rounds blasted through it. The aircraft ejected flares and chaff to confuse enemy radar and surface-to-air missiles.

The anticraft fire and evasive maneuvers continued similarly for roughly the next forty minutes. Midway through the engagement, CW2 Mike Santoro, the ODA executive officer (XO) from 083, heard the navigator shout, "We just lost engine three!" Mike wondered if they could make it the rest of the way with only three engines. Just as they shut the engine down, enemy fire from the second air defensive belt erupted. The aircrews routinely trained on scenarios where their aircraft would be detected or come under attack, and they employ counter measures and evasive maneuvers. No one ever trained for such a sustained period of attack. During one of the hard left maneuvers, CPT Pete Russo from 094 looked up through one of the tiny windows to see red tracer anti-aircraft fire going over the aircraft. The planes were literally flying *lower* than the gunners could hit them.

"So this is how I'm going to die," he thought. "Okay."

It wasn't a panicked thought—more like a casual external observation. He hadn't thought about this possibility. Pete had considered the more likely scenarios of getting shot or blown up, but not this.

On aircraft number four, MAJ George Thiebes saw one of the aircrews monitoring friendly and enemy communications from his suite in the cargo compartment. Thiebes asked what was happening. The dismayed crew member explained, "We just ran out of chaff and flares."

As the aircraft crossed over Saddam Lake, the enemy fire ceased. The Iraqi air defenses were some of the best in the modern world, thanks to years of the US bombing Iraq because of their sanction violations. By some miracle, the formation exited the air defense belt with no one injured, and all aircraft were still flying. The aircrafts' engines were overheated and over-torqued. All the planes had sustained as much as 3 g of torque during the maneuvers, well exceeding the limits. The damage sustained from small arms fire and shrapnel made matters worse.

As the aircraft approached the destination of the two Kurdish airfields, the crews feverishly conducted battle damage assessment of their aircrafts. Aircraft number five, Harley 37, was down one engine and losing fuel and oil at a considerable rate. It was another thirty minutes to the Kurdish airfield. If they could reach the airfield and land, the aircraft would be unable to take back off, essentially shutting the airfield down indefinitely. The crew made the decision to abort the approach and divert to Turkey for an emergency landing at Incirlik Air Base. The aircraft banked hard left and started a steep climb to clear the mountains. US and Turkish air controllers in Turkey were confused by the appearance of an aircraft coming from Iraq. The pilots called Turkish air control and requested permission for an emergency landing.

Turkish air control denied the request, so they replied, "Okay, we're crashing in Turkey. We're just giving you a heads up." The aircraft's radar was malfunctioning, they were leaking fuel, and a thunderstorm was developing to their front.

Harley 37 continued through the storm and made a smooth landing at Incirlik Air Base. Military aircraft have an additive in the fuel that turns the mixture into a foam. The foam has two purposes. It expands the fuel to the size of the fuel cell, which prevents the fuel from shifting in a half-empty tank and changing the aircraft's balance. It also works as a partial sealant for any ruptures in the cells. As the aircraft depressurized from the change in altitude, fuel poured from the numerous holes on the fuselage. In fact, Harley 37 had been hit with a combination of 57 mm, 23 mm, and small arms fire a total of nineteen separate times. The occupants quickly evacuated the aircraft and mustered in a field alongside the tarmac as emergency vehicles surrounded the leaking aircraft. Standing in observation of the spectacle was the US Commander of Incirlik alongside his Turkish counterpart.

At that moment, Turkey realized they had strategically miscalculated by refusing the partnership with America and denying airspace permissions. If the Americans were willing to assume that kind of risk and Turkey looked like they caused problems because they didn't let the US use their airspace, it would be politically disastrous. The Turkish officer quickly excused himself to make a phone call to his superiors. The Turkish military and government had underestimated the situation and American resolve. They feigned surprise and asked why the US wouldn't simply use Turkish airspace. The "misunderstanding" was rectified, and the Turkish military opened their airspace to US overflights. Within hours, at least a handful of aircraft crossed the Turkish airspace.

SULY WEST AIRFIELD

Inside Iraq, the remaining aircraft approached their respective Kurdish airfields. The pilot team had set up infrared lights at the four corners of the runway to aid the pilots in their approach. A contingent of several hundred Kurdish Peshmerga provided outer security. It was cold and very dark. Sound doesn't travel as fast as you might imagine, so when the planes came in, we didn't even hear them until the very last seconds. They were coming in dark and caught us off guard as they emerged from the shadows, seemingly coming out of nowhere. The first aircraft appeared out of the darkness and we didn't even see it until it was slamming down on us a few hundred feet from the runway.

In an instant the night was transformed from silence to roaring aircraft engines wailing to a stop at the edge of the runway. The pilots turned on a few running lights so no one would accidentally run into the propellers. A contingent of Peshmerga were ordered to unload the aircraft as fast as possible. As the ramp at the back of the aircraft was lowered, the shaken Special Forces soldiers collided with a group of enthusiastic Kurdish soldiers. Weeks of meticulous rehearsals for an orderly offload vanished in an instant. It was a flurry of activity as the Peshmerga ripped every rucksack, ammunition box, and weapon system from the floor of the aircraft and stacked them in a large pile off to the side. The plane made a jerking maneuver to help move the pallets off the back quickly. The aircraft was offloaded in what seemed like an instant. However, no one had any idea of where their equipment was in the darkness.

As the aircraft revved its engine for a quick turn and takeoff, CPT Joe Lock jumped into the cargo bay with a flashlight to double-check if anything had been inadvertently left behind. On the floor, he could see a few loose grenades, rifle magazines, plastic bottles filled with urine, and vomit bags that failed to contain their contents. He noted that the Kurds, in their efforts to unload the plane, had also ripped all the fire extinguishers and first aid kits out of the aircraft, but overall, nothing serious enough to stop the aircraft from taking off. Within five minutes of landing, the aircraft was gone. Like the aircraft in Turkey, the soldiers noted the amount of fuel spilling onto the runway from the numerous bullet holes. CW2 Scott Fleming from 094 said he couldn't believe what he was seeing—fuel was everywhere and yet, somehow, the plane still took off immediately at full speed.

In the midst of all the chaos, a Kurdish soldier accidentally discharged a rocket-propelled grenade launcher (RPG) near the airfield. I was nearby in a building briefing the newly-arrived ODAs.

My heart skipped a beat and I instinctively asked, "What the hell was that?" I didn't know if we were getting rocketed, a plane had crashed, or if someone shot at us. Someone informed me it was an accidental RPG discharge. I wasn't prepared for it, and I know for damn sure the guys getting off the planes could have done without that incident.

The remaining aircraft considered their options for returning to Jordan. There was no way in hell they were doubling back along the same route. They decided to climb to maximum altitude rather than retrace the route they had flown into Iraq. The remaining aircraft, now much lighter, climbed to 30,000 feet—above 80 percent of the anti-aircraft weaponry systems' reach—and returned to Jordan along a safer path.

It was a 570-mile low-level infil, the longest in US history since World War II. To describe their mission as utterly astonishing does not do it justice.

The Zargos mountains looking from Iraqi Kurdistan, near Halabja to the Iranian border.

Typical Kurdish Peshmerga of the Patriotic Union of Kurdistan (PUK)

The Sargat valley leading up to the Iranian border.

The rolling terrain around the Green Line border. Oil fires from Kirkuk burn in the distance to obscure coalition aircraft attempting to conduct strikes

Members of ODA 076, the Pilot Team. CW3 Andy Glonlund (center)

The visit to Gurdi Drozna to see the Ansar al Islam defenses.

LTC Tovo meeting with Kok Mustafa and the prong commanders in Halabja.
Note the blank side of his map on the Iranian side of the border.

The UGLY BABY infiltration flight. Members of ODA 094, CPT Pete Russo lower left)

The UGLY BABY infiltration. ODAs strapped to the floor alongside the ammunition.

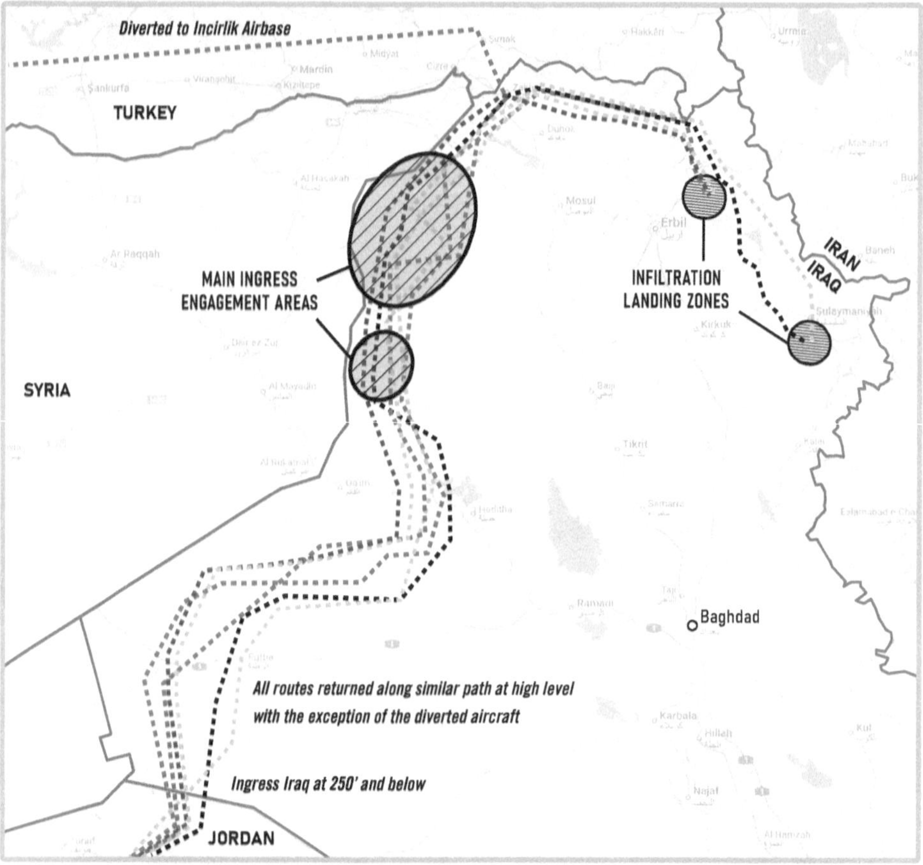

The actual flight paths flown by the six MC-130s of the UGLY BABY infiltration.

Diverted to Incirlik Airbase

TURKEY

**MAIN INGRESS
ENGAGEMENT AREAS**

**INFILTRATION
LANDING ZONES**

IRAN

IRAQ

SYRIA

Erbil

Mosul

Tikrit

Baghdad

**All routes returned along similar path at high level
with the exception of the diverted aircraft**

Ingress Iraq at 250' and below

JORDAN

Karbala

Najaf

The windshield of Harley 37 damaged from 57 mm flake.

The PUK's sand table of the Ansar al Islam defenses.

MAJ George Thiebes (center) oversees the sand table brief for the attack on Ansar al Islam.

*Members of ODA 081.
SSG Blake Kramer, MSG Rich
Sanders, CPT Brian Rauen,
SSG Ken (Happy) Gilmore.*

Members of ODA 081 and 093 on the Green Prong during operation VIKING HAMMER.
SSG Chris Crum takes aim with his Barrett .50-caliber Sniper rifle (lower right)

MSG Chris Hartnett, Team Sergeant for ODA 093, provides fire support from the
81 mm mortars on the Green Prong during operation VIKING HAMMER.

Members of ODA 093 provide fire support from the 60 mm mortars on the Green Prong during operation VIKING HAMMER.

Members of ODA 094 with the Red Prong during operation VIKING HAMMER. CW2 Scott Fleming (left).

CHAPTER 9
THE DECISIVE POINT

There are surprising turning points; there is the straw that breaks the camel's back, and you never know if your action could be the straw.

—FRANCES MOORE LAPPÉ

I SPECIFICALLY ORDERED THAT THE FIRST GUY GETTING OFF THE AIR-craft needed a Stinger missile in case the Iraqis launched fighter jets to intercept us on the airfield. LTC Tovo and I were extremely concerned that if the Iraqis figured out our plan, they would push forward and fire rockets and launch helicopters to disrupt us on the airfield. Thankfully, that didn't happen and the missiles ultimately weren't necessary. Speed, however, *was* necessary and I knew we had to get the teams dispersed as fast as possible. This was the Iraqi army's last chance to disrupt us while we were all together. In military terms, the decisive point is where you've tipped the scales in your favor. Getting the teams on the ground and dispersed was our decisive point. Once we accomplished this, Saddam's ability to stop us, even if he bombed the airfield and the SOTF HQs, would be greatly reduced.

LTC Tovo met the teams as they collected their equipment on the airfield. The guys were genuinely glad to see LTC Tovo as well as to be off the aircraft and on solid ground. They quickly loaded onto buses and drove the ten minutes to the forward headquarters location, where I was waiting for them. When the teams landed, I felt a real sense of relief upon seeing them, but I also knew I needed to get them on their way as soon as possible. They still had a long night and following day ahead of them. I provided a very short update on the situation and then introduced them to the drivers. The drivers spoke no English.

However, earlier that day, I had someone give him explicit instructions to take the teams to the right location. I then introduced the teams to their collection of non-standard vehicles. Since our intended Land Rovers were still in Turkey, we had to borrow whatever was available.

In a typical example, I gave the teams a dump truck, a small bus, and a Kurdish family member's car for the trip. In many of the cases, I received cars with a request to please return the car, since it belonged to someone's father in-law, brother, mother, etc. I then handed each ODA commander a strip of paper with my iridium phone number. I gave them instructions to check in with me when they could, fully appreciating the enormity of their task and making sure they knew my requirements were second to theirs. They knew what had to be done. Tovo and I had complete confidence in each of them. Additionally, I could see them on Blue Force Trackers and could send a coded message via the satellite pagers if there was an emergency. I shook their hands, wished them luck, and then told them to get moving while it was still dark.

The ODAs designated as Green Line teams were pushed out from the airfield within thirty minutes of landing. The first three teams that pushed out were ODA 083 west toward Chamchamal, ODA 075 north toward Tak Tak, and ODA 092 south toward Kifri. Not far behind was the A Company headquarters (ODB 070) with MAJ Tye Connett and his remaining ODAs: 071, 072, 073 and 074. ODA 085 remained at the airfield to assist with security and linked up with MAJ Roberson's Company headquarters, approximately 20 kilometers outside of Sulaymaniyah. MAJ George Thiebes, the C Company Commander (ODB 090), pushed out to Halabja with his ODAs tasked with the attack against Ansar—ODAs 091, 093, 094, 095—where they met up with ODA 081 already on the ground.

During the night, we received intelligence that someone in the ring of Peshmerga security at the airfield was communicating with someone by cell phone, providing real-time information. We also received several warnings—that turned out to be false alarms—that Saddam had launched missiles toward our position. The warnings came in via the satellite pagers: *missile inbound to your position*. In all cases, the

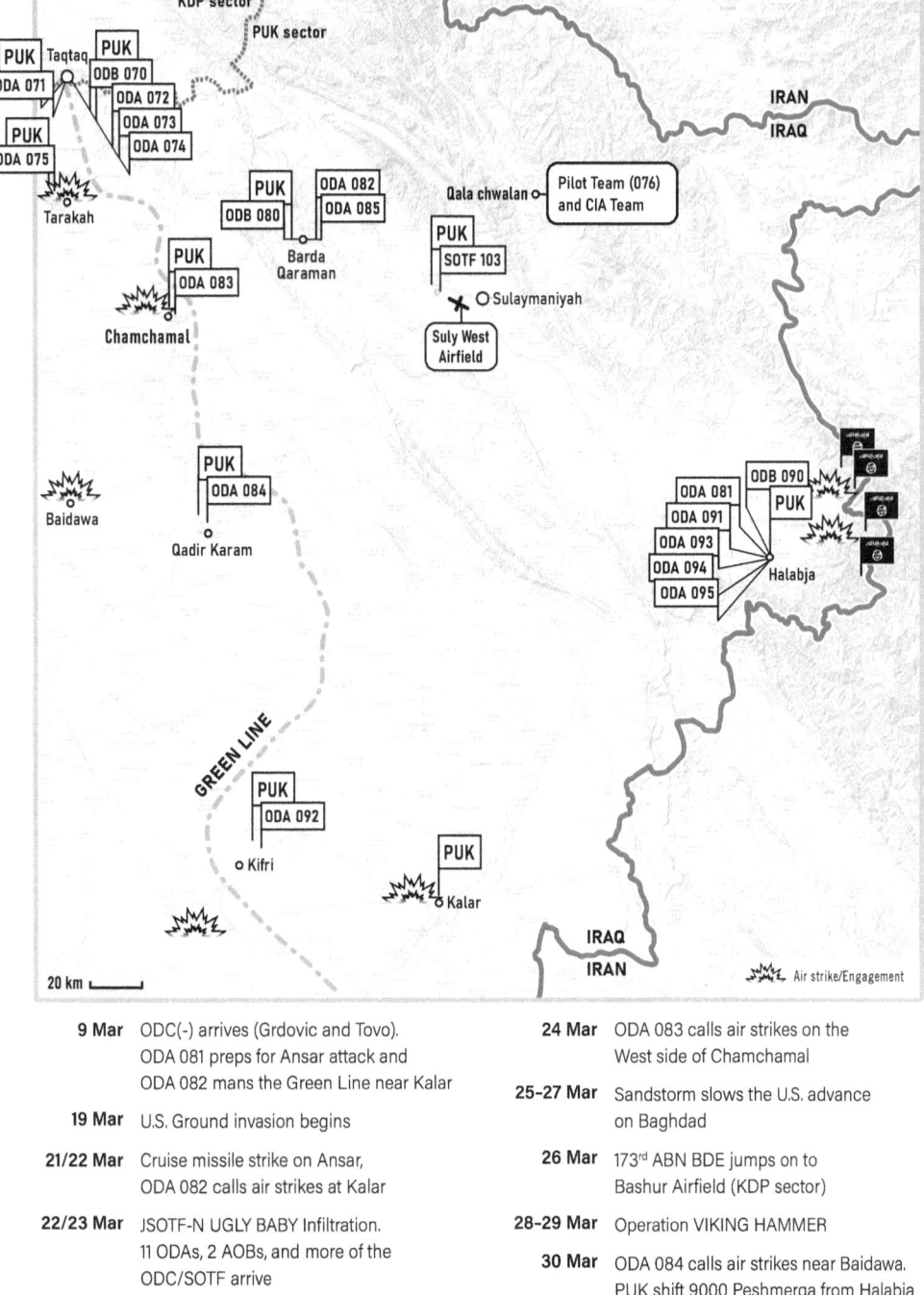

9 Mar	ODC(-) arrives (Grdovic and Tovo). ODA 081 preps for Ansar attack and ODA 082 mans the Green Line near Kalar
19 Mar	U.S. Ground invasion begins
21/22 Mar	Cruise missile strike on Ansar, ODA 082 calls air strikes at Kalar
22/23 Mar	JSOTF-N UGLY BABY Infiltration. 11 ODAs, 2 AOBs, and more of the ODC/SOTF arrive
23 Mar	ODA 092 calls air strikes near Kifri
24 Mar	ODA 083 calls air strikes on the West side of Chamchamal
25-27 Mar	Sandstorm slows the U.S. advance on Baghdad
26 Mar	173rd ABN BDE jumps on to Bashur Airfield (KDP sector)
28-29 Mar	Operation VIKING HAMMER
30 Mar	ODA 084 calls air strikes near Baidawa. PUK shift 9000 Peshmerga from Halabja to the Green Line

Map 2. Disposition of Friendly Forces

missile destinations were transcribed incorrectly from latitude and longitude (or lat/long) into grid coordinates and were, in fact, actually in the southern part of the country. Three-quarters of our forces were now on the ground. All of the forces were either headed toward the Green Line or headed toward Halabja. We only had the equipment we could carry and we still didn't have our vehicles, but our situation was greatly improved from the day before. More importantly, our forces were dispersed, and Saddam hadn't disrupted our airfield. We had achieved the decisive point in this conflict.

ODA 083

The team arrived at the PUK camp on the east side of Chamchamal a few kilometers from the Green Line and the Iraqi defenses. The team leader, CPT Joe Lock, met the PUK Commander, Kok Hewa, and his deputy, Kok Salah. Salah spoke very good English and served as their translator. Both men were in their late forties and very seasoned fighters, evident by the scars from their imprisonment and torture by Saddam's regime. The Kurdish commander was eager to see what the team could do for them, so they took them to a position to oversee the Iraqi defenses. Prior to ODA 083's arrival, one of the advance teams, 082, had identified numerous targets on the ridgeline off in the distance. The team called an air strike, but was unable to determine if it had achieved anything of value. Lock explained he needed to get closer to the front lines. Kok Hewa explained that Chamchamal was a Kurdish town with Iraqi soldiers and defenses, but they knew how to move around them.

The PUK loaded CPT Lock and two other Americans into the back of a pickup truck and covered it with a tarp. They drove through the town and into an enclosed carport. From the roof of the building, Lock had a clear view of the Iraqi defenses. The house was a bit closer than he would have chosen since it was the last house between the Iraqi defenses and the town. The Iraqi positions were along a ridgeline—an unnervingly close 800 meters from the house. Lock and his men spent the day observing and plotting the positions. After hours of observing the defenses, Lock brought the information back to Kok Hewa to describe his plan for a strike. Hewa suggested they bring in a local shepherd who commonly transited back and forth across the Green Line and was familiar with the defenses.

Upon meeting the shepherd, Lock explained the satellite imagery and their understanding of the targets. He pointed out the building with the most traffic, identifying it as the headquarters.

"That building is not the headquarters," the shepherd corrected him.

Lock was surprised and explained that everyone was coming and going from that building.

"That's the water point. The headquarters building is this one," the shepherd clarified, pointing.

Lock adjusted his plan. They plotted the entire length of the ridge-line, identifying each bunker, building, and fighting position.

Kok Hewa had a request when he saw the new plan. He asked Lock, "Can you strike this building first?" He went on to explain that these Iraqi men had recently killed a Kurdish woman at a checkpoint. They caught her trying to smuggle a jar with lamp oil and subsequently doused her with the oil and set her on fire. Lock was more than happy to accommodate the request.

Standing around the radio in the dark of night, the aircraft came on the net, declaring "Bombs away!" Lock explained that due to the aircraft's altitude of 30,000 feet, it would be one minute and fifty-eight seconds of flight time for the bombs. After a minute and fifty seconds of awkward silence, Lock suspected there was some skepticism among the Kurds. As they counted down from five, then reached zero, they saw a bright flash followed by a deafening blast. The bomb had gone through the roof of the bunker, vaporizing it instantly. A moment later the next explosion erupted. The process continued over the next few minutes with over sixty bombs destroying the entire battalion.

It had been raining all night. As a result, most of the Iraqi soldiers were huddled in their bunkers when the strike occurred. The strike was a devastating blow to the Iraqi forces, and it provided an additional opportunity to capitalize on their fears. The next day, several of our Kurds communicated with members of the Iraqi forces along the Green Line defenses. They explained that the Americans destroyed that specific battalion in retaliation for the killing of the woman at the checkpoint, which was a bit of an exaggeration. They also explained the Americans could kill the Iraqis at any time, but preferred surrender.

Since the officers appeared to not be taking us up on our offer to surrender, we took the opportunity to turn the Iraqi soldiers against their officers. The Kurds spread the message asking, "Have you seen your officers lately? They have left you to die. Take matters into your own hands before it's too late." Doing this took minimal effort on our part but greatly amplified the effects of the air strike beyond the range of it physical damage.

Over the course of the week, ODA 083 continued to target and harass the remaining defenses. In desperation, the Iraqi forces responded by firing their tanks and artillery wildly into the town. Each time they did so, it ultimately exposed their forces to more air strikes by Lock and his team.

ODA 075

ODA 075 was the lead team for Alpha Company, which had responsibility for the top portion of 3rd Battalion's sector. They arrived exhausted after the Ugly Baby infil flight followed by a two-hour drive to a small town not far off the Green Line called Tak Tak. Their area was bordered to the north by the Little Zab River, which served as a natural boundary between the KDP and the PUK. The sun was just coming up, and they had all been awake for the last twenty-four hours.

The team leader, CPT Pat Bekurs, was an easygoing but highly competent and experienced officer. Immediately upon arriving in town, the team was taken to the PUK HQs to meet the local commander. Kok Abizaid was a particularly seasoned and well-respected PUK commander. His unit, known as the Cobras, were considered an elite unit within the Peshmerga. Abizaid immediately made it clear that they were very happy that the Americans were with them and supporting them. He also made it clear that he had very explicit instructions to ensure the Americans were not killed, repeating the phrase that he had heard Jalal Talabani say time and time again: "If there is a bullet hole in an American, there had better be two in you." Protecting and retaining American support was critical to the PUK. Bekurs explained his appreciation for their prioritization of the Americans' safety but explained at some point they had to get closer the front lines to do their job.

A couple of days later, after a fair amount of negotiations with Bekurs, Abizaid finally agreed to take the team to find the Iraqi forces to their front. The ODA and the Cobras drove along a dry riverbed in pickup trucks camouflaged with mud until they could observe the Iraqi defenses. As the convoy came in sight of the opposing ridgeline, they came under a barrage of mortar fire. The Cobras and the ODA fell back to the other side of the hill where CPT Bekurs and his JTAC quickly called for air support and coordinated a strike on the ridgeline. Within minutes, a pair of F-14s appeared overhead. Over the next few hours, Bekurs directed several strikes against the ridgeline. The demonstration of firepower caused the Peshmerga to openly cheer and convinced the Iraqi defenders to abandon their ridgeline, which the PUK moved forward to occupy.

As the Cobras advanced, they encountered a hastily laid minefield, emplaced by the Iraqis as they withdrew. Kok Abizaid called for his engineer. An elderly Peshmerga appeared, notably with fewer than ten fingers. The man was well-respected by the others and clearly very experienced with unexploded ordnance. The old engineer slowly worked his way through the minefield, disarming the mines manually one at a time. Once cleared, the Peshmerga engineer collected up the mines and fuses to be repurposed elsewhere, as he'd no doubt done countless times before.

The engagement provided the opportunity the ODA needed to establish a solid working relationship and credibility with their counterparts. Over the course of the next week, the team repeated the cycle several times. The Cobras would take the team to recon the Iraqi defenses, which resulted in more air strikes and the Kurdish lines advancing a few kilometers closer toward Kirkuk every few days.

ODA 092

While the newly arrived ODAs had been traveling to link up with their PUK counterparts near the Green Line, ODA 082 had pushed west to reposition in Kifri. Their intent was to strike the enemy from multiple locations in order to create the appearance of a larger force and confuse the Iraqis during the Ugly Baby infil. Much like the night before in Kalar, the team identified several enemy targets. Aircraft came on station and ODA 082 successfully called several more strikes along the Green Line. ODA 092 arrived in Kifri early the next morning and linked up with 082, who was able to hand them off to the local PUK unit and provide them with a prepared target list. Twelve hours later, during the next period of darkness, ODA 092 was calling in air strikes along the Iraqi positions.

Now that we had infiltrated our teams, all that was left to do was defeat an entrenched fanatical enemy by conducting a daylight frontal attack, uphill in mountainous terrain, with under-equipped Kurdish forces whom we just met. Once we completed that task, we needed to reposition the Peshmerga to the Green Line and advance on Kirkuk before Saddam Hussein decided to use some of his forces in the north to counterattack the advancing US forces in the south.

If it were easy, someone else would have been tasked to do it.

CHAPTER 10
WE ARE RUNNING OUT OF TIME

Most attacks happen where four map sheets meet,
at night, in bad weather.

—British Military saying

The clock started ticking once the US and British forces started the ground invasion on March 20th. If Saddam decided to move his forces south and assume risk in the north to counterattack against the Americans, then our utility would expire. We had only a fraction of the time we had intended to meet our counterparts and revise the plan. Nonetheless, we couldn't postpone it any longer. There were several ways this attack could go—most of them badly—and only one that would yield the desired results.

If we attacked Ansar and the core of the PUK forces were decimated, the PUK would lose the ability to threaten the Iraqi forces and the US–PUK relationship would be over. Saddam would get what he wanted. If we postponed until conditions were more favorable, we risked missing the window to stop Saddam from counterattacking US forces. Our assessment was that the attack had to happen then and the risk of not attacking outweighed the risk of going with what we had.

MAJ Thiebes told his ODAs to get familiar with their counterparts, start planning and preparations, and get familiar with the terrain. He also told them to harass the enemy if the opportunity presented itself during the week— the kind of guidance a commander doesn't need to state twice.

The teams wasted no time. They immediately started preparation and planning with their Kurdish counterparts, who were more than happy to take them to positions where they could observe and kill some of the enemy in their respective sectors. This provided the teams with the opportunity to also get a sense of the enemy's capabilities as well as quickly build rapport with their Peshmerga counterparts. The terrain was very formidable, but surprisingly similar to parts of Colorado. Imagine a mountainous ridgeline that largely runs north and south. Looking east, from the planned starting point of the attack, the terrain starts out as flat open plains that transition to rolling foothills and then finally to ridgelines with steep slopes culminating around 8,000 feet. The final ridgeline, the border with Iran, was still covered in snow. The ground was mostly rocky with very little vegetation. The valleys had numerous small villages with intermittent minefields everywhere. It was as if we were about to initiate an attack in the Rocky Mountain National Park.

While the teams were establishing their relationships with the Peshmerga, the PUK command was starting to get a better understanding of the enemy situation on the ground. In addition to the expected 600 Ansar fighters, there were two other groups considering joining Ansar al-Islam. On Ansar's northern flank was a group called the Islamic Group of Kurdistan (IGK) and on the southern flank was a group called the Islamic Movement of Kurdistan in Iraq (IMKI). These two groups both had approximately 300 to 400 fighters each. This was problematic for obvious reasons. The Kurds were communicating with IGK and IMKI to the extent they could, trying to persuade them to stay out of the conflict.

Sargat village was the location of a facility the US suspected was experimenting with chemical and biological weapons. The PUK were able to provide detailed sketches of the compound, to include the cells where they experimented on prisoners. A few kilometers south the teams found another sight of interest: a suspected terrorist training camp that was believed to house foreign cadre. The camp was located in a small village called Daga Sharkan, which sat in a mountain pass about one kilometer from the border crossing.

The Kurds had devised what they called a five-pronged plan. Each prong would be referred to by a color and have 1,000 Peshmerga and an accompanying ODA. There were also an additional 4,000 Kurds in reserve, so in total, we were a 10,000-man force. From top to bottom, it was the Orange, Black, Green, Yellow, Red, then Blue Prongs.

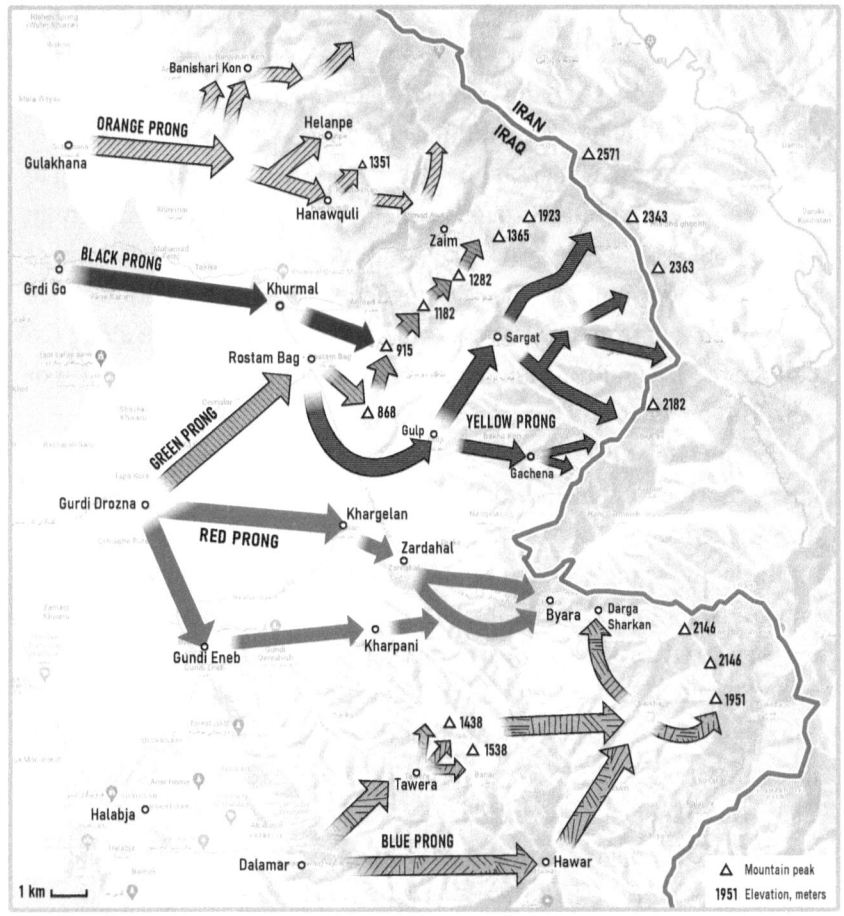

Map 3. The Attack on Ansar al-Islam

MAJ Thiebes had his guys draw the plan's graphic onto Falcon View mapping software. The ODAs' Blue Force tracker icons would appear on the map, allowing Thiebes to track the advance of the attacking Peshmerga units in real time and assist the PUK command in exercising command and control. The incorporation of this new technology provided a previously unimaginable level of fidelity and situational awareness.

The main effort of the attack was the Yellow Prong's direct focus on reaching Sargat. ODA 081 and 091 would move with the PUK forces on the Yellow Prong and the column would split along the way.

ODA 081 would head toward Sargat while ODA 091 would go to the Iranian border. The Green Prong with ODA 093 would support the Yellow Prong. The secondary objective for the attack was the training camp at Daga Shakan. The training camp was about a kilometer from the town of Biyara, which sat on the Iraqi side of the border crossing to Iran. The Red and Blue Prongs, with ODAs 094 and 095, respectively, would both advance up two valleys and meet in the town of Biyara at the border crossing. The Black Prong, supported with a composite of team members from ODAs 093, 091, and 095, would move along the flank of the Green Prong and be prepared to support the main effort or defend the flank of the attack.

Each ODA was equipped with two 60 mm mortars, a small number of mortar rounds, and two MK-19 grenade launchers, which they jerry-rigged onto the Toyota pickup trucks provided by the PUK. Additionally, some teams had an M2 machine gun, anti-tank rocket launchers, handheld unmanned aerial vehicles, CS grenades for clearing caves, and a system known as the anti-personnel obstacle breaching system (APOBS). The APOBS was basically two backpacks that, when connected, fire an explosive line that clears a lane about two feet wide through a minefield. This was a crucial piece of equipment because the valley was filled with minefields.

The PUK collected up many of their available heavier weapons as well. Each prong had three World War II-era US jeeps, equipped with 106 mm recoilless rifles and two Soviet-era BM-21s. A BM-21 is a truck with a pod of 107 mm Katusha rockets mounted on the back bed. Lastly, the main effort on the Yellow Prong had a towed, twin-barreled 23 mm anti-aircraft gun, known as a ZPU-23-2.

MAJ Thiebes was concerned that close air support might not always be available, so he directed his company headquarters to establish two US-only 81 mm mortar crews of three men each. One mortar team would cover the south half of the sector with the Blue and Red Prongs and one would cover the north with the Green, Yellow, and Black Prongs.

To familiarize everyone with the plan, the teams and Peshmerga collectively built a ten-by-twelve-foot sand table. It was impressive, to say the least. Each element briefed their portion of the plan in front of the others. Five days earlier, most of these men had never met. Now they were prepared to conduct a 10,000-man attack. Seeing how quickly the Peshmerga units and the ODAs came together was a testament to the skill of the teams to demonstrate their military competency and value as well as build rapport.

THE FORWARD OPERATING BASE IN SULY

Back at the SOTF forward operating base (or FOB, as we called it), the ODC team was still settling in the influx of additional headquarters members who came in on the initial Ugly Baby flights and the handful of flights that followed from Turkey. As part of the buildup we also now had all three of our company headquarters in theater (ODB 070, ODB 080, and ODB 090). The ODBs would interface with PUK counterparts and provide command and control for their teams. This provided us the capability we needed to command and control the Green Line team and the Halabja fight simultaneously.

A couple of days after the Ugly Baby infiltration, the JSOTF Commander, COL Cleveland, and his J-3 Operations Officers came and visited our SOTF HQs in Sulaymaniyah. We walked them through our operations and showed them how we were managing things. Since the Blue Force Tracker was a new item that most of us had never used, COL Cleveland asked my deputy operations officer, CPT Derek Jones, to show him how it worked. Derek walked him over to the display projected onto a wall. Cleveland noted one icon seemed to be blinking and asked what that meant.

"That appears to be a team in evasion, sir," Derek replied, nonchalant.

Cleveland was a bit thrown off by the response. "What do you mean? Who is it?" Derek right-clicked on the icon, and it showed it was a team from the British SBS who had been transmitting their emergency evasion signal for about an hour. Early in the planning at Fort Carson, a squadron from the British Special Boat Squadron (SBS) had been attached to 3rd Battalion to conduct a raid of the Sargat chemical facility in conjunction with the larger attack against the Ansar forces. The determination was made several months earlier to not conduct the raid for a variety of reasons. As a result, the SBS reverted back to the JSOTF's control for other missions.

When the JSOTF had decided to launch Ugly Baby, the SBS moved to Cyprus and then infiltrated the squadron into the western desert north of the Euphrates River to harass Iraqi forces. Cleveland, clearly concerned, turned to his J-3 and said, "Call back to Romania and find out what's going on," as it was the JSOTF's battle space. The officer, with a sense of urgency, turned to me and asked how he could contact the JSOTF. Of note, this was the same officer who had told me two weeks earlier in Romania that I was wrong about the phone numbers. As the information crisis unfolded, the karmic irony was not lost on me. I directed him to our single satellite channel radio, but it was tied up by 2nd Battalion and we couldn't break in.

The colonel shouted, "J-3! What's the status?"

"Were working on it, sir," he replied. He turned and asked me, "What about the satphones?" By this time, we had learned the number for the Ops Center, but in most cases no one answered. The first time we got through, someone answered by immediately saying, "We're in a meeting. Call back," and hung up. A moment later, the call went through and the J-3 inquired about the evasion event.

The officer on the other end replied, "What event?" It became immediately evident that the JSOTF staff in Constanta had no idea what was going on with the SBS forces.

Unfortunately, we had our own issues to contend with. We were not getting the close air support we had planned for two reasons. With Turkey still out of play for launching aircraft, we were only able to get intermittent support. The available aircraft we could get either came from an aircraft carrier in the south or a strategic bomber, which limited our options.

Complicating matters, 2nd Battalion had developed what they thought was an ingenious workaround for the limited aircraft. The battalion commander explained that if you declared "troops in contact," meaning you were taking fire from the enemy, you would immediately get whatever support you needed. Aircraft from all over the country would divert from their intended missions to come to the aid of US troops in harm's way. This interpretive and liberal use of "troops in contact" as a workaround had a significant negative impact on our planned bombing campaign of the Ansar defenses. As a result, we only received a fraction of the air support we had intended to use to weaken the defenses over the course of the week prior to the ground assault.

MEANWHILE, ALONG THE GREEN LINE

ODA 083

As Kurds cleared Iraqi positions, they pushed forward, often occupying the former Iraqi positions. The team quickly learned that aircraft returning from other missions in Iraq would often come on the air net asking if anyone had a target. Otherwise, the aircraft would jettison their ordnance in the desert before returning to base. Each aircraft had different requirements. Some aircraft needed military grid reference system (GMRS), others wanted latitude and longitude to the one hundredth of the second or one thousandth of the minute. Having a target ready and being prepared to rapidly convert coordinates to the form needed by the specific aircraft made all the difference.

Although ODA 083 was one of the teams that had a JTAC, Lock was clear that the ultimate responsibility for correctly calling close air support resided with him. He instituted procedures to ensure they would not make a mistake despite their exhaustion. The team checked and rechecked coordinates dozens of times. If a coordinate was relayed, three men were involved. One man would read it, the other would state it back, and the third man recorded what was said. In an environment of extreme exhaustion, it worked well.

ODA 083 moved several kilometers west of the Green Line to the town of Qara Hanjir. The team would split in half and work in shifts with the Peshmerga, probing the rolling hills to locate the Iraqi frontline trace and target them with air strikes. One night, as the two halves of the team linked up on the back side of a hill to hand over responsibility, a single artillery round came crashing into their position. The Iraqis often fired randomly into the night as part of their security. The round landed in an existing crater filled with water. The team members were all knocked to the ground and covered with water and mud. Miraculously, the crater and water blunted much of the blast force, and no one was seriously injured.

ODA 084

ODA 084 and a handful of personnel from the battalion HQs were supposed to be on one of the aircraft that would fly from Turkey immediately following the Ugly Baby infiltration. Due to a sandstorm and some maintenance issues, they were delayed an extra day. Soon after they landed at the Sulaymaniyah airfield, the team linked up with their Kurdish contingent and started the movement to their location along the Green Line roughly ten kilometers south of ODA 083's position near Chamchamal. As ODA 084 approached, the team immediately noted the Iraqi positions, especially the T-55 tank at the checkpoint whose main gun was pointed directly at them. The Peshmerga assured the team that it was fine—something they knew since they traveled this route frequently.

About an hour's drive past Chamchamal, the team arrived at a small semi-abandoned town called Gok Tepe. They were introduced to the PUK commander, Kok Usman. None of the Kurds spoke English and the team didn't have an interpreter. However, they quickly leveraged their ingenuity and learned that a handful of the Peshmerga spoke German and Greek from years living abroad. The team leader, CPT John Holevas, was a native Greek speaker, and several members of the team spoke German. As they discussed the situation, Holevas, eager to make up for lost time, asked if they could travel to the Green Line. After a short drive, they arrived at the Green Line to find a series of minefields and destroyed bridges but no Iraqi forces. The Kurds explained the that Iraqi forces had pulled back ten to twenty kilometers a few days before (see Map 2).

CPT Holevas considered the situation and decided they couldn't accomplish their mission from here. They would have to cross the Green Line and locate the Iraqi front lines. Holevas explained his intentions to Kok Usman, who explained that they had men trained as scouts on motor bikes who could go ahead of the main body. The group drove west, fording several streams and navigating across minefields with narrow paths that had questionably been cleared by the scouts. Holevas was immediately struck by the rolling terrain and tall grass. He expected barren dessert and now he was seeing terrain that more closely resembled the Dakota Badlands. Holevas had previously been an Armor Officer and a cavalry scout, as had several of his NCOs. As strange as the situation was, he noted to himself how familiar the tactics felt. The terrain was perfect for forces like the Peshmerga.

After about an hour of navigating the terrain, the group arrived at a small village called Kadir Qarim, about ten kilometers past the Green Line, and set up in the former Iraqi camp. Holevas and Kok Usman agreed that they needed to make the Iraqis think there was a larger force opposing their defenses. They decided to conduct scouting and harassment forays across as wide a front as possible. Their first engagement with elements of the 36th Iraqi Division came on the 30th of March outside the town of Baidawa. The group had been reconning the defenses for a couple of days, which appeared to be a brigade including approximately 3,000 soldiers, artillery, and air defenses. After two days of planning and waiting, a B-52 became available. The bombs struck the Iraqi positions, which erupted in a massive fireball with numerous secondary explosions. The team later learned the position was, in fact, a fuel depot. Hours later, as more Iraqis came to reinforce the position and respond to the casualties, the team bombed the position again.

Like the events to their north with ODA 083, any doubts about our level of commitment that the Peshmerga may have had vanished once the bombs struck their targets. The team's credibility was incredibly high and the working relationship was solidified. Over the next week the team conducted a series of similar operations with their Kurdish scouts, across a 40-kilometer front, specifically incorporating mortars and small arms fire when they could to portray a larger force on the ground.

During a recon to a small village called Qaladiz, one of the team's vehicles got stuck. The Iraqis responded with a barrage of 122 mm artillery fire, forcing the team to abandon the vehicle. Following the artillery, the Iraqis pushed a company of infantry into the field. The group of Peshmerga and half of 084 were cut off from their egress route and were forced to evade the Iraqi patrols on foot while remaining hidden in the rolling hills until the morning. CPT Holevas contacted me later that day to, as he put it, tell me the bad news. I had been John's instructor in the Special Forces Qualification course a few years earlier and knew him quite well. As soon as I saw him, I knew something was up.

"Okay," he started. "Before you ask, everyone is all right, but I have some bad news."

"Go on," I prompted.

Because our vehicles—the Land Rovers—were still in Turkey, we outfitted several of the teams with a mix of vehicles, some of which came from PUK family members. In the case of ODA 084, one of their cars came from a PUK member who borrowed his mother-in-law's car.

"We lost the car," John explained.

I almost laughed. "That's actually not my criteria for really bad news, John. Really bad news would be someone getting killed. So what happened?" I asked.

"Well," John continued, "While we were out in a field the car got high-centered and we couldn't move. We were trying to get the car unstuck when we took about sixty rounds of artillery," he dropped, casually. "We had to evade on foot and leave the car behind."

"*Sixty rounds*?! Jesus Christ, John!" I exclaimed. "Okay, I'll handle the car issue. I'm just glad you guys are *alive*!" Listening to John describe his guys' actions the night prior, I started to grasp the scale of the fire the teams were routinely receiving.

ODA 075

As the foothills opened to a large, flat plain several kilometers across, the Cobras encountered a series of entrenchments and defensive positions. As the team called for close air support, a large firefight broke out. The defenders began firing their tanks, artillery, and mortars, showing no signs of abandoning the position like the previous week's engagements. After several hours of intense fighting and multiple air strikes, the Iraqis finally relinquished the position. As the Cobras advanced across the position, they found what appeared to be a hastily abandoned brigade headquarters. Bekurs noted the maps with the blue and red positions marked in grease pencil. The Cobras translated the Arabic symbols that denoted the Iraqi positions in detail as well as the Peshmerga positions. Alongside the symbols for Peshmerga units, they found an additional graphic: American Special Forces. The Iraqis didn't know their team's number but—chillingly—they did have an accurate depiction of which Peshmerga units had American Special Forces with them.

From the brigade headquarters, Bekurs could see the Koni Domlan ridge approximately 6 kilometers to its south. This wasn't a particularly high ridge, but it dominated the surrounding area. It also ran perpendicular to the Erbil–Kirkuk highway (or Highway 2), making it the last defensive position and chokepoint before entering Kirkuk from the north.

As the Cobras were consolidating after the attack on the brigade headquarters, they came across some Iraqis who wanted to surrender. CPT Bekurs saw the prisoners in the custody of the Cobras and didn't think anything of it until a moment later when he heard the shots. The Peshmerga executed the prisoners. Bekurs immediately protested to Kok Abizad, who offered a token explanation that "things are different here in Iraq than in America." Bekurs explained this was unacceptable.

Kok Abizad countered with his rationale that Bekurs didn't understand how things happen here. Bekurs, not willing to overlook the behavior but also wanting to maintain the relationship, turned Abizaid's points around on him.

"I might not understand things here," he conceded. "But I know this: the PUK is worried about losing US support. You are concerned about what would happen if one of the Americans was killed. Killing prisoners will destroy US support much faster than an American getting hurt." Bekurs made his point well and Abizaid conceded.

The ODAs were holding things together amidst some pretty overwhelming circumstances. The Iraqi forces were heavily engaged with the coalition forces in the south and just starting to experience problems in the north. I imagined Saddam was just starting to get a sense of what was unfolding before him and weighing his next moves carefully. The outcome of our next few days of fighting had the potential to significantly impact the outcome of the entire war.

CHAPTER 11
THE KURDISH WOODSTOCK

To win any battle, you must fight as if you are already dead.

—Miyamoto Musashi

I got up just before sunrise, even though I'd been lying awake for far longer. I felt like I had the weight of the world on my mind, and I felt nauseous—partly from apprehension and partly from lack of sleep. I made a cup of coffee to warm my hands from the 45-degree cold night air and climbed the ladder to the roof of the PUK building headquarters on the outskirts of Sulaymaniyah where we had established our SOTF headquarters. I took ten minutes, admiring the mountains in the distance, centering myself, and preparing my mind for the day ahead.

I thought to myself how beautiful Sulaymaniyah was as its lights sparkled in the distance. The morning twilight highlighted the ring of mountains that surrounded the valley. The short-lived springtime grass transformed the area into a lush green landscape in beautiful contrast to the normal drab gray-brown rocky outcrops or snow-covered terrain. I watched a pack of roughly twenty feral dogs roam the outskirts of the PUK compound, training their squad of new puppies to announce any movement along the perimeter.

As I finished my coffee, I considered how much we had done to get to this moment. I was largely responsible for the plan up to this point. Had we done everything we could to prepare for what was ahead? What was the week ahead going to be like? It was surreal to think about the attack that we were about to conduct. I kept asking myself if we had done everything we could to prepare. Would the attack be successful? I couldn't help but think of the expression I kept hearing the Kurds use: "*inshallah*," if God wills it.

It was time to go. I came down from the roof, and we loaded up in vehicles for the two-hour drive to Halabja.

As we arrived in town, it was impressive to see so many Peshmerga assembled for one battle. Approximately 10,000 Kurdish forces were closing in on Halabja at this point, staging to conduct the attack. No doubt it put quite a burden on the infrastructure to support these people. They all still needed to eat and have water, so there was additional pressure from the logistics of it all—a growing momentum that served as a reminder that the attack needed to happen.

Halabja looked like a Kurdish version of Woodstock—there were Kurdish guys living in every little building and camping out on the lawns next to the buildings with small tarps. When evening came, they built hundreds of campfires with broken wooden trash to warm themselves and cook their last meals of whatever food they found. Everyone stared into the fires, hypnotized by the flames and lost in their own thoughts.

For the last few days, the teams had been conducting some harassment operations with mortars and crew-served weapons and close air support when we could get it. Fortunately, the day before the actual ground attack, we got word that we would finally be receiving the desperately needed lethal aid. The US government had acquired the former Soviet-style weapons and ammunition months ago in Eastern Europe and now the Air Force was finally going to deliver the goods. Not only was it a huge morale boost, but practically speaking, guys had been talking about going into this attack with only a few magazines, which is obviously not what you want to be carrying. Better late than never. The planes landed at the Suly West airfield and our convoy moved the aid by truck. As we distributed the lethal aid at Halabja, morale went sky-high. It was one step closer to where we wanted to be for the attack.

Soon after we arrived, we got bittersweet news. The IMKI was going to stay out of the fight, but the IGK was all in with Ansar. Unfortunately, our missile strike on the 21st had bad timing. One of the missiles struck their headquarters while they were holding a meeting to vote if they should join or separate from Ansar. We learned it also killed

Saddam's liaison officer to Ansar who was in attendance. The IGK alliance created a new problem for us. We had an entire new set of enemy positions on the north flank that we hadn't planned for. A decision was made to split ODA 091 to support the Black Prong and the newly added Orange Prong on the northern flank. The team leader, CPT Eric Fellenz, remained with the Black Prong and Team Sergeant MSG Kevin Cleveland assumed responsibility for the Orange Prong.

Around midafternoon, word reached us in Halabja that Jalal Talabani was trying to broker a ceasefire between the PUK and Ansar with the IGK. When the PUK commanders on the ground heard the news, they did not receive it well. The time for talk had passed. Tovo headed back to Sulaymaniyah to explain why this was no longer an option. He was successful and returned a few hours later.

I was lying on the cold concrete floor, chilled and wide awake. It seemed no one else was sleeping around me, either. Somewhere around 0400 I could hear the first of several people start to stir and check their equipment again. Everybody knew what we were about to do. The air was calm, but the trepidation was palpable.

It felt like we were a medieval army attacking a walled city at first light. You could look out and see hundreds of small campfires. There was a strange calm that was distinctly different from the buzz that had been in the air all week as both sides had sporadic engagements with each other. Now, by contrast, it felt like the night brought a temporary period of uneasy calm over the entire region. It was unsettling.

Everything seemed to almost stop. Suddenly, the world had shrunk and the only things that mattered in that time were what was in your immediate vicinity. The three men sitting near you, quietly checking their gear, trying to eat something or sleep. There was no other world than this one, right now.

As I got myself together and collected my kit, I saw Bafel Talabani. I had developed a considerable amount of rapport with him by this point. I genuinely liked and respected him. He was a critical connector for us because of his English skills, but it's a disservice to him to say he was just an interpreter. As the son of the leader of the PUK, he didn't need to be here, but he was. His cousin Lahur was the same way. They seemed to always be at the most important place at the right time. They felt a responsibility to be a part of this fight. In fact, Bafel's father wasn't happy with him for allowing himself to be in the middle of the danger.

"Where are you going to be during the attack?" I asked.

"I'll be with 081," he responded in his British accent.

I nodded. I knew that meant he'd be with the Yellow Prong.

"How much ammo you got?" I asked.

"Four," Bafel revealed. I had ten magazines for my M4, which did him no good as they were a different caliber of ammunition than his AK-47. I hated the fact that we had different rifles. My mind hastened back to the Cold War era when 10th Group used to maintain AK-47s for every Special Forces soldier, specifically for the unconventional warfare missions in Europe.

Prior to deploying, lessons from Afghanistan were starting to emerge where simply firing your M4 in a sea of AK-47s could put you at considerable risk because they sound very different. In the middle of a huge firefight with AK-47s, as soon as you hear an M4 fire, it's instantly clear an American is shooting. The Taliban in Afghanistan quickly learned that killing an American also meant cutting off the close air support. Back at Fort Carson, I suggested we consider going in with AK-47s for these reasons. As we discussed this, Tovo thought we would really want our M4s because they had superior optics on them. I pointed out that we could put those optics on the AKs, but it didn't matter because it wasn't an option. In 1996, 10th Special Forces Group turned in all of their operational AK-47s because the prevailing belief was that they wouldn't need them again.

Sometime prior to this, I had actually talked to Bafel about getting me an AK-47, because I would have preferred to not stand out as the lone American with an M4 amongst a group of Peshmerga.

When I asked, Bafel shot back, "I would love to give you an AK, but my government is just not that comfortable giving you that type of lethal aid. I'll see if I can get you guys a bolt-action rifle or something." I must give Bafel credit for his sarcastic wit and sense of humor. In all seriousness, he explained that giving me an AK-47 would mean literally taking one out of the hands of a Peshmerga.

Now as Bafel was getting ready to leave the PUK HQs in Halabja and join up with the Yellow Prong, I reached into my ammunition pouch and pulled out a grenade. "I feel bad that I can't give you any ammunition, Bafel, but at least I can give you this. I hope you can give it back to me when this attack is done." I could see the gratitude in his eyes as he accepted the grenade.

His reply spoke to this moment of friendship. "Thank you. Grenades might be a good thing to have," he said simply.

"Good luck," I replied, as he moved out to join 081.

By now, everyone was awake and moving around. The calm was over and we were now bracing for the storm. It was mechanical. Everyone knew what to do and was getting it done. At certain points in life, time either seems to speed up or slow down. This was a fast morning and time sped up and seemed to gain momentum, especially during the last hour. My thoughts raced through all the preparation we had been doing and everything that lay ahead of us. Now, there was simply nothing more I could do. It's like studying for one of the biggest—if not *the* biggest—exams of your life. At a certain point, you have to close the book and hope like hell you've done enough preparation, because it's about to start.

As I looked out across the field at thousands of Peshmerga, any anxiety I had now started to subside. I wasn't sure if we would be able to do this in time to stop Saddam, but I was confident that Ansar's reign of terror over Halabja was about to come to an end.

CHAPTER 12
OPERATION VIKING HAMMER

On difficult ground, press on.
On encircled ground, devise stratagems.
On death ground, fight.

—SUN TZU

IT WAS STILL DARK AS WE MADE THE FIVE-MINUTE DRIVE UP THE DIRT track to the top of Gurdi Drozna. The outpost atop the hill provided a bird's-eye view to the start of the battle. I was standing alongside LTC Tovo, Kok Mustafa and the Charlie Company Commander, MAJ George Thiebes. We watched as the thousands of Peshmerga in long convoys of pickup trucks jockeyed for positions along the narrow roads. A few dump trucks had been converted into makeshift armored personnel carriers with sandbags and steel plates. Toward the front of each prong, a group of approximately one hundred men assembled. These would be the spearheads for each of the prongs.

At 0600 exactly, the single D-30 artillery piece fired a round, signaling the start of the attack.

THE GREEN AND YELLOW PRONGS
The objectives along the Green Prong's axis of advance included hills 868, 915, 1182, 1285 and 1365. The hills on the military maps were named based on the elevation of their peaks, depicted in meters above sea level. The Green Prong started their attack toward the first objective, hill 868. The sun was just starting to rise as the prong started taking some sporadic machine gun fire from the first line of enemy forces. The PUK responded with a volley from their 107 mm Katusha rockets, 106 recoilless rifles, 23 mm anti-aircraft gun, and 82 mm mortars. Within ten minutes the first aircraft was overhead. A Navy

F-14 dropped a single bomb on a position blocking the Green Prong and, in an instant, the fighting position was completely destroyed.

The other defenders higher up the valley had full view of the display before them, like fans watching a sporting event in a stadium. In the distance a B-52 dropped a line of bombs along the length of one of the higher ridgelines. I couldn't help but wonder, now having seen firsthand what was coming, if their extremist fervor was starting to waver as the reality of the situation started to sink in.

At the base of hill 868, the prong's commander, Kok Abdulla, remained crouched behind a rock wall with one hundred Peshmerga and ODA 093. As the fires shifted to hilltop 915, a B-52 dropped its ordnance on the next hilltop behind that, hill 1182. Kok Abdulla blew his whistle and the assault force of Peshmerga and Special Forces, following their commander, went over the wall and started the attack.

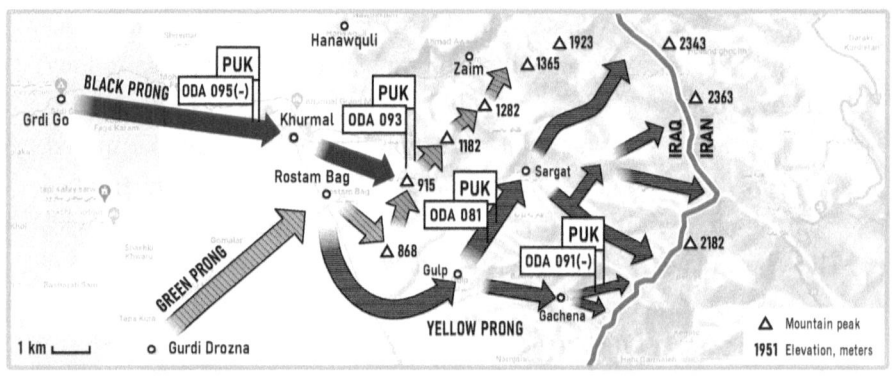

Map 4. The Green, Yellow and Black Prongs

The Yellow Prong, with ODAs 081 and 091, was already moving about two kilometers to the southeast of the Green Prong. The Yellow Prong's objective was to seize the town of Gulp, which sat on a crossroads to the entrance of two valleys—one of which led to Sargat and the other to Gochina. ODA 081 and a contingent of Peshmerga were to seize Sargat and the chemical/biological testing facility and ODA 091 with their Peshmerga would take Gochina.

The Green Prong's advance and subsequent objectives would take them along the north side of the valley that oversaw the Yellow Prong's advance toward Sargat. This would allow the two prongs to support each other with fires. SSG Chris Crum was an engineer and demolitions sergeant from ODA 081. He was one of three men who would move with ODA 093 on the Green Prong to help coordinate their efforts. In addition to the array of equipment the ODA had with them, Crum also had his M82 Barrett sniper rifle. The rifle fired .50-caliber match grade, armor piercing, explosive incendiary rounds. The rounds were originally intended for targeting vehicles and helicopters. The round explodes after penetrating a target, hitting the occupants with burning shrapnel as well as potentially igniting any fuel or ammunition.

With the thirty-pound rifle in hand, SSG Crum followed the Peshmerga. In addition to the rifle, he carried seventy rounds, his radio, a couple grenades, a pistol, and some water. Combined with his body armor he was carrying approximately eighty pounds of gear. The Peshmerga, by comparison, had no body armor, carried relatively little ammunition, and had no radios or water. He knew keeping up with them in the steep terrain would be a challenge.

Within minutes, the Peshmerga closed the distance and were flooding over their position, engaging any enemy who might have survived the air strike. As they advanced up the hill, a young Peshmerga about twenty-five meters away from the Americans exploded. They were advancing across a minefield and the craters from the air strikes slowed their movement. On the top of the hill, the Peshmerga swiftly directed the team members along a path between the small rock piles denoting buried mines. There were hundreds of them.

Looking through the scope on his rifle, Crum could see the Yellow Prong below had already cleared Gulp and was pressing up the valley. The ground around him was littered with dead Ansar fighters. There was little time to take stock as they had to push on to hill 915 to maintain contact with the Yellow Prong's advance. As the group crested the top of hill 915, the convoy from the Green Prong had driven up to meet them. After a quick resupply of ammunition and water, the element decided, in the interest of time, to tactically drive toward hill 1182 until they made contact.

In the valley below, the Yellow Prong was met with a hail of machine gun fire from a small hill near the entrance to the village of Gulp. The Peshmerga instinctively started running toward the fire. Suddenly the charge was interrupted by the sound of a low-flying jet breaking the sound barrier. The group stopped charging to look up and see the aircraft.

When a fighter rips through the air, the sound is more than loud—it's violent. Imagine the sound of tearing paper, only thousands of times louder. You can also tell when a fighter spots its intended target. The way it flies distinctly changes to something much more deliberate and aggressive. Watching the aircraft roaring overhead, it felt like we had brought mechanical dragons with us and suddenly unleashed them on the enemy.

As the hilltop exploded and the machine gun went silent, the screaming Peshmerga charged forward along the road into the village. One of the NCOs from ODA 081, SSG Mark Giaconia, was following the Peshmerga assault. His mind made a note of the gunfire to his far left on the high ground and he could hear the distinct sounds of Chris Crum's Barrett sniper rifle. He wondered how his team was holding up, but then his mind quickly returned to his own situation as he noted the severed body parts of enemy fighters along the road.

As the Yellow Prong entered Gulp and moved among the multitude of buildings, they came upon a mosque in the village center. Several dead fighters lay in twisted positions around the perimeter and inside the building. Among the dead were piles of leaflets in Arabic. On the cover were propaganda images: burning American and British flags and a picture of the World Trade Center collapsing. As the group inspected the mosque, another convoy of Peshmerga from the Yellow Prong, along with ODA 091, broke off to the right and continued toward the town of Gochina, roughly two kilometers from the Iranian border.

The Green Prong advanced to just below the crest of hill 1182. Despite the earlier air strikes, the top was still manned by a handful of fighters. The Peshmerga engaged the positions with their 106 mm recoilless rifle and heavy machine guns, causing the fighters to take cover behind a rock formation. SSG Crum spotted the group of fighters with his Barrett sniper rifle and estimated their range as 1400 meters. His first few rounds hit a few feet to the right. The impact caused the rocks to fragment, trigging the fighters to move farther to the backside of the hill.

As the Yellow Prong advanced up the road in the valley toward Sargat, they came under intense fire from the high ground on their left. The team sergeant spotted the fighters and directed the team to fire their M240 machine gun and MK-19 at the positions. SSG Giaconia was carrying an M21 sniper rifle. Looking through his scope, he could make out the bearded fighters taking cover on the hilltop. He could distinctly see them engaging the Green Prong. He inhaled, then slowly exhaled as he squeezed the trigger. The round struck its target and the fighter fell to the ground.

From hill 1182, Crum recognized the sounds of the MK-19 and realized it was 081 and the Yellow Prong. They were both engaging the same group of fighters from two sides. As the fighters took cover from the MK-19 rounds, Crum sighted in on two of the Ansar fighters. Making the adjustment from his last engagements, he fired one round and then another. This time he hit both targets. Crum and his teammates from the Yellow Prong continued to suppress the remaining enemy as the Peshmerga moved closer for their final assault. After they cleared the final positions, the Peshmerga secured hill 1182.

Continuing toward Sargat, the Yellow Prong had to advance through a curve in the valley that took them out of supporting view from the Green Prong. After the previous engagement, SSG Giaconia started to grow concerned that the columns were beginning to get separated from each other. He had lost contact with the other two elements from his ODA, one under the control of CPT Brian Rauen and the other under the team sergeant's control. He was unable to reach anyone on the radio. Just then, as Sargat came into view, the column came under intense fire from their front. Somewhat channelized by the terrain, the members of the prong had little terrain that provided suitable cover.

He quickly took cover behind a small rock wall. The fire was significantly more intense than anything he had previously experienced. The sheer volume of bullets flying back and forth looked like a horizontal rainstorm. SSG Giaconia, completely exhausted from the twelve hours of fighting, was feeling a dark wave come over him. Despite all his previous brushes with death, this was the first moment when he truly felt like they might not survive. Then CPT Rauen, the team leader of ODA 081, somehow sprinted through the hail of bullets, dodging gunfire to dive next to his guys behind the wall. CPT Rauen was attempting to rally his team, telling them they had to get up, get moving, and press forward to some cover about twenty meters off the road.

Although the situation was incredibly dire, Rauen's surprising calm and positive demeanor triggered something in Giaconia. It reenergized his resolve that they were going to survive this fight, or at least go out fighting. Rauen again took off running amidst the hail of gunfire to his next position. Giaconia realized immediately the captain had dropped his map. A moment later, Rauen returned, running through the fire again. Over the cacophony of gunfire, Giaconia shouted "You're going to get killed! I would have brought it to you."

CPT Rauen shrugged off his concern and responded, "I needed my map."

Giaconia and the Peshmerga with him continued to take fire as they darted from one position to the next, eventually low crawling to get to their final covered position. They were collocated with CPT Rauen, Bafel Talibani, and Randy from the CIA. Bafel was on the satellite phone with his father and Randy joked this would be the last time he would accompany Green Berets on an operation. The valley echoed with the sounds of a heavy machine gun firing from a bunker on the high ground, most likely a Soviet-era 12.7 or 14.5 mm Dshka machine gun.

They realized if they didn't destroy the gun, it was going to destroy them. They hatched a plan to run the couple hundred meters back to their pickup trucks, drive the trucks to the base of a piece of high ground and then carry the M2 .50-caliber machine gun, tripod, and ammunition up the hill to engage the enemy gun. The team's medic, SSG Ken Gilmore, and communications sergeant, SSG Blake Kramer, joined Giaconia and made the mad dash toward the trucks under fire. As they ran with tracers moving past them in both directions, it dawned on the NCOs there was a fair likelihood of accidentally being shot by a confused or frightened Kurd. They started shouting in hopes of not surprising the Peshmerga by running toward them.

As they reached the trucks, the group loaded up and prepared to drive closer to the base of a nearby high ground. As they started forward, a burst of fire hit the windshield and exited the passenger's window without hitting anyone in the cab. They sped 300 meters to the base of the hill and dismounted. With their weapons slung on their backs, Kramer lifted the entire eighty-pound gun and the attached sixty-pound tripod and hefted the entire assembly over his shoulder. Gilmore and Giaconia grabbed as many ammo cans as they could carry and directed half a dozen Kurds to do the same.

Fighting the forty-five-degree rock scree and mud slope, the group clambered 300 meters up the hill. Exhausted and enraged, they dropped their heavy loads to the ground. Instantly, the three-man team went to work. One man straightened the tripod and adjusted the gun in its cradle while another scanned for the target and the third opened the ammo cans and placed a belt into the feed tray. Within a minute Kramer was plunging effective fire onto the enemy bunker 600 meters away. Through his M21 sniper rifle scope, Giaconia watched as bullet after bullet fired from their .50-cal passed through the bunker where the enemy fire was originating. He watched as the bullets entered the building and passed out onto the other side. The sound of their gun echoed across the valley, drawing the attention of the Ansar fighters, who understood the threat it now posed. Despite the barrage of enemy small arms, the three NCOs wisely sank as low as possible and continued to pour fire into the bunker. After 200 rounds, the enemy gun was finally silent. From their vantage point, they now watched as the Peshmerga assault force flooded over the enemy defenses and arrived at the Sargat facility.

As they made their way to back to Sargat to link up with the rest of the team, one of the Kurds named Wahab stopped them. He had been following along during the firefight trying to catch up to the Americans. Wahab presented them with what can only be described as a charcuterie plate of meat and cheese. Mark looked at him in utter disbelief. "What is this?"

"I figured you might be hungry," Wahab offered. "I know Brian [CPT Rauen] likes soda, so I brought him a soda, too."

The soda tasted especially sweet as the group took a short and much-needed break to have some lunch and regroup. They sat a few feet from the facility, which by now was a large pile of rubble with a fence around it. Gunfire several hundred meters away reminded them that fighting was still underway. The trucks that had functioned as personnel carriers earlier were now ambulances. As the trucks stopped, a steady stream of blood flowed off the tailgate and pooled in the road. The team's medics looked at the wounded and did what they could. A casualty collection point had been established near the first objectives of the day and was manned by the battalion surgeon, MAJ Rick Ong, and his surgical team. They dealt with dozens of wounded, some walking miles with gunshot wounds to reach the collection point.

As the trucks departed, the team did a cursory search of the facility. The team leader decided to delay the facility inspection for the exploitation team that would come in the following morning. Hundreds of charred and mutilated enemy bodies lay all around the facility.

CHAPTER 13
THE END OF THE FIRST DAY

*In every battle there comes a time when both sides consider
themselves beaten; then he who continues the attack wins.*

– GENERAL ULYSSES S. GRANT

THE TERRAIN TO THE SOUTH WAS EVEN MORE MOUNTAINOUS THAN THAT
of the other prongs. Both the Red and Blue Prongs split their forces
into two separate columns each, in order to better cover their respective valleys. The Peshmerga and the teams drove on the dirt tracks
when they could and walked when the trails became too narrow for
their vehicles to negotiate. The final objective for both prongs was the
town of Biyara, which the Red Prong approached from the west as the
Blue Prong came from the south. Biyara sat in a mountain pass along
the border crossing with Iran. Just off to the east of the town was the
suspected foreign fighter training camp in a small settlement called
Darga Sharkan.

In his speech at the UN prior to the attack, Colin Powell mentioned
Abu Musab al-Zarkowi numerous times. He was a Jordanian jihadist
who had fought with al-Qaeda in Afghanistan. Although Osama bin
Laden considered him a thug and didn't take him seriously, Colin
Powell's speech elevated al-Zarkowi to a celebrity-like status within
the Jihadist world. It was believed that al-Zarkowi was hiding with the
Ansar fighters. If this was the case, it would most likely be at the Darga
Sharkan training camp.

The Blue Prong, along with ODA 095, started their advance from
Dalamar and cleared Tawera, Balha, Hawar, and numerous other small
villages not even listed on the map. The Blue Prong made surprisingly
fast progress along their route, especially considering the ruggedness
of the terrain and the fact that the majority of their movement was

dismounted. Their final ascent was up the north-south running ridge-line east of Biyara along the Iranian border. The ridge culminated at an elevation of 2,146 meters, offering a clear view into the Darga Sharkan camp. As they reached a vantage point to see the camp, they observed Iranian helicopters dropping off ammunition. While Iran's support to Ansar wasn't a surprise, their willingness to put Iranian helicopters at risk to resupply them was an indicator of how poorly the battle was going for Ansar. They obviously thought the situation was dire enough to warrant such a risky act.

The team reported that the fighters were loading up trucks and evacuating Darga Sharkan. I heard the exchange over the radio because a B-52 bomber arrived onsite. I thought to myself, "We got them." The B-52 explained that they could not drop ordnance because of the proximity to the Iranian border. They said their rules of engagement (ROE) didn't allow them to drop anything within one kilometer of the border. Immediately, I knew they were wrong. I got on the radio and started talking to the B-52's crew. CENTCOM's ROE actually allowed us to pursue and engage targets across the border if needed. As we debated the ROE, the team reported back on the radio to MAJ Thiebes that a convoy of approximately twenty trucks was loading up and preparing to move. After about ten minutes of debating back and forth, we finally determined that they could, in fact, bomb the target, but by then it was too late. The convoy had slipped across the border and out of sight.

While the Blue Prong could see the camp from the ridgeline to the east, the two columns of the Red Prong were still moving along their own axis of advance. One column cleared the towns of Kharge-lan, then Zardahal, while the other column cleared Kharpani and a series of unnamed ridgelines before finally reaching Biyara. Much like the Green and Yellow Prongs, they moved across a series of planned objectives, climbing increasingly higher up the valleys. They encountered resistance, called in air strikes and supporting fires, and then cleared and secured the positions with a Peshmerga ground assault.

By the afternoon, the prong had cleared and secured the majority of its objectives. As they approached Biyara, the terrain narrowed into a series of winding canyons. The ODA commander, CPT Pete Russo, was out of water and exhausted. He was on his third and last battery for his radio and unable to contact the other portions of his team in the adjacent valleys. As the terrain opened back up and Biyara came into view, the column could see fighters loading up trucks from the main mosque to flee across the border. Unaware of the incident between the B-52 and Blue Prong a short time earlier, Russo knew they wouldn't be able to prevent the enemy from crossing if they initiated an assault since the border crossing was less than a 1,000-meter drive for the enemy. He made the decision to call for an air strike. This time, the B-52 dropped several JDAMs, completely destroying the mosque. The enemy had been using the building to store ammunition and the strike triggered several secondary explosions.

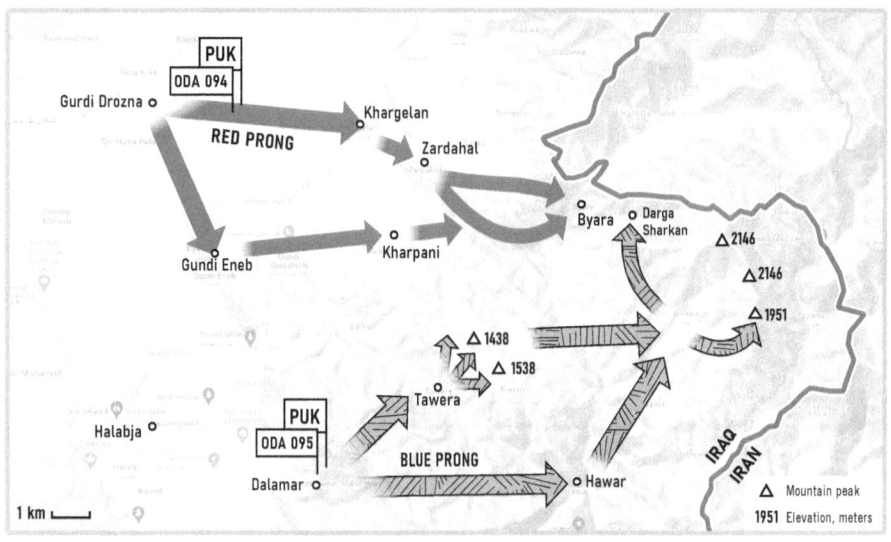

Map 5. The Red and Blue Prongs

Although the Ansar fighters had evacuated Biyara and the Darga Sharkan training camp, in their rapid departure they left more than enough behind to paint a picture of their gruesome activities. Part of the Red Prong moved into Biyara while the other half continued toward the training camp. In the camp, the team found a torture chamber with bloody meat hooks that had been used to suspend their prisoners. The room was stained with bloody handprints and footprints on the walls and ceiling around the hooks. There were bloodstains on the street and curb outside the main building where it appeared they had executed several prisoners.

While conducting a hasty search of the structures, the ODA uncovered a batch of foreign passports from the Middle East—Algeria, Sudan, Palestine, Afghanistan, etc. There were diagrams and formulas for producing chemical agents, workstations for making suicide vests, and laboratory facilities for the production of improvised munitions. The team also discovered several laptop computers, stacks of training manuals, and meticulously handwritten files. The training compound had areas dedicated as classrooms. In one of the rooms was an SA-7 shoulder-fired surface-to-air missile simulator. The SA-7 is the Soviet equivalent of the US Stinger missile, and the simulator was remarkably similar to the one in the battalion's own classroom back at Fort Carson.

As the team's deputy commander, CW2 Fleming, took in the windfall of disturbing material, he watched as the young Peshmerga returned from their own quick survey of the area to present what they had found to Kok Seamond, the prong's commander. The layout included several chickens, some bags of vegetables, a half a dozen eggs, and some other assorted supplies to feed the group. It was a battle drill the Peshmerga were very familiar with. This was how they sustained themselves.

Earlier that day, a young Kurd had handed him a small sack with a hard-boiled egg, two potatoes, and a small drawstring bag containing salt: the equivalent of a Kurdish MRE. He was impressed by the Peshmergas' toughness and their innovation and adaptability. As he sat and reflected on what they had accomplished, he looked at his Garmin GPS. Although they had moved roughly fifteen kilometers straight-line distance on the map, his GPS indicated that they had walked over thirty kilometers, maneuvering from one hilltop objective to the next. He was exhausted but amazed by what they had accomplished.

BATTLE AT NIGHT

As the Yellow Prong reached the easternmost building in Sargat, they came under fire. The previously separated elements of the ODA had all recently regrouped. The ODA 081 Team Sergeant spotted the enemy fire and, like before, picked up their M2 .50-caliber machine gun and carried it to a building for cover. The team engaged in a duel of heavy machine guns, firing roughly 700 rounds. CPT Rauen called MAJ Thiebes and explained the situation: they had taken up a position in a building to defend themselves, but the enemy was counterattacking and they were starting to run low on ammunition.

Standing next to MAJ Thiebes, who was coordinating close air support, I could hear the Air Force explain, "Negative. We have nothing for you. The priority is to 2nd Battalion, who are troops in contact."

A few days prior, I had heard the 2nd Battalion commander brag about the ingenious workaround they had figured out for getting whatever close air support you wanted: just call troops in contact and you get whatever you need. I didn't lose my temper much during this campaign, but this is one of the times I did.

I got on the radio with the JSOTF and started shouting, "I need you guys to tell the aircraft that *we* are the priority!"

The fire support officer at the JSOTF explained, "You are the priority, but 2nd Battalion is dealing with a troops in contact."

I asked the fire support officer, "How long have they 'been in contact'?"

"Uh, for about the last ninety-six hours," he said.

I told him, "Look at their Blue Force trackers and the enemy that they are in contact with. They're miles apart. I've got a team that's about to get overrun! Do you understand that? I need close air support! Right fucking now!"

After a long pause, someone eventually came up and communicated they were sending two Navy F-14s, who quickly showed up on station. At that point, however, it was too late. The team sergeant, MSG Sanders, came back on the radio and explained they were mixed in with the enemy at this point and he couldn't use the air support.

MAJ Thiebes alerted his mortar section to provide 81 mm fires. I got on the radio with our battalion rear back at Sulaymaniyah, explaining I needed them to push all the mortar ammo they had to our position because I expected us to be defending ourselves all night and the one or two mortars we had would be all we could count on to stave off the adversary. Since we didn't have any vehicles, my operations team started making do with what we had and coordinating for guys to bring us what they could in any cars they could find.

To my surprise and relief, a moment later, MSG Sanders called and said they were all okay. The 81 mm mortar fire from ODA 093 on their flank with the Green Prong had broken the enemy's counterattack. A few kilometers to the north, ODA 093 was still clearing hill 1282. A sniper fortified by a rock formation on the high ground was delaying the Peshmerga advance to their final objective, hill 1365. The lead element of the assault called back to the ODA 093 Team Sergeant MSG Chris Hartnett, who had been manning the 60 mm mortars. Chris set five rounds to airburst and fired at the sniper. The rounds landed spot on, killing the sniper.

The enemy seemed to be consolidating around hill 1365. Past this it was a steep climb in snow to the Iranian border. I was on the radio with CPT Steve Stowell from ODA 093, collocated with the Green Prong, who told me the Kurdish guy to his left just got killed by a sniper. A few seconds later, he called again to say the Kurdish guy on his right just got killed by a sniper. I wasn't trying to be flippant about it, but I told Steve he needed to find a better position because I didn't want the next call to be from someone else telling me *he* had been shot by a sniper.

Shortly thereafter, CPT Rauen directed a B-52 strike onto hill 1365. As the aircraft lined up to drop, the Green Prong appeared and was advancing on the enemy positions. CPT Rauen realized the potential fratricide unfolding in front of him, but there was little he could do at this point. Five bombs landed in a row, 400 meters to the front of 093. Amazingly, no friendlies were injured. The team was entering an area that was off limits to all but the most senior Ansar fighters. A ravine opened on the backside of Sargat that contained several caves. It was believed that this was where the senior Ansar members lived. As the team approached the caves, MSG Sanders fired his M203 grenade launcher into one of the openings. Another team members shot a shoulder-fired anti-tank launcher that exploded even deeper into the cave. With little interest in clearing the caves, the team threw in some CS grenades as a final measure.

It occurred to me that, with maybe an hour of daylight left, it was important for the guys to set up a defensible position for the night. Trying to find defendable ground is not something you want to be doing in the dark. MAJ George Thiebes and I were on the radio with several teams communicating that point: pick a spot you can defend and fortify your defenses.

About twenty minutes later, I turned around to see CPT Steve Stowell—who had lost the men to his immediate left and right to sniper fire—standing behind me on Gurdi Drozna. Imagine my confusion as I looked down to see him holding a plate of food containing chicken, rice, and a falafel. I felt like the gears in my brain were breaking as I asked him, "What are you doing here?! How did you get here?"

"Oh," he responded casually. "We came back down for chow."

"What? I...don't understand what you're telling me," I faltered.

The Kurd with him assured me it was fine. "It's all okay. Nobody here fights at night. It's too dangerous with the minefields."

I had never heard of anything like this in all my life. A moment ago I was making preparations with the teams to fortify their positions and use mortars if necessary to hold off the enemy until morning. Now, I could see a hundred guys starting to wander in around me as though we were all returning from rounds of golf after our respective staggered tee times.

While I expressed my concern, the Kurds reassured me it was okay. "No one is going to counterattack at night. We just don't do that."

Everyone left a skeleton crew back at their position, but the majority had come back down to a lower position for chow. For the Peshmerga that remained forward, it was a battle drill. As it started to get dark, they found pieces of scrap wood and built dozens of small fires. It was amazing to watch how comfortable the Peshmerga were in the field and how little they needed to sustain themselves. They shared what food and water they had amongst each other. They huddled together and used their scarves to stay warm around the fires.

It was fully dark now. Our signal intercept teams, referred to as Special Operations Team-Alphas or SOT-As), were picking up all sorts of SIGINT (signals intelligence) from the enemy. The 10th Group SOT-As were exceptionally skilled thanks to the experience they had gained in Kosovo in the last few years. They were able to intercept conversations between enemy fighters discussing their planned rally point where they intended to consolidate that night.

The SOT-A senior NCO told me about the intercepts. That was a pretty amazing piece of work in its own right. A minute later, someone else came on the radio and announced there were four AC-130s in theater, asking if anyone had a target.

I thought, "As a matter of fact, I do." In fortuitous timing, Turkey had started allowing aircraft to come in that day. For the first time in the conflict, the Spooky AC-130 gunships were in theater and looking for something to do. The AC-130 is a modified cargo aircraft with a very specialized array of sensors and weapons. The weapons are fitted on the same side of the aircraft allowing it to orbit in a circle while maintaining direct fire on the enemy. The AC-130 is one of the most lethal killing machines in the US arsenal. Although it doesn't do well in a high anti-aircraft environment, it was perfect for our circumstances. I couldn't imagine the carnage those four gunships were about to cause.

MAJ Thiebes and I all coordinated the grid coordinates with the JTAC for the AC-130s to attack and gave them the green light to strike anything else they happened to see in the Ansar defenses. This was the first night in the war zone for the AC-130s, and they would get to lay waste to the enemy as they tried to regroup and refit for the next day of the battle.

On top of Gurdi Drozna we had a six-man element: LTC Tovo, MAJ Thiebes, me, and three others. We were utterly exhausted, but the options for sleeping weren't great. We decided to take shelter in a small, decrepit dirt bunker with a roof made from a piece of curved corrugated metal. We coordinated a schedule for someone to be on radio watch and security for thirty minutes apiece while the others slept throughout the night. When your half hour is done, you wake up the next guy on the list and it passes down the line. We spent the night in that rotation.

Just prior to sunrise I could hear the radio transmission from the AC-130s that they were Winchester on ammo, the term commonly used by aircrews to convey that they were out of ammunition, and were now pulling off station before the sun came up. Again, I thought, "Good Lord, four AC-130s' worth of ammunition expended on the enemy." Despite our sleeping in shifts, I knew I'd had a much better night than al-Ansar had experienced.

As morning was approaching, the Kurds brought us breakfast and it was almost time to get back to work. LTC Tovo, MAJ Thiebes, and I drove up to join the Green Prong.

CHAPTER 14
RESTARTING THE BATTLE

Hell is empty and all the devils are here.

—WILLIAM SHAKESPEARE, *The Tempest*

AS THE SUN CAME UP, THE BATTLE HAD DEVOLVED INTO A ROUT. THE al-Ansar survivors decided to make a break for the Iranian border. As part of the Green Prong, we could see the fighters fleeing. Exactly as I had been told the evening prior, whenever these guys realized they needed to make the two-kilometer dash for the Iranian border, they didn't start the trek until sunrise. Now they were in knee-deep snow about two kilometers from us. One of the Kurds came running over to the Americans with the Green Prong and explained that a large number of the Ansar fighters were coming out of the caves in the canyon near Zalm, approximately four kilometers to their north. The team quickly followed the Peshmerga to a position to observe the mass exodus to the border.

Within minutes, the team contacted the mortar section with the Green Prong and relayed the coordinates for a fire mission. A moment later several rounds of 60 mm mortars rained down on the fighters. The canyon amplified the effects of the rounds, trapping the fleeing fighters in a narrow corridor. SSG Crum had run out of Barrett .50-caliber rounds and had to start delinking the belt ammunition intended for the M2 machine guns. He had fired so many rounds during the last thirty-six hours that the bipod on his rifle had broken off.

As Tovo and I arrived at their location, the ODA and Peshmerga were in the process of repositioning to engage another group of fleeing fighters approximately three kilometers away. The group of enemy fighters was moving up the final slope, trudging through deep snow. Before the ODA could engage them, the fighters reached the crest of the ridge marking the border and disappeared over the other side into Iran. A moment later, the fighters reappeared with an Iranian flag that they borrowed from the border guards. They stood on the ridge waving the flag to taunt us, assuming they were off limits once over the border.

"Are we allowed to shoot them if they are technically inside Iran?" someone asked.

I looked at the team sergeant from ODA 093 and responded, "What are you waiting for? Shoot those guys."

In a manner of seconds, he adjusted the mortar to an almost direct fire angle, stood on the base plate to stabilize it and fired two rounds. The rounds found their target and the men collapsed in a circle around the Iranian flag which was now lying on the ground. After that incident, the Iranian border guards appeared to have gotten the message and started shooting the approaching Ansar fighters.

As we surveyed the battlefield, we encountered dead bodies everywhere. We inspected several of them for any potential intelligence value. Many of them had diet pills on them, presumably to help keep them awake and alert. At one point, I discovered a dead fighter with a bullet wound in his forehead—except not the normal small round hole you would expect. Instead, the bullet had been tumbling and hit his forehead lengthwise, causing the top of his head to explode, ejecting his intact brain, which I discovered about three feet away from his body.

Prior to deploying, I had been given a burned piece of paper from the World Trade Center by a member of the New York Fire Department, which I carried with me. Since we knew Ansar was affiliated with al-Qaeda, I chose to bury the piece of paper underneath his body as a symbolic gesture in response to the attack of September 11th, 2001. The Kurds asked what I was doing. When I explained myself, they quietly acknowledged and said they understood.

At the Sargat facility, the Yellow Prong with ODA 081 discovered an estimated 150 to 200 dead enemy fighters scattered around the facility perimeter. Following the prong's advance was a chemical recon and site exploitation team. Sifting through the rubble of the facility, they collected various samples that confirmed the presence of hydrogen cyanide at the site. The ODA collected bags of foreign passports, computer drives, gas masks, atropine injectors, various antibiotics for respiratory illness, notebooks with formulas for nerve agent, and a yellow Post-It note with a phone number to a point of contact in al-Qaeda's affiliate in the Philippines, Abu Sayyef. The team also undertook the gruesome task of collecting hair samples from the hundreds of dead bodies for further chemical and biological analysis. As the site exploitation team collected their evidence, local Kurdish residents went about their day as if everything were business as usual. Former residents reoccupied their homes that had been taken by Ansar fighters. Women were sweeping the doorways and men were collecting the dead fighters into piles.

BLACK AND ORANGE PRONGS

As the second day of the battle resumed, the Orange Prong was still actively fighting with some of the IGK fighters. As they approached their final objective, a large open flattop named hill 1351 near the town of Hanawquli, they found themselves in a fairly desperate situation.

The team sergeant for ODA 091, MSG Kevin Cleveland, relayed the enemy was counterattacking and they were out of range of the mortars. The Peshmerga contingent of nearly one hundred men took up a defensive perimeter. MAJ Thiebes moved quickly to get an aircraft on station. MSG Cleveland explained that the enemy was in a group much larger than the Peshmerga and maneuvered to overrun his position.

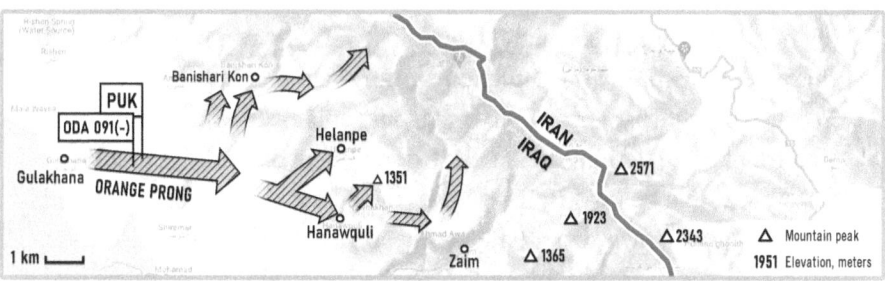

Map 6. The Orange Prong

As the B-52 came on station, Cleveland explained he needed the bombs dropped in a line across the enemy's front. Without the benefit of an Air Force JTAC and under intense enemy fire, Cleveland relayed the coordinates for the drop. The aircraft asked for his initials, a standard practice when bombs are being dropped in an emergency situation with an uncertified controller.

Over the radio, Cleveland announced, "It's my call. Danger close," indicating he knew they were well within the minimum safety range of the ordnance but he was still authorizing the strike. One by one, the 1,000-pound bombs dropped from left to right in a series of five massive explosions that reverberated across the entire valley. When the strike was completed, the valley floor was scarred black in a line stretching two kilometers wide. It was an incredibly brave and risky decision. It worked: the counterattack came to a halt.

Over the course of the next few days, the Peshmerga units with their Special Forces ODAs continued to clear pockets of enemy resistance securing the high ground up to the Iranian border. In total, there were between 300 and 500 enemy fighters killed. Over the course of the two days of fighting, there were no casualties for the Americans, which was amazing. Sadly, about fifty Kurds were killed and at least twice that many were wounded, although it was difficult to ascertain an accurate number. The ODAs called in nearly seventy air strikes during the battle, half of which were called as emergency close air support by the Special Forces team members not certified to drop ordnance.

As we started to get a sense of the scope and sophistication of the enemy's activities, Tovo and I were looking at some of the captured materials. We flipped through one booklet and immediately stopped at an illustration. Although it was in Arabic, we both recognized the picture instantly—a depiction of lima beans in a glass of water. Because lima beans absorb water at a particular rate, they can be used as a timer for a detonator. An electrode attached to a float in a jar of water and lima beans will descend as the beans absorb the water and the level goes down, eventually connecting with the other electrode. We recognized it from a formerly classified Special Forces improvised explosives manual written in the 1970s.

Within twenty-four hours of the battle, the bulk of the PUK units were headed back toward the Green Line. The ranks of the PUK units along the Green Line tripled overnight, as 9,000 motivated and newly-energized Kurdish fighters arrived, equipped with weapons and ammunition recently acquired from the battlefield. ODA 091 remained in Halabja to help the PUK clean-up the remaining pockets of Ansar fighters.

While I was incredibly happy with the outcome of the battle, my mission wasn't to defeat Ansar. They were just a means to an end, albeit one that I was very happy to undertake. My attention could now turn to Saddam and his northern Army.

CHAPTER 15
SHIFTING TO OFFENSE

If the enemy is to be coerced you must put him in a situation
that is even more unpleasant than the sacrifice you call on him
to make. The hardships of that situation must not of course be
merely transient—at least not in appearance. Otherwise the
enemy would not give in but would wait for things to improve.

—CARL VON CLAUSEWITZ, *ON WAR*

A FEW DAYS BEFORE I HEADED TO HALABJA, THE JSOTF ATTACHED A
company from 3rd Battalion, 3rd Special Forces Group to support us.
They hadn't participated in any of the planning and weren't familiar
with the area or the Kurds, so there wasn't time to integrate them into
our plan. While in our area at Sulaymaniyah, one of their teams had an
accidental discharge with the MK-19 grenade launcher, sending the 40
mm grenade exploding next to my aid station. Fortunately, no one was
injured. Incredibly, they did it again a mere few hours later. Thankfully, as luck would have it, no one was injured at that time either.

Now that I had returned to the FOB in Sulaymaniyah, I was considering pushing their teams to link up with C Company and assist in their
mopping up efforts. One of my guys came rushing in and said, "One of
the 3rd Group guys just shot himself in the face with a star cluster!" This
device is a handheld flare in an aluminum tube about the size of the
cardboard tube in the middle of a roll of paper towels. It has a cap on it
that, when removed and placed on the other end of the tube, serves as a
firing pin for the flare. The soldier had removed the cap, configured the
flare to be fired, and stowed it in a side pocket of a pack. While loading
the pack into their vehicle, it fired into his face. Fortunately, I still had
an aid station to treat his injury.

Despite my concerns, I dispatched one of the teams to link up with MSG Cleveland from ODA 091. They were still clearing caves and finding prisoners in the Halabja area. As the 3rd Group ODA made the two-hour drive to the link-up spot, we heard the radio call of "troops in contact."

This immediately struck us as odd because the area between Suly and Halabja is generally enemy-free. The ODA described an enemy position on a hillside about four kilometers from their position. I knew at that range all they could really see were dots on a hill. One of my ops guys looked at the Blue Force tracker and announced, "That's 091 that they are calling as enemy."

We were about to witness a fratricide incident.

A moment later my deputy, CPT Jones, got on the radio with the team's JTAC and canceled the strike. He explained, "That's a friendly position, it's 091." As we stood there shaking our heads, a voice came over the guard net—a backup emergency radio net. Apparently, the team hadn't considered that we were monitoring it as well. The voice on the net again announced they were "troops in contact" and needed immediate air support.

This time I intervened and called off the mission, ordering, "ROUGHNECK 91, return to base. Immediately." When they arrived, it quickly devolved into a yelling match.

They were shouting "Fuck you, we're leaving!" as I hollered back, "Get the fuck out of my sector!" A few minutes later, their convoy headed to the JSOTF at Erbil to link back up with their battalion headquarters.

THE 173RD AIRBORNE BRIGADE

On the night of March 26th, the 173rd Airborne Brigade conducted a parachute jump onto the Bashur airfield, roughly forty kilometers northeast of Erbil in the 2nd Battalion/KDP sector. Nearly 1,000 paratroopers jumped onto the airfield. Soon after, follow-on aircraft landed to deliver the brigade's artillery, counter battery radar, mortar, anti-tank platoons, and a mechanized company consisting of four M1A1 Abrams tanks and nine armored personnel carriers.

Before the deployment to Romania in January, a handful of us from 10th Group traveled to Vicenza, Italy to meet and coordinate with the 173rd commander and his staff. The meeting did not produce the relationship we had hoped. The commander, COL Mayville, was largely uninterested in any of our plans or suggestions. Now that they were in country, we had hoped to incorporate their considerable combat power into our operations. The amount of combat power they brought in country in a short period of time was impressive.

We approached them again with the same offer to join our efforts. Like our meetings in Italy months earlier, COL Mayville was unwilling to have his forces leave the Bashur airfield. Every request for his forces to support or accompany ours were denied. As impressive as their force was, it appeared it wasn't going to be of any assistance to us in fighting the Iraqi army.

YOU WANT ME TO DO WHAT?

As large numbers of well-armed and motivated Peshmerga moved from Halabja to join the PUK units along the Green Line facing the Iraqi army, the JSOTF was increasingly telling us we couldn't cross the Green Line, often bypassing the SOTF and reaching out to our teams directly. On several occasions, I explained to JSOTF officers that we had pushed well past the Green Line days prior. A day later they would come back with a new, revised acceptable limit of advance based on conversations with leadership. SOCCENT was getting guidance from CENTCOM, both of which were located in Qatar. Invariably, by the time the information reached us, the PUK and their ODA counterparts were already several kilometers past the new limit.

On at least two occasions we convinced the PUK to fall back and relinquish ground they had taken the day before, simply to comply with the order. I argued with the operations officers at the JSOTF that following these instructions equated to not accomplishing my mission, so I wanted to know which was more important. I never got an answer.

On ODA 083, CPT Lock explained the odd orders to fall back by claiming that the US had directed aircraft to engage targets past free fire lines and it could put their lives in danger. While a complete lie, it gave Lock the excuse he needed to explain the order that he himself didn't understand. He further capitalized on the opportunity to explain that bombs wouldn't hit the Americans, so when you are assaulting make sure you remain in sight of an American at all times. This provided a useful incentive for the Peshmerga to pay attention and communicate during their assaults. Wherever the Americans went, the Peshmerga stayed close by.

The next wave of guidance was how many Kurds could accompany an ODA. We received guidance that no more than one hundred Kurds could advance with our teams, then it was changed to no more than 500 per ODA. Between the orders to fall back and now the orders restricting the number of Peshmerga going into battle, it felt like we weren't all on the same page as to what we were trying to accomplish. It was difficult to take any guidance seriously that we knew was ultimately being driven by Turkish concerns, especially when accommodating them would have put American and Kurdish lives at risk. As far as I was concerned, Turkey forfeited their vote when they denied us access to the FSB and overflights.

While planning how to take Kirkuk with the PUK leadership, they shared the "traditional way" that they normally attacked Kirkuk, introducing us to what we called the old Peshmerga. These were men who had been involved with various attempts to attack and capture the city dating back to the 1970s. They explained, "You want to start by cutting the north-south highway at Tuz Khurmatu south of the city." So we started to devise a plan to cut the highway and surround the city as much as possible while also coordinating underground activity from within.

ODA 081

In accordance with what the PUK leadership told us, MAJ Roberson tasked ODA 081 to head to Tuz, a town about thirty miles south of Kirkuk. It's the main town along Highway 2 and the terrain provides a natural chokepoint due to the cliffs directly north of town. That makes it very easy to control. The week prior, JSOTF had finally gotten us four white Land Rovers per ODA, which made things a lot easier. With the Halabja fight over, ODA 081 was given back to MAJ Roberson, who had responsibility for the center sector of the Green Line. He chose to send 081 to secure the high ground at Tuz.

As the team traveled to Tuz, they eventually turned off the roads and moved overland to cross the Green Line. During their movement, a Kurdish car hit a landmine. Although no one was seriously hurt, the front wheel was blown off and they realized they had wandered into a minefield. The ODA got out of their vehicles with flashlights and pulled out a bag of small, green chem lights to mark any land mines they saw. They spent the next five hours painstakingly walking very slowly with flashlights through the minefield in front of their vehicles. When they finally set foot on the highway, an enormous sense of relief washed over them as they touched the pavement.

Once they arrived on April 6th, it was evident why the Kurds had recommended taking Tuz. The high ground dominated so much you could see ten miles south along the highway. If a reinforcing military convoy were to come to the Iraqis' aid in Kirkuk, the team would be able to see them forty miles before they got there—accounting for the ten-mile sightline plus the thirty additional miles to Kirkuk.

The team identified Iraqi defensive positions to the north, west, and south of the city. The team carefully plotted the enemy positions and coordinated a strike. The first few strikes hit the positions closet on the west side of Highway 2, devastating the Iraqi forces. The team methodically repeated the same process to the north, then to the south, then to the west again. After a few days, the weather was particularly clear and the Iraqis started to look for the aircraft contrails. As soon as they saw the aircraft contrails start to line up parallel with the highway, hundreds of Iraqi soldiers jumped from their positions and moved several hundred meters from their vehicles and bunkers. For a while, the Iraqis returned to their crater bunkers and burning vehicles. Eventually, the masses determined there was no longer any point to occupying the positions and began stripping off their uniforms and deserting en masse.

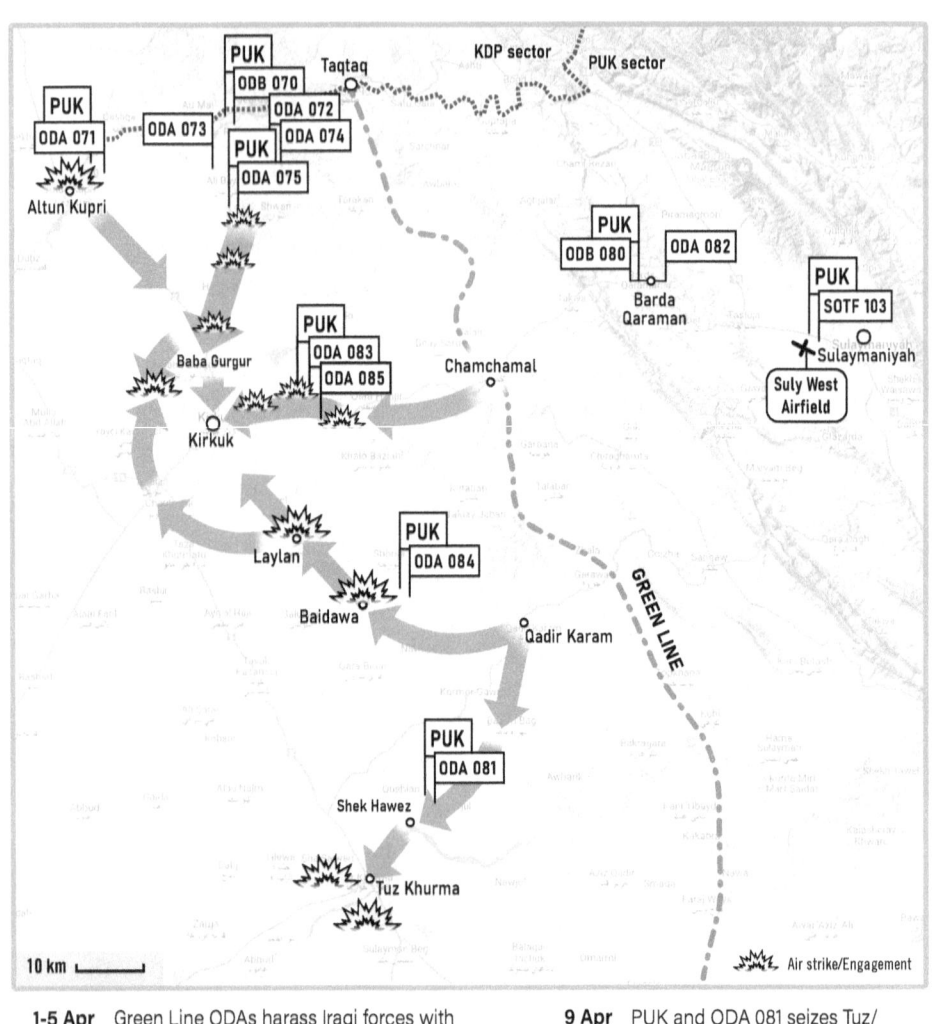

1-5 Apr	Green Line ODAs harass Iraqi forces with air strikes, mortars, and assaults.
5 Apr	Near fratricide incident with ODA 071 and KDP and SOTF 102 at Altun Kupri
6 Apr	PUK and ODA 075 assaults the Iraqi fort north of Kirkuk
7 Apr	U.S. launches ground attack on Bagdad (THUNDER RUN)

9 Apr	PUK and ODA 081 seizes Tuz/ cutting Hwy 2, U.S. Forces enter Baghdad
9/10 Apr	PUK with U.S. Special Forces teams make final assault on Kirkuk, ODA 084 seizes Baidawa, Laylan and Baba Gurgur Oil fields
10 Apr	PUK, with U.S. Special Forces seize Kirkuk
11 Apr	173rd ABN BDE enters Kirkuk and occupies the airfield

Map 7. The Disposition of Friendly Forces (April 1-11)

ODA 071

The KDP were clearly getting concerned about the PUK seizing Kirkuk without them. MAJ Tye Connett, the ODB 070 commander, called me to warn me that they recently had several incidents where KDP Peshmerga had come across the Little Zab River into Altun Kupri. The river is the established boundary between the KDP and PUK. Altun Kupri controls the bridge across the Little Zab River, which is the only crossing point to access Kirkuk from the north. I asked Tye if any of the ODAs from 2nd Battalion were with the KDP. They were not. As Tye put it, "It's only a matter of time before a firefight breaks out between the guys if this keeps up."

My first recourse was to contact the JSOTF Operations team. They assured me I was mistaken in the matter, but they would look into it. A day later, Tye called me again and explained that they had in fact received some machine gun fire from across the river.

This time I reached out to the JSOTF J-3. While explaining the gravity of the situation, I told him the KDP "didn't have any adult supervision with them." He interpreted my comment to mean that I didn't think 2nd Battalion constituted adult leadership. He proceeded to hand the radio to COL Cleveland, relaying his interpretation of what I had said. COL Cleveland didn't want to speak with me and told me to put Tovo on the line.

Tovo, standing beside me the entire time, now replied into the handset, "Sir, that's not what he said. Sir... Sir, may I speak?" Cleveland hung up.

The next day, Connett informed me that 2nd Battalion was planning to attack and seize Altun Kupri that night. I again reached out to the JSOTF Operations team. This time I was less than cordial. I asked them how on earth 2nd Battalion was planning to attack into my battle space and on a position that has Americans with Blue Force trackers on it. The officer proceeded to explain that they had been told that the Iraqis controlled Altun Kupri and they issued a fragmentary order (FRAGO), redrawing the battle space.

My frustration was growing. "What FRAGO?"

A moment later, the officer said, "FRAGO number 23."

Looking at the files, I replied, "Nope. FRAGO 23 is the General Parker visit."

The officer, realizing they had numbered multiple FRAGOs with the same numbers and failed to notify us of the change, muttered the words, "Oh, crap."

Administrative mistake aside, I asked, "How do you not see it's a friendly position from the Blue Force Tracker?" The now-flustered officer had no answer. He assured me they would take care of it.

After the call, I contacted MAJ Connett and the team on Altun Kupri, ODA 071. The team thanked me for looking out for them, but now I told them to pull off the site. The team was confused after listening to the radio exchange. "Sir, you got them to call off the attack," they protested.

"Yeah, I know what they said. Just do me a favor and pull back," I replied.

Later that night, a barrage of mortar rounds came crashing down onto the south side of the Altun Kupri bridge, followed by an assault of KDP Peshmerga and their ODA counterparts. 2nd Battalion had successfully seized Altun Kupri from 3rd Battalion and the PUK.

ODA 075

Around the same time as the growing tension with the KDP in the A Company's sector, the teams from 3rd Battalion, 3rd Special Forces Group, whom I had thrown out of my sector previously for being too reckless and trigger-happy, had regrouped as a company near Erbil and developed a plan to seize the Baba Gurgur oil fields on the north side of Kirkuk. They planned to depart from the KDP's lines, drive across the wide-open area, infiltrate behind the Iraqi defenses, turn south, and seize the oil facility. Frankly, when we heard about their plan, we thought it was ridiculous. The wide-open area they chose is known as the Debecka crossroads. The area is believed to be the location of the battle of Gaugamela, where Alexander the Great's army battled the army of King Darius III in 331 B.C. The code name for their operation was NORTHERN SAFARI.

On that same day, April 6th, in the northern part of my sector, which coincidentally contained the Baba Gurgur oil fields, the Cobras, along with ODA 075, attacked the Koni Domlan ridgeline defenses. Years prior, the Iraqis had built huge rectangular concrete buildings with circular turrets on the corners to defend what they considered the frontier. As the fighting progressed into the day, the Iraqis started to more effectively concentrate their fires against their attackers. While ODA 075 and the Cobras were the main effort, the other four ODAs (071, 072, 073, 074) were also converging on the attack with their Peshmerga units. The situation was starting to turn dire as the Cobras were not attacking from favorable terrain. CPT Bekurs called troops in contact over the net, indicating he needed emergency air support. Moments later, an Air Force Airborne Warning and Control System (AWACS) aircraft, call sign DOOM, came on the radio and directed a fighter aircraft toward his position. As the aircraft approached, another call came over the radio frantically shouting, "This is INCA TANGO. Tanks, we've got tanks!"

The call was from a JTAC assigned to one of the 3rd Group ODAs taking part in NORTHERN SAFARI in the KDP/2nd Battalion sector, approximately forty kilometers northwest of CPT Bekurs team, ODA 075. The ODAs from 3rd Special Forces Group hadn't made it very far past the KDP's front line trace when the Iraqis decided to respond by pushing a platoon of T-55 tanks and infantry into the open area. Subsequently, a large firefight erupted.

The AWACs came on to say, "Stand by, I'm diverting the aircraft to your position."

I grabbed the handset and said, "DOOM, this is NOMAD 43. Negative, negative, I have troops in contact!" DOOM came back and explained that the call with tanks took priority. "You don't understand the situation," I argued. "ODA 075 is dismounted in the middle of a ground attack. The element calling tanks is mounted and has Javelin anti-tank missiles." As I was arguing with DOOM, Bekurs came on the net, with machine guns clearly firing in the background.

"We can fall back," Bekurs said. "If they really need support, give it to them." Bekurs and Abizaid terminated the attack and fell back to their previous position.

Moments later, as we listened to the radio traffic and watched the engagement on the Blue Force Tracker feed, we heard the emergency call for close air support. My Fire Support Officer plotted the grid coordinates in real time in comparison to their Blue Force trackers on our digital map display and called out, "Oh shit! That's behind the KDP lines." As we scrambled to assess the situation, our first thought was that the Iraqi tanks had broken through the Kurdish defenses and were headed straight into downtown Erbil.

A call of "Cease fire! Cease fire! Friendlies hit!" came over the radio. The aircraft had dropped its ordnance on a destroyed tank hull that was being used by the KDP to observe the battle to their west.

As a result of the error, two of the American Special Forces soldiers from 2nd Battalion were wounded, seventeen Peshmerga and several international journalists were killed, and the KDP leader's son, Waji Barzani, was critically wounded. The JSOTF went to massive lengths to save his life and evacuate him, taking him all the way to Landstuhl, Germany.

Unfortunately, beyond killing a company of Iraqi defenders and their vehicles, the operation failed to accomplish its stated objectives. It didn't facilitate US or Kurdish forces getting behind the Iraqi lines or open up a route for follow-on forces to advance toward the Baba Gurgur oil fields, Kirkuk, or Mosul.

ODA 084

ODA 084's efforts to cross the Green Line and find the Iraqi front lines had paid off. They had been harassing pockets of Iraqi forces across a nearly twenty-mile front line trace, creating a deception that there were, in fact, several different Peshmerga units attacking the Iraqis. On April 7th, CPT Holevas attended a sector command meeting with Kok Usman to address the plan going forward. Usman had recently been communicating with the PUK leadership and was getting an idea of the larger plan for taking Kirkuk. Since the attack against Ansar al-Islam, the Peshmerga ranks along the Iraqi front had tripled over about forty-eight hours. Hundreds of motivated and well-armed Peshmerga had now joined their formation. The decision was made to attack Qaladiz on April 8th and then Baidawa on the 10th.

To the PUK's surprise, the Iraqi Army abandoned their positions in Qaladiz that morning. Kok Usman's Peshmerga and the ODA entered the village and occupied the former Iraqi positions. From the roof of the three-story building, the team could see the Iraqis in their new positions approximately two kilometers away.

The team got to work, pinpointing the Iraqi positions for an air strike. After a successful strike on the encampment, the Iraqi artillery responded by firing hundreds of 152 mm and 122 mm artillery rounds in the village. The response was substantially different than the previous engagements. The intensity of the artillery response forced the ODA and Peshmerga to withdraw to their previous camp a few kilometers east toward Kadir Qarim. CPT Holevas started to suspect they had reached the Iraqis' final defensive lines on the outskirts of Kirkuk. The impression he got was that there was a growing degree of desperation among the Iraqi forces and it was going to require a more deliberate attack to dislodge them.

CHAPTER 16
BREAKING THE IRAQI ARMY

*The military value of a partisan's work is not measured by
the amount of property destroyed, or the number of men
killed or captured, but by the number [of the enemy which]
he keeps watching [him].*

—COLONEL JOHN S. MOSBY

THE UNDERGROUND

The relationship we had with the CIA team was particularly strong.
They had been in country longer than us and already had a strong relationship with the PUK's underground contacts. While we could have
performed many of the tasks they managed, the division of labor made
sense. My pilot team, 076, augmented their capabilities, and their attitude of teamwork made our relationship seamless.

The CIA team was particularly skilled in what I would call subversive activities. They helped the PUK with a wide array of underground
actions. For instance, the PUK's underground smuggled satellite
phones and guns across the Green Line. They developed a resilient
intelligence network across the entire country. They delivered our
capitulation message to the Iraqi commanders. They fueled paranoia
amongst the Iraqi commanders by planting satellite phones on loyal
officers. They defaced Saddam murals and spray-painted anti-Saddam
graffiti in loyalist neighborhoods to the effect of: *Saddam is finished.
Saddam's time is over. Thank you, Mr. Bush.*

We directed them to put the graffiti in the *pro*-Saddam neighborhoods, not in the anti-Saddam neighborhoods. When that happened,
the heavy-handed secret police, known as the Fedayeen, would go
there, kick down doors, and rough up the loyalists. This would not

only divert police attention away from the anti-Saddam neighborhoods, but it would also frustrate the pro-Saddam population.

In another example, an underground member delivered a jar of red paint disguised as tomato sauce to a woman who went into the city and threw it on a mural of Saddam as she walked by. The CIA team helped the PUK print anti-Saddam leaflets. A woman could smuggle 300 flyers under her burka, go into the marketplace downtown in a city like Mosul, Kirkuk, or Baghdad, head to the top of the building at lunchtime, and throw them out the window. The anti-Saddam flyers would float down into the marketplace. It was hard to measure, but it made an impact because it inspired others to realize that resistance is possible, and other people in the community were willing to stand up.

The PUK also prepared the underground in Kirkuk to conduct acts of sabotage and rise up in conjunction with the Peshmerga's advance. We broadcast warning the army not to conduct human rights violations or sabotage the oil refineries. We urged the population to protect the critical infrastructure. The CIA team leader, Randy, would constantly come to me and ask, "What can I do for you guys? What's the next area you want to focus on?" For me, his mentorship was a great experience. He and his team helped me more fully appreciate the value and power of the non-kinetic efforts, especially when combined with our kinetic efforts.

NOT THE SIGNAL

Regrettably, we failed to coordinate appropriate timing of our activities. Radio Free Iraq was broadcasting radio messages telling Iraqis, "Saddam is finished." Before any planned coded messages could be broadcast over the radio for resistance members in occupied areas, many Iraqis misinterpreted the toppling of the Saddam statue on the 9th of April as *the signal* to act. It was not. Dozens of Iraqis contacted us, saying they had risen up. We could hear shouting and gunfire in the background of the call, and they'd declare they had risen up and were attacking the police station or the military compound. When we'd ask where they were, they'd be hundreds of miles away—in Tikrit or Ramadi, for instance. Our hearts would sink because we knew those cities weren't getting liberated any time soon and there was nothing we could to help them. Our best advice was for them to go into hiding because we would not arrive in time to do anything. I have no idea what happened to those people, but I have no doubt many brave members of the resistance died as a result of rising up prematurely.

When we realized we weren't getting the response we had expected from the capitulation and surrender efforts, we learned of some of Saddam's attempts to prevent mass surrenders like he experienced in 1991. Our underground contacts told us that during one meeting where Saddam had multiple division commanders present, he ordered everyone to stand up and move to the seat to their left. He then announced those were the new command assignments. In one moment, he changed all of his division commanders. If, for instance, the 8th Division commander had a little scheme going with his upper officers, it was now over. Now, every division had a new commander who, frankly, probably had a scheme going with his previous officers in a different division, but was now terrified of the prospect of asking the existing crop of officers what the plan was. The underground explained they learned of Saddam's restructure because some of the couriers they normally used to deliver the messages back and forth did not return this time.

We decided it was time to adjust our message. We began pushing three important communications to the Iraqi military: 1) do not commit human rights violations, 2) do not commit war crimes, and 3) your officers have abandoned you. After our experience in the Gulf War, America was concerned Saddam would give the order to blow up the oil wells and create a humanitarian disaster. Consequently, we began warning the Iraqi military that if they committed human rights violations or created environmental disasters, we knew who they were and they would be prosecuted when Saddam was gone—and Saddam *would* be gone soon. We made it a point to emphasize that we had an apparatus in the city who knew what happened and who did what. We made a clear case of deterrence, but it was a legitimate threat.

We also had a lot of signal intercepts from our signals intercept teams. They had intercepted numerous Iraqi calls in and around Kirkuk. Iraqi officers were calling each other: *Is this for real? Are we really doing this? Is the attack tonight? Are we going?* We started to get a sense that there would be a mass desertion, a scenario we had honestly not envisioned.

ODA 083

In the last two weeks, ODA 083 had pushed the Iraqi defense back from the Green Line to the Jabul Bur ridge, the last defendable terrain feature before entering Kirkuk. Lock knew this would be a more complex attack than they had conducted to date with their Peshmerga partners, and it was an opportunity to demonstrate a more structured plan. Lock, like most of the officers in Special Forces, was trained at Fort Benning, the home of the US Army infantry. He was intent on showing them a level of planning they hadn't seen before, a Ranger School-style order. The team put together a solid order, built a terrain model to accompany the order, and the briefing went well. As the briefing ended, he turned to his Kurdish counterpart and asked him what he thought.

"Well," the Kurdish commander said, "it's a good plan...it *could* work."

Lock instantly picked up on the cue. He asked twice if there was something wrong. Each time, the Kurdish commander said, "No, no. It's a good plan. It could work." Finally, the commander coughed up the important details. "This just isn't the way we normally attack this position."

Joe asked him, "How many times have you attacked this position before?"

The commander answered, "I've only attacked it once, but some of the others have attacked it more than that."

Joe realized his naïveté and asked the Kurdish commander, "How do you want to do it then?"

The Kurdish commander immediately lit up. He informed Joe, "The depiction of the terrain on the map is wrong. There's a dry creek bed that's big enough to drive down and start our assault from here." The Kurdish commander then went on to brief a whole plan just like it was a standard battle drill. Within minutes, the new plan was briefed. At the end of the brief Lock asked the Kurdish commander if he could please stress to the men to be careful with their muzzle awareness. He was referring to the common but bad habit of not maintaining weapon safety with the gun pointed in a safe direction at all times. Just as the Peshmerga commanders assured Lock they would address the issue, a rifle shot rang out from across the road, twenty-five meters away.

One of the soldiers had an accidental discharge with his rifle and he accidentally shot the other Kurdish soldier right next to him through the head and killed him. The Kurds calmly responded to the shooter by explaining that since he shot and killed the man, his death was his fault. Now, it was his responsibility to go tell the family. The Kurds took one of the rugs they always carry with them for meetings and camping, wrapped the dead soldier, and prepared to drive him back to Sulaymaniyah, his hometown, to inform the family. Other than the accidental shooting, the plan continued as discussed. They would attack the Iraqi defenses on the hilltop at dawn.

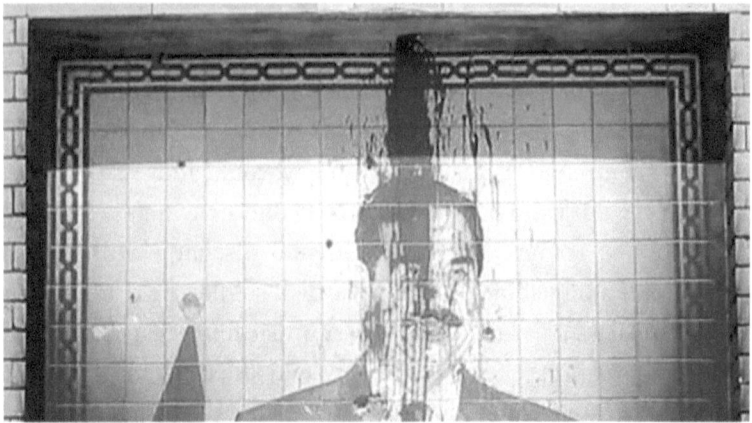

Typical example of the subversive efforts conducted by the Underground in Kirkuk.

Members of ODA 081 pose with their Peshmerga on a destroyed tank near Tuz.

The western edge of Chamchamal looking at Iraqi bunkers along the Green Line from ODA 083's position.

MAJ Pat Roberson (left), MSG Jim Donovan, and CPT Joe Lock, from ODA 083, take LTC Tovo (right) and COL Mayville (Cdr of the 173rd ABN BDE) to see the Iraqi positions outside Kirkuk.

Members of ODA 083 in the final battle for Kirkuk.

CPT John Holevas (right), the Team Leader for ODA 084, pauses during the assault on Bidawah.

CPT Pat Bekurs (left), the Team Leader for ODA 075, at an observation post calling close air support north of Kirkuk.
From March 25th through April 10th, the Green Line ODAs (071, 072, 073, 074, 075, 082, 083, 084, 085, 092) called approximately 1100 close air support missions against the Iraqi forces.

One of the Iraqi army compounds attacked by ODA 075 and the PUK north of Kirkuk.

MAJ Tye Connett, the commander of ODB 070 with his local Peshmerga.

Myself, CW3 Jay Klein, and CPT Scott Riley (the SOTF's S-2 intelligence officer) prepare to head into Kirkuk.

The statue of Saddam Hussein being toppled as we arrived in the city center of Kirkuk.

A member of the SOTF proudly displays a Fedayeen (Darth Vader) helmet found in Kirkuk.

Iraqi Intelligence Services HQs destroyed by cruise missiles in Kirkuk.

A members of ODA 076 poses with a Free Rocket Over Ground or FROG-7 Soviet missile launcher found in Kirkuk. The ODAs found several such missile launchers hidden inside the city.

Fort Carson July 2003, Kirkuk April 2003, Tikrit May 2003.

CHAPTER 17
TAKING KIRKUK

The highest form of warfare is to attack
the enemy's strategy itself.

—Sun Tzu

On April 9, 2003, US forces along with our Kurdish counterparts had Kirkuk surrounded. Highway 2 to the south had been blocked. One ODA (ODA 081) with a Peshmerga force cut the road south of Kirkuk at Tuz; five ODAs (ODA 075, 071, 072, 073, 074) with Peshmerga counterparts advanced from the north; and three ODAs (ODA 083, 084, 085) each with Peshmerga counterparts advanced from the east. Each group had roughly 500 to 1,000 Peshmerga with them.

As our forces encircled Kirkuk from the north, east, and south, we realized we had to do something to close some of the back door to Tikrit. We fully expected the mass exodus was going to flee along the Kirkuk–Tikrit highway. The plan called for MH-53 helicopters to insert ODA 082 to the area southwest of Kirkuk. The plan was for 082 with a very small contingent of Kurds who were fluent in Arabic to fly in and land on the back side of Kirkuk. They would drive off in ATVs and drop off numerous unpacked parachutes intended to look like a parachute drop had occurred. The team planned to deliberately transmit radio messages in the open on multiple frequencies, drop MRE litter, and finally, set off some explosions to make noise and create a diversion. We agreed to launch the mission in the next period of darkness.

During a follow-up meeting with COL Mayville from the 173rd Airborne Brigade, we took him to see ODA 083's and 075's positions, where we showed him the Iraqi army. We shared our intelligence about the defenses of Kirkuk. He confided in us that he, in his words, "slow rolled us" in Italy.

Tovo politely laughed and said, "Yes, sir, we knew." We told him we felt if American tanks appeared it was likely to break the defenses. We recommended bringing the tanks to Sulaymaniyah and then pushing them along the main highway into the city, which offered significant maneuver space.

Against our advice, he dispatched the armor convoy over the mountain by Koi Sanjaq, which included secondary dirt roads and switchbacks. We told him it was a terrible idea, but he didn't listen. The tanks broke down, one by one, every ten kilometers, starting ten kilometers from the airfield. Every time a tank broke down, two of the armored personnel carriers had to stay with it to guard it. Consequently, the tanks and personnel carriers—largely the reason for the jump—wouldn't be taking part in any attack on Kirkuk.

After the meeting and learning the fate of the tanks, a young member of my two-man Tactical Psyops Team (TPT) explained he had a backpack loudspeaker and a recording of various "tank sounds" that could possibly be used to intimidate the enemy. I hadn't been aware of this capability prior to his comment. We didn't know if it would achieve our goal, but it certainly wouldn't hurt, and it cost us nothing, so with nothing to lose, we figured we'd give it a shot. I dispatched him to the front lines where the two men walked the up the ridgeline and positioned the loudspeaker facing the Iraqi forces. He played the sound of tanks driving around back and forth on repeat all night. I have no idea if that had any real effect, but I suspect it contributed to the panic the Iraqis were starting to feel, and, again, it cost me nothing.

Between the Peshmerga closing in on the city from the north, east, and southeast, and the subversive efforts being conducted by the underground from within, there was no doubt pressure was building. We had methodically positioned our forces and prepared the city to collapse in on itself. With the momentum from Baghdad falling the day before, it was just a matter of time.

ODA 083

At 0430 on April 10th, elements from ODA 083 with several hundred Peshmerga were moving into their assault positions to begin the attack. The team's warrant officer, CW2 Mike Santoro, would serve as the senior American alongside the PUK assault force leader and Lock would remain positioned to the rear with the PUK commander to coordinate close air support.

Now, in the dark of morning, as the assault force crept forward over the open rocky slope, the ridgeline to their front erupted with machine gun fire. The Iraqis had pushed forward in the night and caught the Peshmerga moving into their positions. Lock heard the shooting and immediately knew something had gone wrong. The assault force was now caught in the open and exposed. CW2 Santoro immediately called for the force to fall back to better covered positions.

Responding to the enemy fire, SFC Kelly Hornbeck immediately returned fire from his MK-19 grenade launch mounted on one of the team's Land Rovers. Santoro shouted to Hornbeck, "We've gotta go now!"

Hornbeck called back, "No, I've got these guys." Hornbeck unloaded his MK-19 right on top of the advancing Iraqis. Dozens of 40 mm grenades exploded across their positions, killing several of the Iraqis and stalling their advance. Santoro was able to take advantage of the lull in fighting to rally the assault force at a more defendable position. As the Iraqis recovered from the initial shock of Hornbeck's MK-19 fire, they started to target the Peshmerga with machine gun, tank, and artillery fire.

Lock was already calling for close air support, this time as "troops in contact." The first aircraft to respond was a single Navy F-14 with a single bomb. The aircraft dropped onto the ridge and then strafed the positions for the next few minutes until he was out of rounds and low on fuel.

The air strike created another lull in the Iraqi fire. The ODA's team sergeant, MSG Jim Donovan, directed the team to set up their 81 mm mortar. The team only had eight rounds of ammunition, but Jim knew they might as well expend what they had. He asked Santoro for a target and range. Santoro eyed the enemy positions and quickly counted the number of telephone poles between himself and the target to determine their range. There were twenty poles, each fifty meters apart. He quickly did the math and called on the radio to Jim, "One thousand meters, fire for effect!" Jim promptly dropped eight 81mm mortar rounds—right on target.

By now the Iraqis were directing any remaining artillery in Kirkuk to fire forward of the ridgeline. The Green Berets and their Peshmerga had taken positions in old Iraqi trench lines. Artillery was raining down all around them, often within twenty-five meters and splattering the men with mud from the blasts. Fortunately, the trenches provided excellent protection.

Lock was on the radio with multiple aircraft lining up to drop their ordnance. He was also in communication with MAJ Roberson, fifteen kilometers east of his position. Roberson quickly loaded up what ammunition he found, which included the last twenty-four 81mm mortar rounds in the battalion and raced forward to their position. As Lock directed and deconflicted the air strikes and mortar fire, he noted two Kurdish males standing behind him, not in Peshmerga uniforms. Lock had never met Bafel or Lahur Talabani. Lahur was on his cell phone with the Peshmerga contingent pinned down with Santoro. In his British accent, Lahur said, "They like what you are doing, but would like it more to the left."

Lock shot back, "Who the hell are you and to whose left? You know it doesn't work that way?" Bafel and Lahur quickly introduced themselves and relayed their information from the men forward. At this point Lock had sixteen aircraft all in line waiting to drop ordnance. After approximately an hour of bombing the ridge, the Iraqi positions went silent. Lock directed a team to move up and check the ridge. Before anyone could stop him, Hornbeck jumped in a vehicle and raced to the ridge. Ten Kurdish vehicles, following their instructions to stay near the Americans, followed.

As Hornbeck's vehicle crested the ridge, he reported to Lock, "Holy shit, it looks like an Iraqi 10K race!" Hundreds of Iraqi soldiers were shedding their uniforms and running the four-kilometer stretch of road into Kirkuk.

As the fleeing mob of Iraqi soldiers fled toward Kirkuk, they were met by the Kurdish underground, who were waiting for them. The melee of gunfire could be seen and heard from the ridgeline. As Bafel had claimed weeks earlier, the underground was already inside the city. It was literally the PUK's fifth column.

ODA 084

That same morning, ODA 084 and their Peshmerga counterparts approached the town of Baidawa. As they reached the outskirts, Iraqi forces opened fire on Peshmerga. The Peshmerga quickly engaged the Iraqi soldiers, who were caught off guard by the size of the PUK force. After a few hours, Iraqi soldiers began to strip their uniforms and drop their weapons. In several cases, Iraqi soldiers opened fire on each other as some of their members attempted to surrender.

From Baidawa, the PUK expressed a concern to CPT Holevas over the Baba Gurgur oil fields on the north side of Kirkuk. Holevas suspected their concerns were as much about the KDP reaching the facility as they were about the Iraqi forces destroying the infrastructure. In any case, he decided to split his team and have half accompany a contingent of the PUK to the oil fields while the other half remained with Kok Usman's forces and advanced on Laylan.

As they advanced into Laylan, the PUK encountered surprisingly stiff resistance from the Iraqi defenses. Some of this may have been due to the Iraqi forces being aware what was occurring to their rear in Kirkuk and a growing sense of desperation. During the fighting, a particularly seasoned PUK commander who had recently joined them from Halabja was shot and killed by a 12.5 mm machine gun as he stood next to Holevas. The sight of his death shook the group. The Peshmerga assault stalled and started to retreat. CPT Holevas took control of the group, shouting commands in English and what broken Kurdish he could muster. As the Peshmerga fell back, Holevas was able to regain control of the group and prevent the situation from deteriorating into complete chaos. Moments later, a barrage of artillery rounds landed where the Kurdish commander had fallen.

The ensuing fight lasted another twelve hours. Eventually, the combination of Peshmerga fighters and air strikes broke the defenses. Holevas received a report from Roberson telling him that Kirkuk was falling and they were headed toward the city center. He could see the southeast side of Kirkuk from their position in Laylan, and the Kurds were already advancing in that direction. As they entered the city, thousands of civilians packed the streets, cheering. Through the crowd, Holevas spotted the recently acquired white Land Rovers from another ODA. Pulling alongside, it was MSG Jim Donovan, the team sergeant from ODA 083. In his typical, half-laughing gruff voice, Donovan smiled and said, "What took you so long, Johnny?"

ODA 075

As CPT Bekurs awoke on the morning of April 10th exhausted from the previous day's battles, he looked around the camp and noticed it seemed strangely quiet. He grabbed a Peshmerga and asked, "Where is Kok Abizaid?" The young Peshmerga pointed toward Kirkuk. Bekurs quickly realized that Abizaid had learned that the Iraqis on the Koni Domlan had abandoned their positions in the night and now nothing stood between him and Kirkuk. Not sure how much of a lead Kok Abizaid had on him, Bekurs alerted the team and told them to get ready to move.

He called Connett to alert him of the situation and then headed toward his vehicle. "We are going into Kirkuk, now!"

The teams from A Company raced along Highway 2 and over the ridge. They could see the Baba Gurgur oil field complex to their right and Kirkuk ahead of them. Discarded Iraqi uniforms littered the roadway. Before long, the team caught up to Abizaid, who had been engaged in some minor skirmishes with the last of the city's defenders. Just behind 075 were MAJ Connett, his headquarters, and the other four ODAs, all with their Peshmerga counterparts.

INTERRUPTED PLANNING MEETING

That same morning, LTC Tovo and I drove up to Dokan Lake, about two to three hours away from Sulaymaniyah, to meet with the 173rd Airborne Brigade and conduct a joint planning meeting. The PUK brought some of the old Peshmerga to the meeting. They were in their uniforms and came with several maps under their arms, which they rolled out and proceeded to depict every single enemy position inside the city. They had done some pretty good military work largely based on the Kurdish underground in the city and then transposed the intelligence onto a map to explain the situation.

The 173rd wanted absolutely nothing to do with this information or the old Peshmerga. As they had tried to do previously on multiple occasions, they wanted to run the show. They were fully prepared to explain how they would conduct the attack. They began their briefing by stating they anticipated executing the attack in about two or three weeks because they wanted time to prepare. Immediately, the Kurds pushed back and thought it was ridiculous. They were *not* waiting two to three weeks.

During the meeting—which wasn't going well—LTC Tovo noticed that a lot of the Kurds were receiving calls on their cell phones, leaving the meeting, and not returning. "Do you see what I see?" he quietly asked me. "See if you can find out what's going on." I stepped outside and quickly called MAJ Pat Roberson, who informed me that Kirkuk was collapsing.

He relayed that ODA 083 and the Peshmerga were assembled on the ridgeline with a clear view into the city. Lock had stopped their advance, telling them, "We don't have orders to enter Kirkuk." He then tried to reuse the excuse he had used previously about the dangers of the "free fire lines" to keep the Peshmerga from advancing past his position. However, slowly, one at a time, civilian cars navigated the barricades on the highway to enter to the city, in full view of the Peshmerga. Lock could see the analysis going through the young Peshmergas' heads in real time: "How are they not being killed if there are American free fire lines?"

Lock turned to Roberson and said, "Uh, we may have a problem."

I told Roberson we would head his way.

"I'll do what I can to hold the Kurds back, but it's not going to last much longer," Roberson replied.

I returned to the meeting and quietly conveyed the message to LTC Tovo, who promptly asked where the trucks were and declared we needed to go.

COL Mayville saw that we were leaving and asked, "What's going on?"

"We're going into Kirkuk," I explained.

His face revealed his surprise. Wide-eyed, he asked me, "Are we going to postpone the meeting?"

"We've got to cancel."

COL Mayville was searching for words, clearly uncomfortable with losing control of the situation. "When are we going to hold the next session?"

"I don't know," I said, starting for the door. "Maybe next week?"

"Where?" he asked.

"Probably in Kirkuk," I quipped. He looked at me like I was crazy. I explained that Kirkuk was falling. "We have to go. Now."

"Do they really think they can win this fight?" he asked, seemingly bewildered at the events transpiring before him.

I turned and faced him and, in a particularly cheeky response, said, "They're not picking the fights they know they can win. They are picking the ones they believe need to be fought." I whipped my scarf around my neck, turned around, and hastily walked out.

LTC Tovo and I got in the truck and started racing south to try to link up with the B Company elements and MAJ Roberson.

LIBERATION

LTC Tovo and I raced back at top speed from Dokan. MAJ Pat Roberson, his B team, and ODA 082 were all on the main highway going into Kirkuk waiting for us. 082's mission to infiltrate behind Kirkuk was now overcome by events. We all linked up a few kilometers outside the city. The highway was already packed with civilian vehicles trying to enter the city. It looked like every picture I've ever seen of Paris or Antwerp getting liberated in World War II. The streets were absolutely bursting with thousands of people everywhere who were overjoyed at our presence. Complete jubilation rained around us. I've never experienced anything quite like it—before or since. There were so many people packed around us celebrating that we couldn't even properly drive our seven vehicles.

As we slowly neared an intersection, Randy jumped out of his car carrying a box and asked for my help. I peered into the box to see thousands of handheld American flags—the ones on sticks that you wave at a 4th of July parade. He gave me two fistfuls and several of my guys grabbed their own handfuls. We ran around the intersection, passing out hundreds of American flags on the street. The international media journalists who surrounded us not only saw this powerful optic but could palpably feel the ecstatic energy from the crowd, just as we could. I can't speak to what may have happened elsewhere in Iraq, but I can say with certainly that we were welcomed as liberators in Kirkuk.

We quickly made our way to the governor's palace, which we established as our center of operations after we consolidated forces and linked up. As we were pulling in, the crowd was toppling the Saddam statue in the center. When they saw we were Americans, they started laughing, crying, and cheering simultaneously. Although most of us still looked like Peshmerga with our mustaches, green camouflage uniforms, and neck scarves, we wore our US flags on our sleeves for the population to see that we were, in fact, Americans. Ready or not, the city was now ours.

CHAPTER 18
NIGHTFALL OVER KIRKUK

Conquering the world on horseback is easy; it is dismounting and governing that is hard.

—GENGHIS KHAN

NIGHTTIME IN THE CITY FELT VERY APOCALYPTIC. THE JUBILATION OF the day dissipated as the sun started to go down. The streets suddenly became deserted. There was no electricity, and the city was black and covered in shadows. There were several fires burning and the atmosphere seemed unnerving. Even though there wasn't much enemy fighting happening, there was still ongoing shooting in the distance, always a few blocks away.

Iraqi uniforms littered the roadside. The soldiers had literally just ripped off their uniforms and fled. The local townspeople brought us captured and isolated soldiers who couldn't get away. We collected approximately one hundred prisoners and held them in the governor's building. It was a mixed bag of men—some were legitimate threats and others were just innocent old men. Others appeared to be foreigners who had nowhere to run. The situation was such that Sunni Arab Iraqi soldiers who had relatives in a city elsewhere could simply remove their uniform and run to that city. However, Iraqi soldiers who came to join the jihadi fight from Syria, Jordan, Palestine, or wherever had nowhere to go.

My real concern in all of this was that I had about a hundred prisoners in a hallway in the governor's palace with no lights or electricity. Meanwhile, there were fewer than ten Americans acting as jailers. Although they were all sitting with their hands tied behind their backs, I didn't tie their hands personally, and I didn't see their hands being tied. In short, I had no idea what the condition of their hands might be, and I certainly couldn't see to check. We knew we had to process them and get them out of the hallway—fast.

Sure enough, one of them started shouting. "Fuck you, Americans! *Fuck you!*"

Before anyone could do anything, one of the particularly burly guys from ODA 083 who stood about 6'1" came flying out of nowhere with his ridiculously large open hand to smack the guy right across the face. "No one told you to speak!" he shouted. The prisoner immediately shut up.

For all of us who have attended military SERE school—with its simulated POW training camp—it was a flashback moment and a reminder that everyone is a badass until they get smacked in the face. That simple gesture reestablished order. Everyone's eyes went to the floor, and, just like that, everyone was quiet and compliant once again.

At one point, we made our way to the old intelligence services building, which was exceptionally creepy. To start, there were two holes, clear as day, through the entire five-story building down into the basement from the cruise missile strikes. While we were there, several civilians were milling about with pioneer tools—shovels, picks, and the like. Our Kurdish colleague explained they were looking for the secret entrance to Saddam's infamous torture chambers. He explained that everybody has relatives who have been in the torture chambers but no one knows exactly where they are, and they were concerned their relatives might be trapped underground somewhere. Although we didn't find them, seeing people looking for them was eerie.

SECURING THE CITY

As the sun rose on the morning of April 11, 2003, Kirkuk was in our hands. The 173rd was still not in the city. I had been in communication with them during the night and planned to link up with them on Highway 4 on the east side of the city in the morning and escort them to the airfield. I was at the link-up point waiting to make contact as a few US Army Humvees pulled up and stopped about 100 meters from my position. A patrol dismounted and cautiously approached me.

I waved a VS-17 blaze orange panel. "Where is the brigade? Where is everyone?"

They explained they were only the advance party. They would have to return, debrief the commander, and escort the brigade back in the afternoon. I was notably frustrated and told the patrol I needed them to move faster and call me when they were on their way back to the city.

When I returned to the governor's building, I told Tovo the 173rd would not be entering the city until that afternoon at the earliest. We both agreed that if the population knew how few of us there actually were in the city, it could be a problem. Somehow, we needed to make it seem like there were more of us in the city. We made the decision to shave our mustaches and change into Army desert uniforms, to create the appearance of more—or at least different—US soldiers.

I instructed the teams to drive up and down every street at least once a day. I told them we needed to make sure every resident of Kirkuk saw an American at least once a day. As the teams explored the city, they came across several military vehicles that had been cleverly disguised to look destroyed. Their tarps were deliberately sliced up and pieces of twisted metal were attached to the sides, making them look destroyed. The unit identification on the bumpers was from the Nebuchadnezzar Division. Finding their vehicles in Kirkuk confirmed the Iraqis hadn't counterattacked south, but had instead abandoned their equipment in Kirkuk.

We leveraged the media to spread rumors of American forces in the city. We deliberately shouted to each other in earshot of journalists, who came running to us asking if we were American soldiers. We acted flustered, like they caught us. We then proceeded to tell them a fantastic story about the airborne brigade that had taken the city.

We'd say, "Three *thousand* US paratroopers! Didn't you see them?" No matter where the reporters had just come from, we'd say, "You *just* missed them." Before long, everyone in the city had secondhand knowledge of this US paratrooper brigade in Kirkuk.

The ODAs all pushed out to find a suitable house to establish a base of operations. Each team took a different section of the city. A Company would control the east side and B Company would take the west side. The ODC was set up in the governor's building in the center.

In some cases, teams occupied houses with Kurdish families. One of the A Company teams occupied one of Chemical Ali's houses in the northern part of the city. Although Iraq was a relatively new environment for the teams, operating from houses in dense urban areas was very familiar from the years of operating in Kosovo and Bosnia. The teams knew exactly what to do to establish their houses.

ODB 070 AND 080'S SECTORS IN KIRKUK

They wasted no time setting up their communications and security as well as developing support networks with the local population. As they patrolled their areas, we found hundreds of abandoned Iraqi uniforms, abandoned trucks, tanks, rocket launchers, and other assorted military equipment. The teams also made some odd discoveries. In several warehouses, they uncovered hundreds of plastic helmets that can only be described as Darth Vader helmets.

I couldn't help but imagine movie night in the Hussein house, with Saddam and the boys watching *Star Wars*, thinking, "Finally, here is a guy who gets it! Vader is trying to create a weapon of mass destruction to bring stability to the universe but annoyingly, he has to deal with rebel scum!" Maybe Uday chimed in to say, "Hey, dad, we should make helmets like that for our secret police!" and Qusay agreed, "That's a really great idea!" Whatever the case, they quickly became a hot commodity for the guys to bring home to their children.

Not surprisingly, Saddam's rule left a lot of people disenfranchised. We called several meetings at the governor's building for anyone who had a grievance. After being suppressed for so long, people were clamoring to take advantage of this service. We wanted to bring stability, but the grievances looked more like "he shot my donkey five years ago," than something that would really affect the population at large. There were thousands of people who (understandably) all wanted to be heard.

In the midst of the crowd, my guys noticed a man who was dangling a gigantic set of keys, akin to what a janitor of a high school might carry. He explained that he was the guy in charge of the power plant and we needed to go with him to restore the power so people didn't

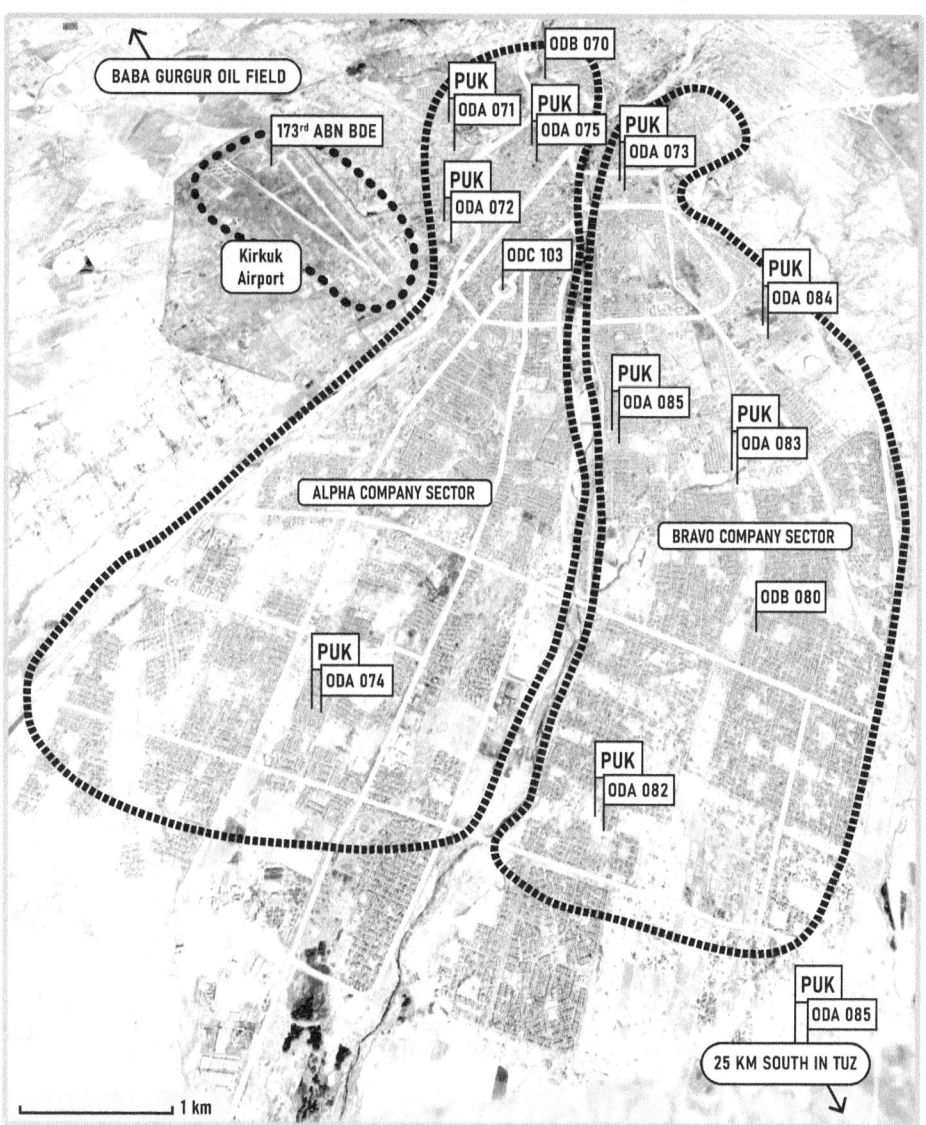

Map 8. *The Occupation of Kirkuk*

loot it, because Iraqi looting is different than what Americans envision. First, Iraqis had a notion that they were owed war reparations. Second, because of the poverty, they would take whatever they could get their hands on. Iraqi looting was more like salvaging. So when he was concerned about looting, he meant they would literally rip the metal wiring out of the walls and take it home and then nothing would function.

Four of my guys accompanied him to the power plant, where he took them to a huge switch, the likes of which you might expect to see in a cartoon. He flipped the switch and power immediately came back to 75 percent of the city—all within twenty-four hours of taking the city. As soon as he restored the power, it felt like the tension dissipated. Now, because there was power, people were far less aggrieved. Soon after, the three-man civil affairs team attached to the SOTF established the Civil Military Operations Center (CMOC) at the governor's building to address infrastructure issues like this. They served as a critical link to address power, water, sewage, oil infrastructure, and a host of other factors that directly related to government services and stability.

We did see evidence of retaliation. We found the body of a police officer on the outskirts of town who was not only murdered, but someone had also taken the time to duct tape a grenade to his head. We announced that the "rule of law" would be fully enforced starting tomorrow. This was an indirect way of saying if anyone had a score to settle, they had twenty-four hours to do it. It might seem completely inappropriate, but honestly, we didn't have the ability to enforce it immediately and frankly, you could feel the pressure within the population. This transition or grace period was the only way to get them back to a manageable level of stability. There were several Arab neighborhoods along the south end of the city. They had been Arabized by Saddam a decade earlier. I'm sure there were numerous violent clashes as Kurdish families returned to their ancestral homes to find Arab occupants. The first order of business was restoring some basic semblance of order and then expanding outward.

We hoisted an American flag at the governor's building. Shortly thereafter, LTC Tovo came to me and told me to remove it. When I asked why, he explained we had just received a message from Donald Rumsfeld that said we were not occupiers and we could not fly the US flag.

This was a complete misreading of the situation. It was a decision made in a vacuum by people thousands of miles away. Although I maintain that the capitulation blunder was the top mistake, this was a very close second. The Iraqis *needed* us to be occupiers, at least for a short while. By sending the message that Americans were not occupiers, however, we also communicated an unintended message: *no one is in charge.* It was utterly insane. People in the city even seemed to give us a grace period where they still respected our authority and, without voicing it, were asking: *Are you sure you want to go with this?* Apparently, we did, even though we were collectively at a loss as to why.

By complete contrast, the PUK leadership back in Sulaymaniyah had anticipated this exact scenario of a vacuum of leadership, law, and order. Brilliantly, they knew that commerce was the key to stability. If essential services were restored and people could sell their wares and buy necessities, the citizens would have stability in a city. The Kurds brought maybe fifty buses to restore transportation, along with approximately 400 uniformed—but unarmed—police officers. Basically, men with a white sash, a white helmet, white gloves, spats on their shoes, and a whistle. They stationed them at every intersection, and it was absolutely shocking to witness the effect it had on the rule of law.

BG Parker, the SOCCENT deputy, flew into Kirkuk at noon that second day, April 11th. We took him to the governor's building for a briefing and then took him on a tour of the city. The marketplace was open and if you hadn't seen the city the day before, you might think nothing had even happened. The Turks were once again opposed to the Kurds and so they had told CENTCOM the Kurds were looting in the city and causing problems. Turkey told the US it was a red line to have *any* Kurds in Kirkuk. Following CENTCOM orders, BG Parker ordered the PUK out of the city, along with the unarmed police. The city was happy and calm, even though the Turks claimed it was in flames. BG Parker clearly didn't understand the situation in the same way we did. We loosely complied with the orders. We might have sent the unarmed police home, but we didn't really have the Peshmerga leave the city. We minimized their numbers but still maintained their presence in the city because we knew it would completely fall apart if we sent the Peshmerga home.

During a meeting at the governor's building with the local community leaders, we introduced them to BG Parker and COL Mayville. Parker had told me to keep the PUK out of the meeting. Right off the bat, the meeting turned hostile. Arab, Kurdish, and Turkoman community leaders where shouting accusations at the Americans and each other. COL Mayville tried to calm the group in a scene that looked like a substitute teacher who had lost control of his class. The more he yelled at them, the worse it got.

Outside the building, Bafel called me and told me Dr. Barham Salih was there and wanted to join the meeting. Against the general's orders, I escorted Salih through the back of the building and into the room. As he entered the room, the shouting immediately ceased and the entire group rose to their feet. To instantly go from pandemonium to complete silence was impressive. Dr Salih was universally recognized and respected as an honest man by all the ethnicities. He calmly addressed the room, and you could feel the tension dissipate.

A day later, we met with two retired American generals: LTG (Ret.) Garner and GEN (Ret.) Schoomaker, from the Office of Reconstruction and Humanitarian Assistance (ORHA). Garner was a veteran of the Provide Comfort operations in the 1990s and Schoomaker was the former USSOCOM Commander and a legend in the special operations community. They were fantastic. They understood the environment, they knew all the names of the key players, they knew all of the towns and cities. In short, they were squared away and we were eagerly anticipating working with them to further our stability and reconstruction efforts. The PUK were bringing us the right people to restore the essential services in the city. I felt like our plan for stability was on track.

SURPRISE HANDOVER

On the morning of April 18th, I headed to the 173rd Tactical Operations Center at the airfield to attend their daily update. The S-3 for their brigade, a major, had the names of the paratrooper battalions written on the map in sectors that were under my control.

"Hey, those aren't their sectors. Those are my sectors," I told him.

His eyes lit up. I could tell he'd been eagerly anticipating this moment. "No, they're my sectors now," he countered.

"What are you talking about?" I asked.

"4th ID has arrived in theater," he explained, referring to the 4th Infantry Division that was supposed to come through Turkey. "They were diverted to Kuwait and have driven all the way across Iraq and arrived in Tikrit, so this is now their sector. We've been chopped to them,"—meaning the operational control of the 173rd had been reassigned from the JSOTF and transferred to 4th ID. "This is no longer your battle space," he concluded with a wide grin. He was obviously feeling quite pleased with himself and dropping this news on me.

LTC Tovo and I both shrugged our shoulders. "Okay. Well, good luck with this. You guys take care." We turned and started to walk out of the room.

The major was agitated. "Wait! Where are you going? What do you mean?" I'm sure he was crestfallen that he didn't get the fight he was hoping for out of us.

"We're going back to Sulaymaniyah," I clarified.

"No, no. I've got tasks for you!" he exclaimed.

"*Nah*," I countered. "We don't work for you. This is your battle space. We don't automatically come with the battle space." I could see the concern on his face since we had done nothing to coordinate a handoff. In the week they had been on the airfield, they had not participated in any patrols with us and subsequently knew almost nothing about the city. The reality of his monumental task was probably flashing before his eyes. "I wish you guys had spent a fraction of the effort you used to secretly get control of the battle space to actually learn about the city. Anyway...good luck with that."

In our final meeting with COL Mayville, he was really excited to show us his plan. He explained that he was going to tell the population that the airfield was the center of gravity, and therefore, he needed to declare Kirkuk a gun-free zone.

As kindly as we could, we told him that didn't make sense, and no one would support that plan. "Center of gravity" in military terms is the source of strength, balance, or stability necessary to maintain an operation. In other words, without the center of gravity, your operation will fail. The airfield in Kirkuk was *not* the center of gravity. In fact, that airfield was important for COL Mayville but meant *nothing* to anyone in Kirkuk, and we told him as much. Telling the Iraqis they couldn't have guns because he wanted an airfield to stay open meant absolutely nothing to them.

We could tell he was frustrated by our response and questioned our reasoning. I told him the actual center of gravity was the support of the population. LTC Tovo and the Civil Affairs officers said the same thing. To achieve that center of gravity, we needed to be doing things to support governance, stability, and security. The airfield was the least of our concerns regarding the support of the population, but it was his task to sort out now. After the meeting, we left the city and returned to Sulaymaniyah.

I was greatly worried that what we had worked to build was going to be destroyed not by deliberate choice, but by ignorance.

CHAPTER 19
IF WE'RE NOT CAREFUL WE'RE GONNA WIN THIS WAR

It is unfortunate when final decisions are made by chieftains headquartered miles away from the front, where they can only guess at conditions and potentialities known only to the captain of the battlefield.

—ATTILA THE HUN

AS I SMELLED THE AROMA OF WINE WAFTING ACROSS THE ROOM, I FELT like I had been living as a feral animal for the last week—and now, I was back among civilization.

In stark contrast to the chaos of the past few weeks, LTC Tovo and I were sitting with Dr. Barham Salih in his elegant home in downtown Sulaymaniyah. About ten minutes after we returned to Sulaymaniyah, he called us to meet with him. Dr. Salih, dressed in a smart-looking, pressed suit, graciously offered us a glass of wine as classical music played softly in the background. While we declined his offer, my heightened sense of smell underscored the contrast between battle and civilization. It was an odd feeling.

We discussed the situation in Kirkuk and what he thought the PUK should do next. Dr. Salih wasn't intentionally name dropping, but he said, "Let me check with Paul." By "Paul," he meant Paul Wolfowitz, the then-Deputy Secretary of Defense, whom he dialed up on his cell phone. They were clearly on a first-name basis. Paul answered the phone. "I'm sitting here with Ken and Mark, and by the way, they're doing a fantastic job," Dr. Salih said as he winked at us, clearly impressed with the favor he was doing by talking us up to the Deputy SECDEF. I suspected Wolfowitz must have thought Ken and Mark were odd names for two Kurdish guys and no doubt had no idea who Ken and Mark were. Most likely, he couldn't have cared less. I appreciated the gesture, nonetheless.

A day after we returned to Sulaymaniyah, we learned that there had been a disagreement between the Secretary of Defense and the Secretary of State regarding who was in charge of reconstruction and stability operations. The team we met last week from ORHA had been a Department of State initiative. They were now being thrown out of country. Secretary Rumsfeld made it clear that the Department of Defense wasn't going to allow the Department of State to execute their stability plan. Retired Generals Garner and Schoomaker stopped by Sulaymaniyah to tell us the bad news. To say we were stunned was an understatement.

THE MEK

With Kirkuk now under the control of the 173rd Airborne Brigade, our focus shifted southward. The war wasn't over and we intended to maintain pressure on the remaining Iraqi units. C Company, now with all five of its ODAs, each with their own Peshmerga contingent, started to push south past Kalar. They quickly liberated the towns of Jalula and Khaniqin. The JSOTF told us we had advanced too far outside of traditional Kurdish territory, and we needed to fall back. When I spoke with MAJ Thiebes, he explained that when they entered Jalula, Mullah Bakhtiar had gone straight to his childhood house to find his mother, whom he had not seen in over ten years. When they arrived, she prepared them a reunion dinner. George said simply, "These are Kurdish towns and they aren't giving them up. Either way, I'm not going to ask them to."

As the PUK and ODAs continued to advance, they encountered the remnants of the 3rd Armored and 34th Infantry Divisions. They also encountered an Iraqi unit that appeared to be something different. Most notably, it fired back more rapidly and with greater accuracy compared to most of the units they had previously encountered. The skirmish led to several PUK casualties and two men from ODA 094 receiving minor injuries from artillery shrapnel. The ODAs called in

APR 12-MAY 10 2003

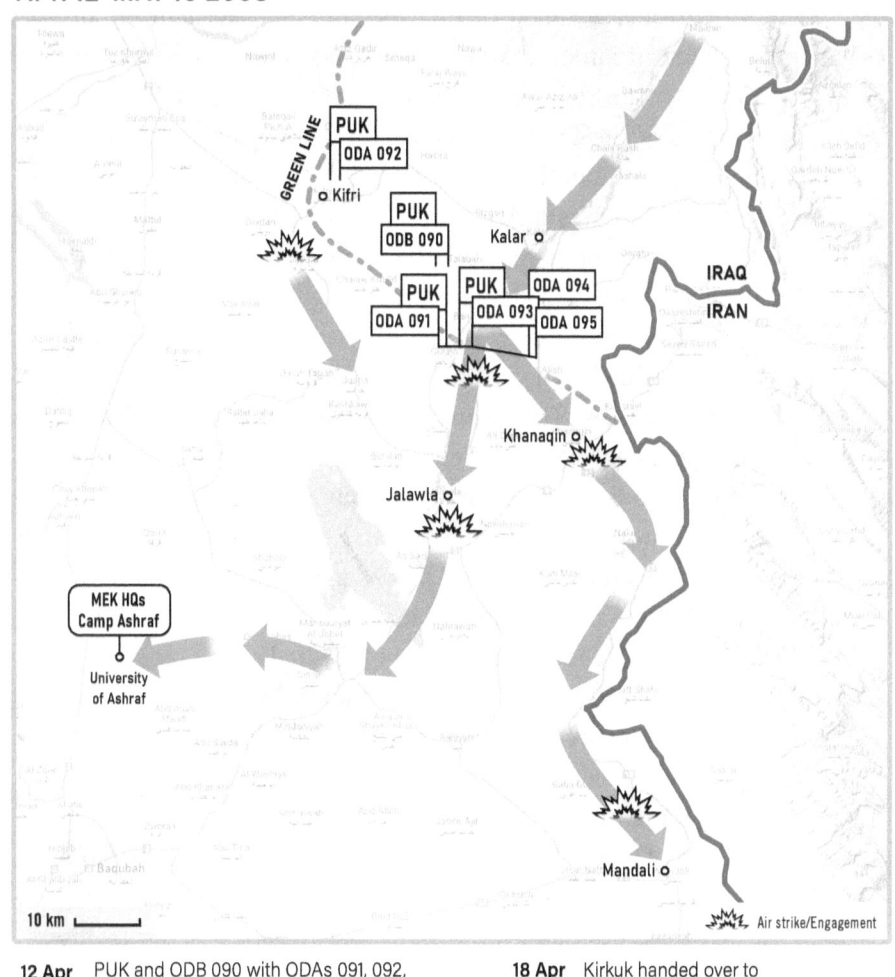

Map 9. The Disposition of Friendly Forces (April 12–May 10)

12 Apr	PUK and ODB 090 with ODAs 091, 092, 093, 094, 095 seize Jalawla, Khanaqin, encounters the MEK
14 Apr	PUK and ODB 090 seize Mandali
15 Apr	LTC Tovo and MAJ Thiebes meet the MEK at Camp Ashraf and broker the capitulation agreement
18 Apr	Kirkuk handed over to the 173rd ABN BDE
4 May	LTC Tovo, MAJ Grdovic and the PUK LNO travel to Tikrit to meet the 4th Infantry Division Commander
10 May	TF 103 redeploy to Ft Carson Colorado

an air strike on the Iraq force and the skirmish ended. Soon after, the PUK explained that this was in fact the Mujahedeen-e-Khalq, or MEK, and they were asking for a ceasefire.

The Mujahedeen-e-Khalq (MEK) was an elite, mechanized, brigade-sized force of fanatical Iranians—ethnic Persians—who found exile in Iraq after the Shah of Iran was overthrown in 1979. They are mortal enemies of the Iranian Regime, who views them as traitors. Oddly enough, they found a new benefactor in Saddam since they were outsiders to the Iraqi Arabs and Kurds and had no potential allies with whom to conspire. Thus, Saddam used them to fight Iranians during the Iran-Iraq War. They were a great asset for Saddam since they had no political or ethnic allies among the population. They were well trained, with a cultlike discipline and better equipped than other Iraqi forces. They were more than eager to fight Kurds, Arabs, or Iranians at Saddam's behest. The MEK had a saying that captures their mindset quite well: "Use your tank tracks to kill the Kurds and save your bullets for the Iranian Revolutionary Guards."

On the first meeting, Tovo and Thiebes met with the MEK leadership at Camp Ashraf, near Mandali. They claimed they were trying to avoid fighting with US forces, and in fact they had sent a message to a US politician months earlier explaining their willingness to change sides. A few weeks later we were able to verify that claim as legitimate. At the subsequent meetings we brought our surgeon, MAJ Ong, to tend to some of the wounded from the air strike.

On the 15th of April, Tovo and Thiebes successfully negotiated a capitulation agreement with the MEK. Once they signed the agreement, the MEK were actually quite amenable and some of our teams moved into their compound with them. They were an odd lot, no doubt, but they weren't the problem. To give some perspective of how fanatical they were, they assumed the US would be continuing its attack into Iran as Iraq was pacified. They requested the honor of leading that attack.

About this time 3rd Brigade of 4th ID was heading our way from Tikrit. We got word that they were intending to attack the MEK. We intervened and explained the situation: they had capitulated and there was no need for an attack. Instead of being grateful for a peaceful turn of events, the brigade essentially accused us of stealing their opportunity to fight.

It got so heated that the brigade told us if we didn't leave the camp, they were still going to open fire. We informed them that on behalf of the United States government, we had signed an agreement with the MEK, and legally, according to the agreement, they were required to provide twenty-four hours' notice prior to resuming any hostilities so they could disperse their equipment so it would be a fair fight. The brigade challenged our authority to enter into such an agreement. At one point, we pulled the ODAs out of the compound for their own safety—from an American attack. Fortunately, their lawyers eventually conceded that the agreement was, in fact, valid.

If the situation with the 4th Infantry Division and the MEK weren't complex enough, there was another complicating factor, the BADR Corps. The BADR Corps are a Shia paramilitary group of the Islamic Revolutionary Guards Corps (IRGC) of Iran. They are the archenemies of the MEK. Their hatred is so deeply rooted that they saw the collapse of the Iraqi army as an ideal opportunity to attack the MEK in their camps. During the period of confusion as the 4th Infantry Division had to figure out what to do with the MEK, they also had to contend with attacks from the BADR Corps.

PESHMERGA MONITORING OPERATIONS (PMO)

As the conventional forces increasingly took control of the battle space, the JSOTF was developing the concept for the next phase of operations. When Tovo and I arrived for a routine meeting, the staff was jokingly talking about "getting back to Colorado in time for the last run at A Basin," referring to Arapahoe Basin ski resort, which habitually stays open into June. Their comments felt very weird and disconnected. The JSOTF headquarters was a very different world than that of the SOTF. There were no Kurdish counterparts; it was solely an American headquarters.

We asked about the recent changes to the battle space ownership with the 173rd and 4th Infantry Division. No one could explain the rules for movement and LTC Tovo and I voiced our concern that Dr. Salih might get detained at a US checkpoint. In response to our concern, one of the majors at the JSOTF made the comment: "You guys sound like you're getting Stockholm syndrome." Another JSOTF major told us we needed to let it go, because the Kurds are the regular Army's problem now. That comment set LTC Tovo and me off. LTC Tovo didn't anger easily, but things got a bit testy. We never viewed the Kurds as our problem; they were our *partners*.

The purpose of the meeting was to hear the concept for how the JSOTF's operations were going to evolve. They came up with an idea to intern all the Peshmerga in containment camps and the ODAs would monitor them. They called it Peshmerga Monitoring Operations (PMO).

We needed to "monitor" the Kurds? I couldn't believe what I was hearing. One of the operations officers from the JSOTF asked me what my problem was with their concept. I immediately responded, "You want to know what my problem is? We are still fighting Iraqi units, we are still looking for Saddam and his top officers, and we are still looking for weapons of mass destruction, but you guys think the thing we should focus on is placing the Peshmerga in internment camps!?"

It's fair to say that my patience was wearing thin for ideas that seemed to be counter to our mission, and my frustration was becoming increasingly obvious. Fortunately, I was able to convince COL Cleveland to at least change the name to Kurdish Cooperative Council (KCC). The KCC would be a forum where the US forces, KDP, and PUK could periodically meet to address any concerns. This was much improved from the PMO concept.

THE KURDISH COOPERATIVE COUNCIL (KCC)

At the first KCC meeting, we were asked to provide a complete list of the PUK's forces and locations. At my request, the PUK provided a comprehensive list within twenty-four hours. The KDP was not as forthcoming. The Turks were conducting their own special operations to restrict the growing Kurdish influence in the region. They were fabricating crises in Kirkuk and sending false reports to CENTCOM of Kurds attacking the Turkoman population as a pretext for sending troops into the Kurdish territory. A Turkish armor division had preemptively deployed to the Turkey–Iraq border, awaiting the order to cross. On more than one occasion the Turkish Special Forces were caught smuggling weapons to the Turkoman population and promoting acts of violence. We learned of this through the Turkoman in Kirkuk.

The KDP was not going to allow the incursion, and they certainly weren't going to accept being contained into camps while it happened. Despite the 2nd Battalion teams, which included an attached company from A Company, 3rd Battalion, 3rd Special Forces Group, having conducted some very good operations with the KDP, the battalion commander's relationship with Masud Barzani, the KDP's leader, was becoming increasingly strained following a series of disagreements that culminated with the previously mentioned fratricide incident involving his son, Waji. The CIA team collocated with the KDP did what they could to correct the misperception, but not without a degree of friction between the 2nd Battalion commander and the CIA team chief. The KDP's unwillingness to confine their Peshmerga to camps that would be monitored was being misperceived as a lack of compliance as a partner.

While at one of the KCC meetings with the 101st Airborne Division, they were discussing staging one of their brigades in Sulaymaniyah. I told them it was completely unnecessary and would be a waste of resources since there was zero threat there. It was friendly territory. They began speaking about the KDP and the 101st G-3 was being somewhat disrespectful. Consequently, Kok Brushka from the KDP was very upset and refused to sign an agreement.

After the meeting, I approached the officer and pulled him off to the side so no one would hear our conversation. "Sir, you should consider treating these guys like they're general officers."

"Are you kidding me?" he shot back.

"You're right," I continued. "They're not like American general officers. They've actually been fighting since they were teenagers. I'm just telling you; you would do well to treat these guys with a little bit of respect."

The American colonel largely dismissed my remarks and walked off. I didn't realize, however, that Kok Brushka could hear me or how much English he understood. In reasonably good English, he came over and said, "Thank you very much for saying that. I appreciate it."

He followed it with the hand-over-heart gesture where they put their right hand over their heart. It's a way of saying hello, but with respect. They do it constantly. As he put his right hand on his heart, I mirrored his gesture with my own.

The growing frustration felt by the KDP was evident. They were being pushed aside and left out of discussions regarding their own territory. While I was significantly concerned about this growing dynamic, little did I know how much stranger things were about to get.

CHAPTER 20
RELUCTANT ENEMIES

We have met the enemy and he is us.

—WALT KELLY

SURRENDER OR DIE

The new American position that came down from the Secretary of Defense via CENTCOM for the Iraqi commanders left no room for the capitulation agreements we had been brokering.

Many Iraqi commanders at the division and brigade level had fled to Syria or to the Syrian border somewhere in the desert. I was still coordinating capitulation offers with the CIA. While the commanders were in hiding after deserting, the question of their future still loomed. In the middle of my communications with the commanders, we got the message from CENTCOM that capitulation was no longer acceptable. The only option was surrender—or die. A month ago, when we were overly polite in our request, our wording had to change. It made sense in the context of cultural differences to adjust our approach accordingly. Now, it seemed like I was just sending mixed messages for no good reason. The reality was none of the context was different. The commanders I was attempting to force to surrender weren't even physically near me. This was essentially a long-distance phone call telling them to surrender or die. Of course, they knew I couldn't kill them, so it was a hollow threat.

On top of that, capitulation was a completely acceptable path. It allowed them to maintain their job, rank, and status and gave the same to the soldiers in their command. If they were an Iraqi colonel or general and capitulated, they would still be an Iraqi colonel or general the following day. They could still have a job, their dignity, remain with their families, and move on in life. Surrender, however, required them to be disbanded from the military, unemployed, and put in a prison camp until we could reconcile what to do with them. They no longer maintained their dignity or remained with their family—a completely unacceptable outcome.

I had been brokering a deal with one particular Iraqi commander and his 5,000 soldiers. He was concerned for their future, looking out for their welfare, and trying to negotiate a good deal for them. Before we were able to finalize the agreement, however, the US policy abruptly changed. Wahab, my Kurdish bodyguard, was on the phone with him wherever he was, likely near Tikrit. Although I wasn't speaking directly with him, I could hear the commander's voice coming from the cell phone. I had to tell him the policy had changed and capitulation was no longer valid. He asked what the new offer meant. I explained I couldn't guarantee he wouldn't be sent to a detention camp away from his family and I could no longer offer that he would be a paid member of the Iraqi army after this. There are things that transcend language barriers, and his pain was one of them. I could sense his confusion, and it was amplified by my own. There really wasn't anything I could do or say other than apologize.

"I'm sorry for this change. I'm sorry I can't make this arrangement anymore," I offered.

"You understand what this means?" he asked.

"I think I do," I said with a heavy heart.

Our conversation was not that of two adversaries. It was two professionals speaking, man to man, both beholden to our circumstances but not wanting the inevitable outcome. If we had only finalized the deal just three days ago, we would have been on the same side.

"You understand, the next time we meet it will not be as friends, and I regret that," he said.

"I understand, and I regret that as well." What had we just done? I couldn't believe this was our policy, but it was and I was powerless to do anything about it.

"Peace be upon you and your family," he graciously offered.

"Wa alaykum as-salam," I replied. I could see the devastation in Wahab's face. I could feel the emotion welling up inside of me. I walked away, choked up and stunned.

Instead of bringing them to our side, we had just pushed the bulk of the Iraqi military and exiles into an insurgency that would haunt us for years, needlessly costing untold amounts of money, pain, and suffering. And why? I had no good answer. We had all been working to convince the Iraqis to join us. There's no telling how differently the future would have been if this one policy hadn't changed.

THE FREE IRAQI FORCES AND AHMED CHALABI

During one of our meetings at Dokan Lake with the JOSTF and the KDP, which were now held weekly, we met Ahmed Chalabi. Years prior, Chalabi had fallen out of favor with the CIA because they discovered they couldn't trust his intelligence and regarded him as a deceptive con man. Now, he was back playing the DOD, who had embraced him as their new guy in Iraq.

The KDP and the PUK leadership were clearly not comfortable with this man. Chalabi arrived at the meeting along with an American colonel who said he was representing the Pentagon and a former State Department guy who was sporting a new camo uniform that still had its creases from the PX. The latter was clearly out of his element.

Collectively, Chalabi, the COL, and the ex-DOS guy were here to tell us all about the Free Iraqi Forces (FIF), who, as they put it, represented the resistance inside Iraq. They brought some of the FIF with them, who looked like a collection of malnourished criminals, standing there in fatigues with patches on their shoulders that said "FIF" in English.

The Colonel explained that the Pentagon was very excited about this program and wanted to put "an Iraqi face" on the conflict. He was from the Army's Training and Doctrine Command (TRADOC) and the Pentagon had selected them to create this resistance force.

I couldn't believe what I was hearing. *Are you kidding me?* I wondered. The FIF were, plain and simple, mercenaries—and not very good ones.

The Pentagon had been funding Chalabi based on his claims of ties to a resistance force inside the country. Since the start of the program he had only been able to find a few hundred volunteers. But now in country, with the assistance of the Pentagon funding, his plan was to raise an army of willing volunteers. Chalabi didn't announce the FIF pay rate in front of the KDP and PUK leadership, but they were acutely aware that he was offering *$1,000 per day* for prospective volunteers—a princely sum by Iraqi standards.

During the meeting, one of the PUK commanders, Mullah Bakhtiar, raised an objection to Chalabi's presence at the meeting. Bakhtiar, who looked every bit like a classic guerrilla commander, was having none of Chalabi's claims. In Kurdish he said, "This man is no leader, and he has no army. He is a liar here offering money to our soldiers to desert, and I'm not going to tolerate that." To emphasize his seriousness, he simultaneously put his hand on his pistol. The implication was pretty clear and he was looking directly at Chalabi when he said it. Although his statement was in Kurdish, I understood. I also apparently failed to hide my own facial expressions, which demonstrated my approval of his leadership style.

After the meeting was over and we broke for lunch, he walked over and silently handed me a plate of food. He gave me a sturdy thump on the shoulder in solidarity. I thanked him and we had a wordless moment of connection. Later, I was discussing it with Bafel. I noted, "Mullah Bahktir seems like a really good commander."

He agreed. "He's one of our best. He really appreciated you backing him up at the meeting."

"Absolutely," I concurred. "I really like his style."

"Me too," he said. "Actually, he's my father-in-law."

We didn't know anything about the FIF prior to the meeting, but now, suddenly, these guys were uniformed and credentialed by the US military. They even had US military-issued ID cards (CACs). The US forces treated the FIF as a legitimate partner because the word had gone out that these were the real Iraqi resistance forces. They had special privileges that we were unable to coordinate for our Kurds.

The PUK forces were getting stopped at checkpoints and harassed. The Americans would routinely point guns at the Kurds, get them on the ground, and even put them in flex cuffs. The soldiers confiscated their weapons more than once and even crushed them under the track of a vehicle. We tried to get CENTCOM to issue guidance that the PUK and the KDP were to be treated as partners. Tovo even traveled to Baghdad to make the case in person, but was ultimately unsuccessful. In the end, the Department of Defense wasted somewhere on the order of $60 million on the FIF program with absolutely no return on investment while simultaneously minimizing the 60,000-man-strong resistance that had actually supported the invasion.

THE STAY BEHIND PLAN

Around the first week of May we got word that the majority of the force would be redeploying soon. A decision was made to attach three ODAs to a company from 2nd Battalion with three of their own ODAs as the force that would remain in Iraq in the north. The 5th Special Forces Group would do the same in the south and provide a SOTF headquarters to command both companies.

The 2nd Battalion commander came to our forward operating base (FOB) to brief us on his intent for the operation as the major in charge was from his battalion. "We need to come up with a quantifiable metric for success," he explained. "Something that we know we can't accomplish, and that way we will demonstrate that we're not value added and get sent home."

I was absolutely furious listening to what he was saying in front of my guys. Even though I was just a major, I pulled him aside and said, "Sir, if you don't mind, don't ever say that in front of my guys again." He looked at me like I had lost my mind by addressing him that way. I reiterated, "I'm serious. Don't say things like that to my guys again."

TYING UP LOOSE ENDS

Tovo and I were both concerned that the JSOTF's departure was premature. We considered what we could do to mitigate some of the nonsense we were seeing. We chose to go to Tikrit and meet with the 4th Infantry Division Commander, MG Raymond Odierno. We brought Amanj, the PUK member who was going to accompany 082 on their mission behind Kirkuk with us, to stay on as an LNO to the PUK. He was fluent in Kurdish, Arabic, and English.

I presented a briefing to MG Odierno that outlined everything we had been through with the PUK and what they had done for the US. We made it very clear that the PUK had been incredible partners. The meeting went extremely well, and MG Odierno was grateful for the information and for his new LNO. Tovo and I flew back to Sulaymaniyah feeling like we had done as much as we could.

The next day, Bafel, Lahur, and Kok Mustafa gave Tovo and me a gift as a memento of our time together. They presented us both with a hand-carved wooden chess set. It was as much a beautiful gift as it was a symbolic gesture of our adventures. We spoke about our concerns for the future, and I offered some suggestions.

I ended up departing the next day, one day sooner than expected. Thankfully, I had the opportunity to say goodbye to Wahab, the Kurd who had loyally served as my bodyguard. We were both choked up. He saw me as a man willing to help liberate him and his people and I saw him as someone willing to risk his life to protect me. In his broken English he said, "Thank you, Mark" and placed his hand on his heart. I did the same.

Unfortunately, I didn't get the chance to see Bafel or Lahur before I left, but I did leave them a letter. I offered a list of recommendations that would help protect the PUK's position with the US forces. I also told them how much I valued their friendship and respected them. I said that it had been my great honor to fight alongside the Peshmerga in pursuit of such a noble cause. I wished them well and hoped the Kurdish people would find the peace and prosperity they so deserved.

It was difficult to leave. What we had accomplished was frankly hard to believe, especially in the face of what often seemed like insurmountable odds. I couldn't have imagined a better ally than the PUK. It was like we were walking off the field in the third quarter because we were so impressed by our performance, blissfully unaware that the ball was still in play. It felt like we hadn't finished what we came to do and not enough people seemed to care.

I left Iraq on May 8, 2003. Forty-eight hours later, I was back home in Colorado Springs.

CONCLUSION

Strategy without tactics is the slowest route to victory.
Tactics without strategy is the noise before defeat.

— Sun Tzu

In the spring of 2003, there was an optimism about Iraq within the US military. On April 15th, US forces found eleven buried or concealed laboratory facilities in and around Karbala. A month later, in Mosul, a mobile lab was discovered that matched the description provided by GEN Colin Powell at the UN in February. A week later, a second mobile lab was discovered at a KDP checkpoint. It appeared the evidence of WMDs was starting to surface. In July, Saddam's notorious sons, Uday and Qusay, were killed during a raid in Mosul. Over the next five months, coalition forces tirelessly searched for Saddam Hussein, which eventually resulted in his capture on December 13, 2003 outside of Tikrit.

Looking back on the war, it's difficult to draw a single conclusion, and it's not my intention to attempt to justify or invalidate the invasion. I would, however, offer some perspectives about its execution in the hope of contributing to a more comprehensive history of the invasion and provide the benefit of those experiences—good and bad—for future military planners and special operators.

THE IMPORTANCE OF THE SECOND FRONT TO THE INVASION PLAN

To this day, I'm not sure the US military appreciates how critical the second front was to the success of the attack from the south. As the 2nd Brigade of the 3rd Infantry Division closed on Baghdad, in what became known as the Thunder Run, they engaged in some of the fiercest fighting in US military history. The incredibly bold strike, to pierce the heart of Baghdad and crush the enemy's will, succeeded by the narrowest of margins. That comment is in no way meant to be a slight to the bravery and skill of the Armor and Infantry task force that conducted the attack, but more a comment on the realities of the limitations of logistics. As the forces reached the palace complex in the capital, their vehicles were critically low on ammunition and fuel. Had there been additional Iraqi forces capable of counterattacking in and around Baghdad, the outcome could have potentially been very different.

SURRENDER AND CAPITULATION

Arguably, when it was time to convey the message for surrender, the Pentagon was too soft. In their message of capitulation, they overcompensated and were too heavy-handed. How differently would things have gone if, after the seizing of Baghdad, the US military had multiple Iraqi brigades intact working alongside our forces. Those Iraqi forces could have told us where all the remaining holdouts were hiding. Iraqis could have compelled the rest of their army to come in from the cold. It could have demonstrated that our fight was not with the Iraqi people or even the army.

THE FREE IRAQI FORCES (FIF)

The entire concept of the FIF was ill-conceived and even more poorly executed. Resistance forces—effective ones—*cannot be manufactured.* There was no need to create a force to put an Iraqi face on the resistance when there were already 50,000 Kurds fighting as a resistance. Additionally, if the Pentagon wanted to put more of an Iraqi face on their coalition, it could have placed more emphasis on the capitulation efforts. They could have identified Arabic-speaking special forces to be prepared to link up with and integrate capitulated units into the coalition. This would have been a massive windfall of local and cultural knowledge for the coalition and would also have created legitimacy with the population.

THE ORDER THAT WE ARE NOT OCCUPIERS

The guidance to not fly the US flag or portray US forces as occupiers was a huge mistake. This one command completely undermined all efforts by the military forces to establish some semblance of order and stability. It was a last-minute addition and not part of the original plan. It not only authorized a large amount of looting, but worse, it created an absence of control. That vacuum allowed enemy forces to exploit the situation. Had we established a clear but temporary martial law, we could have more quickly established a baseline of governance and rules for the populace. This would have led to a degree of collaboration and cooperation from the population.

Instead, the population remained confused and concerned about the uncertainty of their future. This dynamic offered an opportunity for the insurgency to grow like an infection in an open wound. How different would things have been if we had communicated to the population that we were establishing martial law (with rules) but would turn over control to Iraqi officials as soon as possible?

THE RECONSTRUCTION AND RECONCILIATION PHASE (PHASE 4)

The debate between the Department of State and Department of Defense and the subsequent removal of ORHA was a devastating blow. What if we had followed the structured Phase 4 plan for reconstruction and reconciliation? Imagine if we had placed a premium on getting Iraqis back to work, repairing power stations, water treatment facilities, ports and waterways, sewage treatment, roads, bridges, and oil infrastructure. What if we had not banned all former Ba'ath party members from serving as government workers, which largely disenfranchised every Sunni adult male? What if we had followed a model like the experience with the Marshall Plan in 1946? Would the population have supported the rise of the insurgencies in the Sunni and Shia areas?

In hindsight, the chaos that ensued and the rise of the insurgencies was not a forgone conclusion. It was due to a perfect storm of bad military planning combined with ideal conditions for the enemy, plain and simple. The conditions for a much more favorable outcome were entirely present but not seized.

THE DEBATE OVER WEAPONS OF MASS DESTRUCTION

The question of whether Saddam had WMDs remains understandably polarizing since it was the stated basis for the invasion. There seems to be little doubt that the normal analytical process of the intelligence community was corrupted to support the expected or even desired conclusion. While it's easy to apply judgment in hindsight, it's also worth noting that this took place in the immediate aftermath of the 9/11 attack, fueled by a decade of defiance and deception by Saddam (as I covered in the overview of history in Chapter 1).

On September 30, 2004, the Iraqi Survey Group, which had replaced the United Nations inspection team, produced its final report on Iraq's WMD programs. The report, known as the Duelfer Report, outlined the following conclusions:

- Saddam Hussein deceived his own army and the best intelligence agencies in the world into believing he still had WMDs because he believed he needed to maintain a deterrent against his enemies, most notably Iran.
- Iraq destroyed the majority of its chemical weapons stockpile in 1991.
- Saddam Hussein's regime abandoned its nuclear program in 1991 and its biological weapons program in 1995.

As the war devolved into a full-blown counterinsurgency, the prevailing opinion regarding WMD seemed to be best case, the Bush administration was wrong. Worst case, the administration deliberately misled the public. However, by 2009, the US military in Iraq had recovered and destroyed more than 4,500 previously unaccounted-for chemical weapons. The argument has been made that the vast majority of these munitions, which contained a variety of chemical agents, were generally in poor condition and dated from the 1980s. Therefore, their existence didn't constitute proof of an active program.

In the end, advocates and opponents can both shape arguments to support their cases. I personally suspect the truth regarding Saddam's alleged WMD capability was somewhere in between.

MY FINAL THOUGHTS

An aspect that I still find interesting is that the argument for going to war was based on the alleged threat Saddam posed if he had weapons of mass destruction. The Western powers still debate about the validity of the intelligence that influenced and ultimately compelled the United Nations to authorize the use of force. For the Iraqis, this was an irrelevant argument. They were not concerned about what he might do as much as focused on what he had done.

Saddam Hussein was tried and found guilty of genocide and crimes against humanity by an Iraqi Special Tribunal consisting of five Iraqi judges. During his time as the president of Iraq from 1979 to 2003, it's estimated that he was responsible for the deaths of anywhere between 100,000 and 250,000 Iraqis, mostly Kurdish and Shia. By all accounts, this was a deliberate and methodical campaign of genocide. Between 1983 and 1991 he employed chemical weapons over nineteen times, mostly against Iranian forces, but also against his own population on several occasions. He was sentenced to death and executed on December 30, 2006. The Iraqi government has since uncovered evidence of over 250 mass graves dating to his rule.

These details have a tendency to fade into the background as the West debates amongst itself. It's a very different perspective on the ground in Iraq. The generational trauma with which decades of oppression have imbued the population is always present. It's hard to see at a glance, but if you spend any amount of time among the population, whether Kurdish or Arab, the memories of that oppression are readily evident. When you travel to remote areas and see the remnants of former villages wiped off the map or the sight of mass graves, it is horrific. It's hard to fully comprehend.

In his final interview with the FBI, Saddam explained that they had destroyed his stockpiles without the UN inspectors' knowledge and that was a mistake. He explained that it was cost prohibitive to include the inspectors because they insisted that all their expenses were paid. He conceded that it was a bad decision that later caused concern by the inspectors. Saddam also explained that he was, in fact, a friend to the Shia Marsh Arabs and only drained their marshes to improve their health conditions.

Hopefully, given time, the scars of the Saddam era and the decade of instability and conflict that followed will heal, allowing Iraq to assume its rightful place in the world.

Iraq has all the components it needs to be a thriving nation and source of stability in the region. It has unquestionably one of the richest histories of any nation on the planet. It was the home of Abraham and Noah from the Old Testament. It was the seat of the Akkadian, Sumerian, Babylonian, and Assyrian empires, which gave the world numerous inventions that became the basis for modern civilization. Examples include the wheel, algebra, writing, written laws, maps, modern time based on 60 seconds and minutes, many aspects of advanced medicine, chemistry, architecture, sailing, astronomy, and math. It has an unrivaled economic potential in the region based on its oil reserves, agricultural capacity, and archeological and religious tourism. The fate of Iraq, for the first time in a century, is now in the hands of its people.

Lastly, the operations conducted by 10th Special Forces Group in Northern Iraq serve as a remarkable example of how special operations, and more specifically, unconventional warfare, can contribute to a broader campaign. A relatively small number of Green Berets and CIA officers, totaling around 1,000 personnel, spread over an area the size of West Virginia, were able to tie down thirteen Iraqi divisions—over half of the Iraqi army. The 3rd Battalion, or SOTF 103, with the Patriotic Union of Kurdistan (PUK), seized Kirkuk, the first city taken in the north, and the only city captured without the support of conventional forces. The remarkable success of the operation, in the face of overwhelming odds, serves as a testament to the professionalism of the men and women of the 10th Special Forces Group and the bravery and courage of the Kurdish people to persevere against tyranny.

THROUGH THE LOOKING GLASS

Do not try to do too much with your own hands. Better the
Arabs do it tolerably than you do it perfectly. It is their war,
and you are to help them, not to win it for them.

— T.E. LAWRENCE

A VERY DIFFERENT KIND OF WAR

It wasn't long before Iraq started to devolve into a state of chaos. The Department of Defense was in a state of denial, insisting that Iraq was not facing an insurrection, but rather just criminal activity. In fact, they were dealing with two distinctly different but overlapping insurgencies: a Sunni-based insurgency in the Arab areas (predominantly north and west), and a Shia-based insurgency (predominantly in the center and south). The Sunni insurgency was a mix of former Ba'ath regime members and foreign fighters. Before long, the foreign fighters gained influence over the movement, which eventually became categorized as al-Qaeda in Iraq, or AQI. The Shia insurgency was comprised of Shia Arabs with support from Iran, generally categorized as Jaysh al-Mahdi, or JAM.

By October of 2003, large numbers of US forces started to return to Iraq. The newly established Combined Joint Special Operations Task Force Arabian Peninsula (CJSOTF-AP) was established in Balad, about sixty miles north of Baghdad. The CJSOTF rotated every nine months between 5th and 10th Special Forces Groups. It included two Special Forces battalions and a Navy SEAL equivalent. The two Special Forces battalions made up SOTF North and SOTF Central, while the SEAL team made up SOTF West. In total, the number of Special Forces ODAs and SEAL platoons was usually between forty and forty-five, with a presence in nearly every major city in Iraq.

In order to survive in these communities, the teams needed to find people who were willing to work with them, locals who understood the nuances of the neighborhoods. Teams found willing volunteers from former police, former soldiers, or even ordinary citizens. Over time, the teams transformed their indigenous security forces into well-trained fighting forces. This, coupled with their local support network that would provide early warnings and intelligence, proved to be a powerful combination.

In 2004, elements of 5th Special Forces Group developed an Iraqi special operations unit comprised of Sunni, Shia, and Kurdish volunteers. This new unit was called the 36th Commando Battalion. At the same time, 3rd Special Forces Group developed the Iraqi Counter Terror Force (ICTF). The ICTF was trained by the 3rd Group's Crisis Response Forces (CRF). At that time, each active-duty Special Forces Group had a single company specially trained in direct action and hostage rescue operations. They were called the Crisis Response Force (CRF in the case of 3rd and 5th Groups) and the Commander's In-extremis Force (CIF in the case of 1st, 7th, and 10th Groups).

Both the 36th Commandos and the ICTF quickly proved their immense value and were combined into the Iraqi Special Operations Forces (ISOF) Brigade. Regardless of the Special Forces Group that was on rotation, manning the CJSOTF, the CRFs and CIFs from 1st, 3rd, 5th, 7th, and 10th Special Forces Groups rotated to provide the bulk of the training and advisors for the ISOF Brigade. In 2005 the ICTF and Commandos started to conduct raids in areas previously considered inaccessible to coalition forces, such as Karbala, Najaf, and Sadr City. In some cases, during particularly complex operations, the Green Berets advising the ICTF or Commando battalions wore the same uniforms as their Iraqi counterparts and mixed in with their forces.

In addition to the CJSOTF-AP, there was also another special operations headquarters referred to as Task Force 714. The task force included various units focused on unilateral raids against high value targets. With its headquarters collocated at the Balad airfield, the task force maintained strike forces on airfields in Balad, Mosul in the north, and Al-Asad in the west. To augment this force, the Special Forces CRFs and CIFs that had been supporting the ISOF Brigade were split in half. Half would continue to support the ISOF Brigade and the other half would function as a unilateral strike force under the control of TF 714.

By 2006, most of the CJSOTF's partner forces started to transform into Iraqi Special Weapons and Tactics (ISWATs), under the control of the local provincial government. In all, the CJSOTF-AP's Iraqi partner forces included roughly thirty ISWAT units, each comprising a company or battalion of soldiers, the new Emergency Response Unit (ERU), and the ISOF Brigade, which now included its two Baghdad-based battalions, a special reconnaissance company, a training academy, and two regional Commando battalions in Mosul and Basra.

As the partner forces matured, CJSOTF was able to focus on the development of Public Affairs elements embedded in the provincial ISWAT units to counter enemy propaganda after successful operations. They also pioneered procedures that transformed classified US intelligence into Iraqi warrants for raids. These types of initiatives provided an unprecedented degree of legitimacy with the population, a dynamic that US unilateral strikes, regardless of their tactical effectiveness, couldn't match.

RETURN TO A VERY DIFFERENT IRAQ

In 2006, I was promoted to lieutenant colonel while serving in the White House Military Office. The war had gone on longer than expected and was going badly. Most of my peers had served one if not two rotations during this time and I felt an obligation to get back to Iraq after four years away. To my surprise, I was selected for an overseas assignment outside of the Special Operations community. Accepting the assignment would have kept me out of the war for another two years and placed a huge burden on my family. I chose to decline.

Tovo, now a colonel and in command of 10th Special Forces Group, was rotating into Iraq to command CJSOTF-AP. He asked if I would be willing to serve as his J-3 Operations Officer. I immediately said yes. After contacting my assignments manager, he explained that these were career-enhancing positions and they needed to be careful who they gave them to. He went on to explain that there were a lot of great officers who hadn't had the chance to go to Iraq yet and he needed to take care of them. My request to rejoin the war was denied.

Over the next few months, I continued to submit requests and finally received word that I could join 5th Special Forces Group as the Chief of Staff (COS) during their next rotation. Soon after, I headed to Fort Campbell, Kentucky to join the Group during their final preparations for deployment. On my first day there, I met with the commander, COL Chris Conner. I didn't know him other than by his reputation, which was quite good. Within the first few minutes, we were interrupted by a phone call. It was a general officer calling to explain that one of his guys had recently had an accidental discharge in Afghanistan and was consequently sent home. The general explained that this officer was a really good guy and needed a strong evaluation. He was sending him to join the CJSOTF as the COS.

Conner looked at me awkwardly and explained they would find a position for me. I politely replied that I didn't need them to find me a position. If they didn't have a position for me, I could return to the White House Military Office. I could tell Conner didn't like the situation any more than I did. During that time, I met the J-3, LTC Mark Mitchell. Mark was a long-time member of 5th Group and a very smart and down-to-earth officer. Had I been the chief of staff, Mitchell would have been my main counterpart in the CJSOTF. He and I spoke, and I asked him to find me a position where I could help the CJSOTF the most.

Upon arriving in Iraq in October of 2007, I was assigned to MNF-I headquarters located in the embassy compound in Baghdad (what was called the "Green Zone"). The CJSOTF rarely briefed the MNF-I headquarters, whereas TF 714 briefed their operations each morning. This was due to a misperception that the CJSOTF's operations were merely tactical and more appropriate for the three-star, Multi-National Corps–Iraq (MNC-I) headquarters. As a result, planners in MNF-I developed an unbalanced perspective of the value, scale, and scope of special operations being conducted. This was the type of opportunity that LTC Mitchell and I had spoken about weeks earlier.

One day in February, the British major general I was working for invited me to accompany him to visit the TF 714 HQs. Upon arriving, we were greeted by the TF commander, LTG McChrystal. He explained how they had harnessed the vast resources of the US interagency to enable their Find, Fix, Finish methodology, which had gained popularity among the American planners. It was an impressive briefing. As we flew back to Baghdad, the major general expressed how useful and informative the visit had been. I asked if he would be interested in visiting a Special Forces team on the ground. He immediately said yes, and I started the coordination.

A week later we were traveling to Hillah to visit one of the ODBs from 5ᵗʰ Group. Their partner force, the Hillah SWAT, was an exceptionally good unit. As we departed, the general's aide asked what the name of the airfield was at our destination.

"There is no airfield," I said. "Just a field."

His expression showed a hint of concern as my comment sank in. As the helicopter approached the open field in the middle of a dense urban area, a man looking somewhat like a homeless person stepped into view to guide the aircraft down. The bearded sergeant, in civilian clothes, directed us to follow him inside.

Once inside, MAJ Pat Duggan introduced himself and his men. Looking around the city from the vantage point of the roof, the general asked awkwardly, "I don't mean to be rude, but how are you all still alive?"

MAJ Duggan smiled. "Well sir, that building next door is the Hillah SWAT. At least twice a week I have dinner with the commander. Once a week I have dinner with the mayor. The local people here like us. We buy our food from them. They see us as a benefit to their community."

The general asked if the major spoke Arabic. Coincidentally, Pat's Arabic was excellent. The general turned to the senior NCO and asked if he, too, spoke Arabic. He replied, "My Arabic's not that great. I'm a Farsi speaker."

A short while later we departed and headed to Najaf. The nearest coalition forces were based forty miles away. As the helicopter made its approach, a small, walled earthen compound in a barren field appeared ahead. The aircraft landed inside the compound and a group of bearded Special Forces soldiers greeted us. The senior NCO introduced himself and, like the previous brief, he explained their relationship with the community, specifically, the local tribes. This time the general met members of their Najaf security force. Several of the Iraqis explained they had been with this team since 2004. After about an hour of conversation over tea, we headed back to Baghdad.

During the flight back, the general's mood was notably different than the previous week's trip. He was somewhat taken by the stark contrast he just observed. While the tour at TF 714 was, without question, very polished and impressive, this visit was messy and personal. He thanked me for arranging the visit and remarked, "Now I understand how you seem to know what's going on all over this country." He was referring to the executive summary I compiled each week based on the CJSOTF's weekly SITREP and to the fact that he had now seen two of the CJSOTF's nearly forty outposts across the country.

BREAKING THE SUNNI INSURGENCY

By early 2007, al-Qaeda in Iraq had overplayed their hand.

They had increased their campaign of intimidation and violence against the population, particularly the western Anbar tribes. Various Special Forces teams that maintained relationships with the tribes were attuned to their frustrations. Many of the team members had learned hard lessons over the years, persuading village members to stand up to the insurgents, only to find their mutilated corpses at the village entrance the next week. The teams knew that making this concept work would require their presence on the ground, demonstrating commitment and sharing the risk. They proposed an initiative to train, arm, and pay members of the tribes to protect their own neighborhoods.

The program was named the Sons of Iraq (SOI). It was actually very similar to what 5th Special Forces Group had done during the Vietnam War with the Civilian Irregular Defense Group program. The SOI program ran into some initial challenges. While the program paid the volunteers a weekly salary, providing the required weapons proved problematic. Despite the destruction of numerous caches of weapons each week by coalition forces, the decision was made that any weapons or ammunition should be the responsibility of the volunteers. This caused many volunteers to turn to the black market to purchase their weapons, which unfortunately was controlled by the insurgency. Regardless of these flaws, the program still mobilized a significant portion of the population onto the side of the government. At its height, the Sons of Iraq included over 100,000 volunteers, predominantly in the west.

During a visit to an outpost about an hour south of Baghdad, I spent the day with a handful of volunteers. They stood at their post, wearing blaze orange reflective vests, no body armor or helmets, holding rifles with two magazines of ammunition. One man told me that the insurgents were offering $100 payments to emplace an improvised explosive device, which was twice what we were paying. I asked him why he volunteered. With his nine-year-old son standing by his side, he said he was doing this for his son's future. I asked him how the nights were, and he admitted they were scary. "The insurgents have more guns than we do." I was incredibly moved by his bravery and sacrifice.

A second phase of the SOI program was the incentive for government service and transition to stability. The program was intended to offer free vocational training for six months of service. This seemed brilliant to me, as Iraq was desperate for professional electricians, plumbers, carpenters, etc. After I returned to the embassy, I met up with two US officers managing the budget for the SOI program. The officers, an Air Force colonel and Navy captain, said they thought this program was "nothing more than paying these people to not attack us." I disagreed, but they were not interested in my opinion. To my disappointment, the vocational training phase never materialized.

Around the same time, MNF-I had developed a plan to incorporate additional US forces from the United States. An additional 22,000 soldiers arrived from the United States, predominantly to secure Baghdad. This became known as "the surge." While the surge was an important component during this time, it was the Sons of Iraq that made the real difference. The Sunni population was now on the side of the government and that was too much for the insurgency to overcome.

OPPORTUNITY AMIDST CHAOS

In March of 2008, the situation in Basra, one of Iraq's southernmost cites, was growing desperate. The city had devolved into complete chaos and a stronghold for Jaysh al-Mahdi. Numerous prominent Iraqi officials had recently either been killed or kidnapped in the city. Basra had been the responsibility of British Forces since 2003. For political reasons, British coalition forces had withdrawn from the city a year earlier and positioned at an airfield about ten kilometers outside the city. Iraqi Prime Minister Nouri al-Maliki was convinced the Americans misunderstood the situation, and in a show of defiance, he insisted on visiting Basra personally. Although the MNF-I Commander, General Petraeus, tried to convince him of the gravity of the situation, Maliki insisted that his information was wrong and declared he would travel to the city in the morning.

With little ability to stop the prime minister, Petraeus directed the CJSOTF to send someone with him to ensure he at least remained in contact with the headquarters. As the only CJSOTF member in the headquarters, it was easy to predict how this was going to play out. In the morning, I received a call from LTC Mitchell letting me know I was to accompany the prime minister, with the additional guidance, "Do your best to keep him alive." I grabbed my weapon and a small pack with a radio, some ammunition, and water.

I linked up with two Air Force officers, a captain and a major, both of whom were Intelligence, Surveillance, Reconnaissance (ISR) platform specialists. Someone thought it would be a good idea to send them along, which in hindsight made no sense since we had no ISR platforms supporting us. The major had just lost the knife which was strapped to his vest with the handle facing down, and the captain asked if I thought it would be all right if he wore a CamelBak water bladder on his kit. I just looked and them both and said, "I'm not sure you guys are mentally grasping where we are headed." They both turned out to be very good officers but were a bit out of their element.

We loaded on to two British helicopters, along with the PM and his staff. As we approached the city, it looked like a scene from a post-apocalyptic movie. The city was in ruins and deserted. As we landed in an abandoned British base on the south side of the city, I could see fires burning in the distance and hear sporadic gunfire. The city had no electricity or running water. In the abandoned compound, the outside of every building was riddled with bullet holes while the insides were covered with human urine stains and feces. The helicopters quickly departed, and Maliki's group quickly shuffled into one of the main buildings.

On board the other aircraft was a British lieutenant colonel, Ian Cave, who had brought three enlisted communications specialists with him. In addition to our small team, there were also two South African contractors who advised Maliki's security detail. They were ex-military and very experienced. We all occupied a building one down from Maliki's building. The compound was walled but there was no guard force beyond us. I briefly met with the prime minister, who made it clear he had no use for me. I reported to MNF-I that the situation was very serious, and the PM and his staff did not grasp what was going on in and around the city. I called the CJSOTF and told them I needed some additional help. That night LTC Mitchell sent a helicopter with four personnel from the CJSOTF: Major Seth Krummrich, CW3 John Bryant, and two communications sergeants.

The next morning, the PM wanted to see me. He started by reminding me that he didn't need my help, but then asked if I could arrange for a fighter aircraft to fly over the city in a show of force. He assured me this would break the enemy's spirit. I told him I would see what I could do and placed a call to MNF-I. Sometime later I was summoned again to explain why the aircraft never appeared. I learned that it had in fact flown over the city as I requested, but at 20,000 feet. That one was on me for not being specific. Now the PM wanted another fighter to fly along the river, firing its machine guns into the water. I did not accommodate that request.

By the evening, I was being told to "bomb the white pickup truck next to the tall building." After a lengthy discussion on how military grid coordinates worked, I was handed a piece of paper with some writing and the insistence that I drop a bomb on this position, now. Before I could respond, my Iraqi interpreter, a former military officer himself, pointed out that the grid coordinates only had seven digits. Maliki's chief of staff quickly explained, "Ah, yes, that's the telephone number of a man who knows where to drop the bomb. Call him." This surreal dance of increasingly bizarre and frantic demands continued for the next twenty-four hours, culminating with "US forces must attack the city immediately."

Meanwhile, over the course of the two previous nights, the Basra Commandos, with their 5th Group counterparts, had conducted several incredibly daring and successful raids. In response, the enemy made the mistake of telling the population this was the American 82nd Airborne Division. The CJSOTF psyops elements wasted no time capitalizing on the mistake, informing the population that this was in fact Iraq's own special operations forces. The news was as stunning to the population as it was to the enemy.

Maliki, pleased with the raids, ordered the Hillah SWAT and emergency response unit to head to Basra. Unfortunately, any advantage of surprise enjoyed in the last few nights was now gone, and the commandos knew if they continued to press their luck, it would run out. On the previous night, the enemy launched a coordinated response. Fortunately, the British garrison, positioned a few miles away on the outskirts of the city, violated their standing orders and responded with a tank platoon. The platoon broke the counterattack, but one tank was severely damaged.

While the raids had succeeded in disrupting the enemy thus far, they were not a long-term solution. As a result, the PM was persuaded to order additional forces to support the effort. However, the order did not go to well-equipped army units that had been receiving equipment and training from the coalition but rather to lightly armed police units from Baghdad, to which the PM had a tribal affiliation.

The next morning around 0430, the attack of Basra—now called Operation Charge of the Knights—began. The conglomeration of police and army units executed a surprisingly well-coordinated start to the attack. Unfortunately, by late afternoon, the situation started to turn. Soldiers and police were running low on ammunition. Almost once an hour, one of the Iraqi policemen would have an accidental discharge with their AK-47, frequently resulting in a gunshot wound to their own thigh. Casualties were being collocated in rooms with corpses. No one had any food or water. Men started to fill water bottles and pull fish from a local lake. It wasn't the enemy that was breaking the attack; it was the lack of logistics.

Lt. Col. Cave and I continued meeting with Maliki's staff to hear their increasingly desperate demands for action. "You must send forces into the city now. Our forces are pinned down!" Cave and I both suspected this was deliberate theatrics for the PM's benefit. They expected we would explain this wasn't possible and then explode in a gesture of solidarity with the PM's frustration.

Lt. Col. Cave calmly took out his map. "Okay, show me," he said. "Where do you need our force to go to save your men?"

The group froze like deer caught in headlights. They had not anticipated this response. One of the staffers responded. "Just have your forces start moving south," he said. "We will get the information."

As the battle started to culminate, the prime minister's former attitude of self-sufficiency seemed to give way to what I can only describe as a combination of desperation oddly mixed with conditional demands. He wanted a substantial coalition ground force to come to their aid and they wanted it within the hour, but not from the British. After PM Maliki stormed out of the room, his chief of staff intended to continue berating us.

I leaned in and commanded, "Enough! The prime minister gets to yell at me, but you do not." I explained how the British troops saved Iraqis yesterday and continued, "I don't care about your history with them; we are a single coalition. There is no Iraqi, American, or British. There is only *us* and the enemy. The sooner you accept this, the better our chances of surviving the week will be."

The next morning, I received a call on the satellite phone. It was a brigadier general from Multi-National Corps Iraq (MNC-I) insisting that he was now in charge. He ordered me to go find the most senior Iraqi official I could and establish a secure video teleconference (VTC) with him ASAP. He then asked who the senior Iraqi that I had been dealing with was. I told him I'd been dealing with the Prime Minister. I could tell that it caught him off guard.

I then said, "Sir, let me explain the situation here. I'm in a burned-out building. There's no power and the city is literally under siege. There are no offices or VTCs here and I don't work for MNC-I. I work for MNF-I."

As he began shouting, my attention shifted to the series of explosions outside my window. They were significantly larger than the explosions I had become accustomed to. I shouted into the handset, "Sir, I'm getting shelled!" and hung up. I shouted to the team to get to cover, grabbed my Tough Book laptop and slid under a table. By now the fourth round had impacted and I awkwardly typed to the CJSOTF, "Contact, 120 mm fire, enemy is walking rounds onto our position. Grdovic out."

I grabbed my kit and rifle and went to the roof to assess the situation. We had received six rounds of 120 mm mortar fire. The rounds were methodically walked onto Maliki's building, striking the entrance and killing the head of his security detail. The attack triggered wild automatic gun fire from the Iraqi police in all directions. Soon after the shooting stopped, I got on the radio to let Mitchell at the CJSOTF know we were fine and warn him of a likely call from an angry one-star general. He said, "Yeah, thanks, that's already taking place as we speak."

Eventually the MNC-I Commander, LTG Austin, flew into to assess the situation. Before his helicopter landed, I received a call instructing me to have four armored SUVs for the commander at the landing zone and a few secure workstations. I tried to explain the situation, but the officer didn't want to hear it and simply said it was an order and hung up. To my amazement, I was able to muster a single unarmored SUV from the Iraq police, complete with bullet holes in the windshield for the general and an old school bus for the rest of the group.

On the landing zone, one of the officers from his entourage irately explained this wasn't what was coordinated for and demanded an explanation.

"We need to get off the landing zone and inside before we get shelled," I explained. A few minutes later, the group arrived at the PM's building for a meal and some tea with the prime minister. By all accounts it was a fine meeting.

As General Austin exited the building, he asked one of his colonels, "Who has my helmet?"

I watched as that colonel turned to another colonel literally next to him and asked the same question. This process was repeated between six officers and two sergeants major, all standing within ten feet of each other. Finally, the question reached the last member of the group, a CW2, who then relayed the question to me as if it were somehow my responsibility.

I had had enough of the nonsense. "How the fuck should I know where his helmet is?"

The CW2 shouted, "You need to watch your tone!"

Standing there in a uniform so filthy you could no longer see the camouflage pattern, I reached up and grabbed the top of my body armor to pull it down and expose the LTC rank I was wearing and said, "I don't really give a fuck what you think, chief." I could see the collision of anger, confusion, and frustration on his face.

He turned to the other Special Forces soldier with me and angrily asked, "And what rank are you?"

John quietly replied, "Chief Warrant Officer 3."

The frustrated warrant officer mumbled under his breath, "Fucking Special Forces."

I learned the general had left his helmet in the vehicles from the landing zone. I somewhat laughed as I explained, "You know those vehicles weren't mine? They belong to the police and are in the fight as we speak."

My interpreter got on his cell phone and performed his usual magic. A few minutes later, a young Iraqi police officer was frantically running toward me with the helmet. After less than three hours on the ground and one meeting, the group departed for Baghdad, convinced that the situation was well under control.

It was becoming increasingly obvious that Maliki's presence in Basra was problematic. His very presence was causing his generals to exaggerate their reports. No one would convey any bad news despite any obvious facts to the contrary. He would look to his staff and commanders, and they would all agree with whatever he proposed. From his perspective, Lt. Col. Cave and I were the ones being problematic. Eventually the South Africans who supported his security detail persuaded him to return to Baghdad.

As the PM departed, I conveyed to MNF-I in my last report that Maliki was under the misperception that he had been right, and his intervention was the key to the reestablishment of any semblance of security. Despite being the opposite of reality, General Petraeus chose to deliberately reinforce this message and image, and it was a brilliant decision. Maliki landed at Baghdad airport and was met by a cheering crowd and media. He was hailed as a powerful and charismatic Iraqi leader who stood up to the Americans and got things done. The Iraqi population found a new pride in their government.

BREAKING THE SHIA INSURGENCY

I returned to the MNF-I headquarters on March 29th, hoping for some much-needed rest. Unfortunately, my return coincided with the decision by JAM's leader, Muqtada al-Sadr, to unleash a wave of violence against the south, which included an unprecedented rocket campaign against the Green Zone. During a meeting with the CJSOTF, TF 714, and MNC-I, General Petraeus said he wanted to put more pressure on JAM in the south. It was determined that Maysan province was a major source of support for the insurgents due to its border with Iran. There hadn't been an Iraqi army or coalition presence in Maysan province for several years.

MNC-I explained they could divert a battalion from Nasiriyah, but it would take three to six months. TF 714 explained they could establish a new location potentially as far south as Kut, but it would require significant resources in terms of aircraft, ISR, manning, and, best case, it would take several weeks. LTC Mitchell briefed that CJSOTF forces were already fighting alongside Iraqi partner forces all across the south and could increase the pressure now. In addition to the fighting in Basra, multiple Iraqi SWAT units and commando forces had recently been engaged in fierce multi-day battles in Kut, Hillah, Nasiriyah, Najaf, and Diwaniyah.

Petraeus asked what the CJSOTF would need.

"A pallet of printer paper and another box of soccer balls should do it," Mitchell said with a shrug.

One of the MNF-I staff officers snapped, "This isn't a joke!"

General Petraeus, as usual, was calm. "Okay, Chris [referring to Colonel Conner, the CJSOTF Commander], do what you can now, tell me what you need, and everyone else: start planning for what you can in the near future." He then told his staff, "Okay, enough is enough. Wall it up," referring to the rocket attacks emanating from Sadr City, the thirteen square kilometer ghetto, which sat a mere four kilometers from the Green Zone. Sadr City held somewhere on the order of two million residents and had been a safe haven for the Shia insurgents and predominate source of the rocket attacks.

A stunned staff officer said, "Sir, that would take thousands of T-walls," referring to the 12-foot-tall concrete barriers.

"I don't want to hear it's impossible," the general replied. "If there are T-walls in this country that aren't being used, get them moving in this direction."

As the massive effort to blockade Sadr City was underway, huge firefights broke out in the streets, resulting in hundreds of JAM fighters being killed.

Coalition aircraft began a continuous overwatch above the Green Zone, reducing the response time to enemy rocket attacks from twenty minutes to less than five. The same week, PM Maliki directed the Iraqi Counter Terror Battalion to conduct night raids inside Sadr City, an area previously regarded as too dangerous to penetrate. Driving in blacked-out vehicles under night vision googles, the ICTF with their Special Forces advisors entered Sadr City several times, fighting their way to the objective, attacking their targets, and then fighting their way back out.

The CJSOTF started to prepare the environment by broadcasting television and radio messages across the south. They dropped 10,000 leaflets in Amarah, with a picture of an ISOF soldier that read, "Justice is coming. Surrender now or face death." Several photos of prominent insurgent leaders appeared on the leaflets. It was an aggressive message that resonated with a dejected population. In response, the enemy ordered sympathetic government officials to get those leaflets off the streets. The next night the CJSOTF dropped another 10,000 leaflets that now included the government officials' faces.

The Nasiriyah ISWAT was the first unit to conduct a raid into the heart of Amarah. The helicopter assault was deliberately planned against a target that was in full view of the city and would generate paranoia among the enemy. After the raid, a nervous enemy frantically started to communicate in hopes of gaining some sense of what was happening. The CJSOTF leveraged informants, tip lines, rewards programs, and signal intercepts. The Commandos established checkpoints all around the city, passing out flyers and soccer balls and removing any doubt of who they were. The increasingly frayed enemy started receiving messages interrupting their communications to taunt them: "We are coming for you," feeding their fears until it became a self-fueled panic. Signals intelligence indicated JAM fighters in Maysan wanted to fall back to Sadr City and the fighters in Sadr City were hoping to fall back to Maysan province.

A month later, the US and Iraqi Armies cleared Sadr City. JAM never fully recovered and remained in a defensive posture for the remainder of the war.

The changes to the security environment in 2008 gave new hope to the Iraqi population and coalition forces. As a result, President George W. Bush signed an agreement that US forces would begin working toward a deliberate withdrawal with a deadline of December 31, 2011. In accordance with that agreement, in December of 2011, President Obama ordered the withdrawal of all military combat forces.

For the first time in the nation's history, control of the country was formally turned over to the elected government of Iraq. What they make of that opportunity will be up to the Iraqi people. I remain profoundly honored and proud to have played a part with the 10th and 5th Special Forces Groups, and the roles they played in creating and preserving that opportunity.

De Oppresso Libre: to free the oppressed.

WHY WE WERE SUCCESSFUL IN OUR SPECIAL OPERATIONS

WHEN I REFLECT ON THE EXPERIENCE AND CONSIDER WHAT MADE OUR efforts successful, I draw the following conclusions.

Leadership. Leadership was the foundation for all other efforts. The leader's character and actions (much more than their words) will set the tone for professionalism, ethical behavior, open communications, adaptability, stress management, risk tolerance, and decision-making across the entire organization. The relationship among commanders at the battalion, company, and team level needs to be such that all levels feel connected by purpose and intent. LTC Tovo created and promoted an exceptional environment with his subordinates that empowered them to make decisions and take action in accordance with his vision. The direct and indirect impact of his leadership on the organization cannot be overstated.

The Experience of the Force. Every solider knows they could be sent to war. If they are sent, they will deploy to a forward US base and eventually move forward with the rest of their unit. During this period, it's fair to expect there will be a mental adjustment over time. Sending a special forces solder to infiltrate into denied territory is an entirely different situation. This scenario doesn't come with the same grace period and transition time. It is an extremely high-risk environment with no real US support infrastructure: no medical evacuation, no quick reaction forces, and potentially no close air support (depending on the status of the conflict). The stress associated with this can degrade or incapacitate a person's ability to function. It can manifest in a number of ways—some are minor and some are severe. This can include irritability, nervousness, impaired judgement, and/or hyper-emotional states.

There are several ways to mitigate some of this dynamic. The first way is with training. While quality training can provide some experience and skills that mitigate some of these effects, it can only provide so much.

The second way is by gaining regional experience. The culture shock of being completely immersed in another culture is a very real thing. The language, the smells, the food, the customs, and of course the enemy are unfamiliar. There is no reprieve for your nervous system. Sending soldiers overseas on training deployments to target regions reduces much of this unfamiliarity. Eating the local food, struggling with the language, and gaining some insights to their regional perspectives and nuances helps. In June of 2002, Tovo and I, along with ODA 083, spent a month in Turkey, training with the Turkish special forces for this exact reason. These types of training deployments also allow the teams to become more accustomed to operating without the support apparatus I mentioned previously.

The third way to mitigate some of this is by gaining operational experience. I would estimate 25 percent of the battalion had operated in support of Provide Comfort. Ninety percent of the battalion had conducted deployments to Kosovo or Bosnia, probably multiple times. It also seemed like a third of the force had served in the first battalion in Germany, with many of us having served in C/1-10 or what was formerly known as the EUCOM Commander's In-extremist Forces (CIF). The CIF maintained forces on alert to respond to various crises in the theater, which, at the time, included Europe and Africa. These experiences reduce the mental gap that exists between peacetime and wartime. It helps soldiers make the psychological transition required to operate in denied territory without being overwhelmed. Without these experiences among a significant portion of the force, the concept of inserting special forces into enemy territory would have been unrealistic, as the psychological leap would have been debilitating.

Planning. The decision between Tovo and me to develop a plan and write an operations order for our subordinates without receiving an order from higher up was critical. It is all too easy to rationalize not following good procedures that we were all taught in our military education and training, particularly the higher up the chain you go. Suddenly everyone is justifying their actions, or lack thereof, by saying that this is the "real world" and it's too complex to follow those procedures. That is a grossly false rationalization.

Planning needs to be a priority, and all other distractions fill in around it, not the other way around. Planners need to respect the process and work through the analysis before drawing conclusions that prematurely lead to courses of action. If this is not done, this is how plans become a compilation of tactical activities that sound good but collectively accomplish little to nothing of real value.

If commanders can accomplish this, they should then vehemently protect their plan. That is not to say they should rigidly force the plan against a changing situation, but rather keep the plan afloat by adjusting to the changing situation, all the while maintaining the objectives, the purpose, and the end state. This provides context when the situation requires the forces on the ground to adapt and change their plans. Because we were able to do this, our plan became our North Star and served us well when the circumstances took us off course. Good planning doesn't guarantee success, but bad planning guarantees failure.

Pre-mission Training. The innovative use of our time with training concepts was critical for two reasons. It would have been incredibly chaotic if the company and teams were all trained to develop these concepts without knowing how much time we had left before deploying. It would have likely resulted in a lot of wasted time and energy. The way we approached it maximized our time and provided some unique training opportunities that would have been difficult for the teams to coordinate on their own.

In addition to some of the rehearsal and training events mentioned previously, we also conducted two weeks of language training and three days of Middle Eastern/Kurdish history and cultural orientation. The top three leaders on each team traveled by bus to Fort Leonard Wood, Missouri for live chemical agent training. While the leadership was in language or live agent training, we sent the NCOs to shadow conventional forces conducting training at the Joint Readiness training Center (JRTC) and National Training Center (NTC) to gain experience in large-scale attacks.

We visited an oil refinery outside Denver to familiarize ourselves with the unique and significant dangers of such a facility. The oil fields in Iraq suffer from what is called "sour oil." This means it has a high concentration of hydrogen sulfide, which is heavier than air, colorless, odorless, and highly toxic. The Denver facility showed us hydrogen sulfide alarms that the workers wore that were about the size of a pack of cigarettes. While a useful and somewhat terrifying orientation, when we brought the information back to the Group staff to consider purchasing some, they assured us the facility was wrong and no such thing as hydrogen sulfide detectors existed.

One of the last training events we conducted was having the teams all utilize the Battle Simulation Center on Fort Carson. Their task was to fight the Iraqi Army as if they were their Kurdish counterpart on their actual terrain. It was a chance for the teams to experience and practice command and control, separated into small teams in different rooms. While the simulation itself was underwhelming, the exercises demonstrated a critical dynamic. All of the teams fought the Iraqis with a focus on attrition, not survival. They fought like American military and not like guerrillas. Tovo and I took the opportunity to reiterate our conversations from the brief backs and stress how their success was not based on enemy attrition, but on maintaining a continuous threat. It was a particularly valuable training event that allowed Tovo to reinforce his intent with the teams.

Decentralized Command and Control. Our ability to employ decentralized command and control with our teams was critical. This was only feasible because we knew and trusted our teams and they were indoctrinated with and empowered by the commander's vision and guidance during planning. The leap to do this in combat wasn't dramatically different than how the teams were treated in garrison. The teams were familiar with operating off plans and intent.

As part of the decentralized command and control, we treated the companies and ODAs as battle space owners. We didn't expect them to ask us if they could conduct operations. We certainly didn't require briefings to be sent up to the chain of command for approval. This is a dynamic that was largely not the case during the nearly two decades of counterinsurgency operations in Iraq and Afghanistan. The reason I said we treated them like the battle space owners is because we recognized that the PUK were the actual battle space owners.

The Iraqis Were Vulnerable. It should be noted that while the Iraqis were a formidable army, they had significant vulnerabilities that we were able to exploit. Their army had been significantly degraded from the Gulf War. This, coupled with the No-Fly Zones, caused them to lose some degree of control over the ethnic Kurdish and Shia populations. Without this loss of control and the favorable terrain of the mountains, the establishment of safe havens would not have been feasible for the Peshmerga. Without safe havens, the PUK would not have been able to establish such a large guerilla component. Most of the Iraqi Army's equipment was at least thirty years old and in a poor state of readiness. T-55, T-62, and T-72 tanks are relics from the Cold War. As a result, our margin of error was much greater than would have been the case against a contemporary peer adversary.

The PUK Were Great Partners. The PUK were excellent partners. We developed a strong working relationship based on mutual objectives. We respected and treated them as partners. It should be noted that the PUK were very well-structured. They had a robust guerrilla component and favorable terrain on the east side of the Green Line. This allowed them to establish a viable safe haven, which is largely what enabled US forces to operate inside the territory, unlike the situation 5th Special Forces Group faced with the Shia resistance in the south. They had a supportive population on both sides of the Green Line and a robust underground across the Green Line. The combination of these factors gave them a very substantial capability.

The CIA Were Great Partners. The attitude of the CIA team was one of collaboration and teamwork. Their team leader was a positive influence in every endeavor. While I feel as though—theoretically—we could have performed many of the same functions that they provided, my sense is that we wouldn't have done this as well as they did. In hindsight, our SOTF didn't have anywhere near the psychological operations capability we should have had to accomplish our mission. As a result, the complementary nature of our relationship brought the most holistic approach possible to the operation.

APPENDIX B

OBSERVATIONS FOR UNCONVENTIONAL WARFARE

OVER THE COURSE OF MY CAREER AS EITHER A SPECIAL OPERATOR OR instructor, there have been several key observations that shaped my understanding of unconventional warfare.

The Potential for Unconventional Warfare. The successful execution of UW is contingent on certain prerequisite conditions in the environment, some of which are beyond control and some that can be influenced. If these factors are not clearly understood by planners or are overlooked by decision-makers, the likelihood for missed opportunities, inappropriate application, or unintended consequences will be high.

The requisite criteria include:

- Weak government control over the population
- Goals and ideology compatible with those of the United States
- A population with a strong national or ethnic identity
- Favorable terrain
- Capable and skilled indigenous leadership

It is essential that leaders and planners maintain objectivity in their analysis of these prerequisites. US military doctrine has traditionally stated, "Special Forces do not create resistance movements, they support them." This is not due to a lack of authority, but rather the reality that resistance potential can be enhanced if it exists, but it cannot be manufactured.

Understanding Resistance and Insurgency. Although the concepts of resistance and insurgency are very similar, there are some important distinctions for military professionals, and they should not be used interchangeably. There is a degree of clarity that comes with deliberately distinguishing *insurgency* as a movement that forms and revolts against the indigenous government and a *resistance movement* as a movement that forms in response to an external occupier. The distinction is important to military planners because there are significant and unique requirements, whether supporting or countering, for each of the two.

It is worth noting that these terms are also often used to convey a more positive or negative image, regardless of their correct technical categorization ("resistance movement" being the more positive and "insurgent" being the more negative connotation). Military planners and practitioners need to understand and accept this nuance and demonstrate some mental flexibility when speaking internally to peers and externally in public forums.

Developing a Concept for Resistance. At the inception of any concept to "enable resistance," it's critical to clarify the intent and scope for any resistance activities as a common reference point for further planning. This must be done between the Geographic Combatant Command (GCC) and the Theater Special Operations Command (TSOC) before an order is issued to "conduct unconventional warfare." There are many things a resistance can do to contribute to a campaign effort. However, these potential contributions are not necessarily intuitive or obvious. This is why a feasibility assessment must precede any tasking and must be conducted at the GCC level of command. GCC planners may not understand the potential value of enabling resistance or may inadvertently task special operations forces with unrealistic missions that are not appropriate for resistance forces.

Theater special operations planners need to be prepared to speak to these scenarios with a high degree of familiarity while also maintaining an objective and realistic perspective. Any concept for resistance should include the anticipated scope of the proposed actions for the guerrillas and the underground that correspond with the campaign objectives. If this is not done, there is a potential for various levels of command to develop divergent perceptions of exactly what "resistance" or unconventional warfare includes.

If the concept includes providing lethal aid to guerrillas or elements of the underground, this should be quantified with a description for the type of activities to be conducted and the type of material that is acceptable and available. A similar example could be made for the conduct of subversion through the underground. If this is not articulated clearly during the theater planning process, it will lead to a breakdown in planning, categorized by the units continuously submitting requirements back to their higher headquarters, requesting authorities for the very tasks that they have been assigned. This dynamic has a potential to cause concepts to become overly *guerrilla-centric* and substantially less effective.

The Role of Armed Conflict and Subversion. There is significant benefit for personnel to understand the relationship of armed conflict and subversion with regard to the broader concept of resistance. Understanding this dynamic mitigates the concept of resistance being overly focused on purely guerrilla operations and consequently limited in effectiveness. This is most easily understood as two halves that collectively make up the concept of resistance and generate the greatest effects. The armed conflict, normally in the form of guerrilla warfare, reduces the host nation's security apparatus and subsequent control over the population. Acts of subversion undermine the government's or occupier's power by portraying them as illegitimate and incapable of effective governance in the eyes of the population. The combined effects are exponentially greater than the sum of their parts.

As a young Special Forces officer, I often read accounts from the OSS in World War II that emphasized the power of psychological operations. I didn't fully appreciate this until witnessing it firsthand.

Defensive vs. Offensive Posture. Depending on the capabilities of the resistance, they will most likely be in a defensive posture (fighting for survival). Theater planners need to be aware of this dynamic and avoid superimposing unrealistic operations on the resistance. In certain cases, a resistance movement that is in a defensive posture can undertake limited offensive operations, e.g., in support of a pending liberation event, but these are one-time, high-risk events that need to be deliberately and carefully coordinated.

Guerrilla Warfare and Mobile Warfare. Depending on the degree of control over the local environment, the size of guerrilla forces can range anywhere from squads to brigade-sized groups. In the early stages of an insurgency or resistance movement, the guerrilla force's offensive capability might be limited only to small stand-off attacks—what would traditionally be considered guerrilla warfare. At some point, the guerrillas may achieve a degree of parity with the host nation forces. When this occurs, the guerrilla force may start to act more infantry-like, employing tactics less like traditional guerrillas and more like a mobile infantry column or militia.

Advisors need a firm grasp of guerrilla tactics and light infantry tactics (not merely small unit patrolling) and an ability to recognize the limitations of the guerrilla force and not allow them to get into situations for which they are not trained. It's not uncommon for guerrillas to inaccurately assume that the addition of US air power will mitigate all of their shortcomings as a maneuver force. This is a dangerous dynamic that advisors need to be aware of as they operate with guerillas. Guerrillas are not infantry. To inadvertently push them in that direction when the conditions are wrong would be irresponsible and unrealistic on the part of the advisors. Additionally, the US personnel should not turn into a close air support team and the guerrillas devolve to the team's security party. Air power has limitations and it's a limited resource. In the context of a large campaign, using air power to destroy a single machine gun position becomes counterproductive.

Partners vs. Surrogates. It's very important to understand the distinction between partners and surrogates. In the simplest terms, a surrogate is someone who conducts activities on my behalf, almost like an employee. In special forces, the employment of surrogates is a normal tactic applicable to any special operation. During counter-insurgency operations, teams frequently developed local surrogate forces to conduct operations and reconnaissance. Generally speaking, these forces were under the control of the US forces. With a partner force, they exercise their own chain of command. It's important they be treated as an equal, even if they are very accommodating and looking to the US forces "for the next move." Referring to these forces as surrogates would be derogatory.

The techniques of working with surrogates and partners are distinctly different. Each also comes with associated requirements with regard to reporting, vetting, degree of control, authorized activities, etc. US Special Forces personnel involved in these types of efforts need to have a clear distinction of the two methodologies and not mix the associated procedures and governing requirements. Even if it seems to be operationally expedient, applying the wrong procedures will yield an undesirable result.

Planning and Decentralized Command and Control. Operational elements conducting unconventional warfare are expected to operate under a system of decentralized command and control, largely due to the unique constraints associated with operating from denied territory. This implies they must be empowered to determine the specific resistance activities that would achieve the required effects. To enable subordinate units, orders need to focus on the required effects rather than overly specific tasks (such as specific targets for attack). Specific resistance operations cannot be determined from friendly territory and without consultation with the actual resistance force.

Similarly, when operations are conceived from within the denied territory, their coordination cannot be conducted in the same manner as those during an unrestrictive counterinsurgency environment (e.g., submitting detailed CONOPs for approval to the higher command).

Without the required detail at the start of planning, such as sectors with delegated levels of authority, subordinates will be unable to develop a realistic plan.

Signature Management and Command and Control. Commanders need to be aware that the techniques for command and control (C2) used in other special operations will potentially not apply during UW. Units conducting UW risk some degree of exposure with every communication. Communications encryption should not be confused with not emitting a communications signature. The US military's insatiable appetite for computer-based briefings, real-time communications, and large headquarters needs to be managed in relation to the operational environment. Units engaged in UW should always operate under the assumption that the enemy is conducting direction finding for unusual signals in urban and rural areas. Additionally, every member that infiltrates an operational area increases the signature on the ground as well as creates an additional logistics burden on the host nation partners. In this scenario, more is not always better.

The Size and Location of the Headquarters. Unlike conventional operations, the acceptable size and optimum location for headquarters for units engaged in UW changes as the mission progresses. The early phases of UW are often conducted in a low-visibility manner with a minimum footprint in denied or enemy controlled territory but includes a minimum HQs footprint at the FSB in a neighboring country to avoid unwanted attention on the operational effort. As the conflict becomes increasingly overt and conventional in nature, the environment may accommodate larger headquarters and types of units without a risk of compromise or degradation to the mission by their exposure. The size of forces that the environment can accommodate is the signature threshold. The size and signature of the headquarters will be dictated by the signature threshold and evolve in a manner that is commensurate with the changing operational environment.

The Operational Detachment Bravo (ODB) and Operational Detachment Charlie (ODC). During the conduct of unconventional warfare, Special Forces company and battalion headquarters have some unique roles. For special operations that involve infiltrating elements across an enemy border, Special Forces company headquarters don't have the means to provide command and control. Having them in the chain of command would add an unnecessary layer. This is distinctly different from other types of special operations, such as foreign internal defense, where the company HQs is established in relative proximity to its teams.

If the decision is made to insert the ODB into denied territory, the primary reason isn't to provide command and control to the teams but more likely to interface with the appropriate resistance counterpart. An infiltration is not like a deployment. Every person sent into denied territory raises the operational signature and associated risk to the operation, as well as placing an additional logistics burden on the resistance forces.

Having the battalion task the teams and retain control until the ODB infiltrates and gets established is a better way to manage this process. It also allows the ODBs to plan and rehearse like a tactical unit without the burden of simultaneously trying to control their teams, either in isolation planning or operationally in the denied territory.

Like the ODBs, the decision to send the ODC forward into denied territory wasn't based solely on a need to have C2 of the teams. It was based more on a need to interface with the PUK leadership. We somewhat anticipated this requirement early on in planning. Based on some lessons from Afghanistan, we also wanted to ensure we didn't hamper what the ODAs were doing by falling in on top of them, inadvertently becoming the team leader.

We started to train a small command element, the ODC. This would be a mobile forward version of the Battalion or SOTF HQs, similar to what the conventional Army calls a tactical action center (TAC). The Tactical Operations Center (TOC) is the main headquarters and the TAC is able to move around the battlefield while retaining its C2 functions.

While the teams were undergoing their planning and rehearsals, we identified an eight-person ODC that rehearsed its own battle drills, such as breaking contact or reacting to an ambush from a vehicle and infiltrating by static line parachute. While we didn't execute the concept exactly as planned, the preparation allowed LTC Tovo and me to function pretty close to how we intended and not repeat what occurred in Afghanistan. Once the remainder of the ODC came forward, our concept for the ODC was utilized exactly as intended for the seizure of Kirkuk.

GLOSSARY

Al-Qaeda – an Islamist terrorist organization established by Osama bin Laden in 1988. Sometimes referred to as AQ.

Ansar al-Islam – An Islamist terrorist group established in 2001 in Northern Iraq and loosely affiliated with Al-Qaeda.

FSB – Forward Staging Base

IRGC – Islamic Revolutionary Guards Corps

Jaysh al-Mahdi – an Iraqi Shia militia created by Muqtada al-Sadr in June 2003. Sometimes referred to as the Mahdi Army or JAM.

JSOTF – Joint Special Operations Task Force. A tactical configuration when a US Army Special Forces Group or similar special operations unit deploys to a forward location to conduct operations. The term Joint is used to denote components from more than one service (Army, Air Force, or Navy). The term Combined is added to denote multinational components (e.g., CJSOTF).

KDP – the Kurdish Democratic Party, established in 1946, is one of the two main Kurdish Groups inside Northern Iraq.

KDPI – The Kurdish Democratic Party of Iran, established in 1945, is the main Kurdish group in Iran.

Multinational Corps Iraq (MNC-I) – the US-led three-star coalition headquarters, located in Baghdad, Iraq from 2004–2011.

Multi-National Forces Iraq (MNF-I) – the US-led four-star coalition headquarters, co-located with the US Embassy in the Baghdad Green Zone from 2004–2011.

ODA – Operational Detachment Alpha. An ODA is a 12-man unit within US Army Special Forces. Sometimes referred to as an SFODA (Special Forces Operational Detachment Alpha) or an A-team. In 2003, US Army Special Forces battalions consisted of 15 ODAs.

ODB – Operational Detachment Bravo. An ODB refers to the headquarters portion of a US Army Special Forces company. Sometimes referred to as an SFODB (Special Forces Operational Detachment Bravo) or a B-team.

ODC – Operational Detachment Charlie. An ODC refers to the headquarters portion of a US Army Special Forces battalion. Sometimes referred to as an SFODC (Special Forces Operational Detachment Charlie) or a C-team.

PUK – The Patriotic Union of Kurdistan, established in 1975, is one of the two main Kurdish Groups inside Northern Iraq.

PKK – The Kurdish Workers Party. A Turkish based insurgent group established in 1978, that has, on various occasions, taken refuge inside Northern Iraq and Syria.

Peshmerga – A term for Kurdish fighters; translates to "those who face death."

Redeploy – A military term used to denote returning to home station from a deployment.

Scud – A tactical ballistic missile developed by the Soviet Union during the Cold War and employed by the Iraqi military.

SOCCENT – Special Operations Command Central based in Tampa, Florida

SOCEUR – Special Operations Command Europe based in Stuttgart, Germany

SOTF – Special Operations Task Force. A tactical configuration when a US Army Special Forces Battalion or similar special operations unit deploys to a forward location to conduct operations.

USCENTCOM – United States Central Command based in Tampa, Florida

USEUCOM – United States European Command based in Stuttgart, Germany

USSOCOM – United States Special Operations Command based in Tampa, Florida

UW – Unconventional Warfare consists of activities conducted to enable a resistance movement or insurgency to coerce, disrupt, or overthrow an occupying power or government by operating through or with an underground, auxiliary, or guerrilla force in a denied area. (Joint Pub 3-05)

ACKNOWLEDGEMENTS

I WOULD LIKE TO ACKNOWLEDGE AND THANK THE MANY INDIVIDUALS who graciously shared their stories and experiences, and in some cases their journals, maps, and pictures. Without their contributions, this story would have been incomplete. Specifically I would like to thank LTG (Ret.) Ken Tovo, Derek Jones, Andy Gronlund, Serge French, Sid Crews, Pat Bekurs, Kirk Windmueller, Tom Hoshule, George Antonino, MG (Ret.) Pat Roberson, Kirk Liddle, Todd Black, Brian Rauen, Blake Kramer, Chris Crum, Mark Giaconia, Tim Fuller, Ken Unbewust, Tim DeNio, Jim Cossey, BG Joe Lock, Mike Santoro, Matt Apel, John Holevas, Eddie Licon, George Thiebes, Mendy Cleveland, Pete Russo, Scott Fleming, Cordell Johnson, Chris Hartnett, Matt Goldberg, Cory Peterson, Rick Ong, Eric Lyons, Mike Oppedal, Tom Vogel, Ray McPeek, Mark Mitchell, Duane Mosier, Seth Krummrich, John Bryant, Burt Glover and Pete Vutera.

I would also like to thank Nicole Jobe from Copper Mountain Books (*CopperMountainBooks.com*) for helping transform my disorganized collection of anecdotes and turning them into a coherent story.

ABOUT THE AUTHOR

LTC (Ret) Mark Grdovic served with the US Army for over 23 years, including 19 years as a Special Forces officer.

He served with the 10th Special Forces Group, the US Army John F. Kennedy Special Warfare Center as a Small Group Instructor and Company Commander at the Special Forces Qualification Course and as the Chief of Special Forces Doctrine. Additionally, he served as the G3X at US Army Special Operations Command (USASOC) and Deputy Commander of the Joint Operations Group Central (JOG-C) at Special Operations Command Central (SOCCENT).

His experience includes numerous deployments to Bosnia, Iraq, and Afghanistan and crisis response operations in Europe and Africa.

Since retirement in 2012, he has served as a defense consultant and contractor supporting USSOCOM in a variety of capacities.

LTC (Ret) Grdovic holds a Master's degree in National Defense Studies from King's College London. He lives in Florida with his wife, Gretchen.